Also by Tim Mulligan

The Hudson River Valley: A History and Guide

VIRGINIA

VIRGINIA
A History and Guide

Tim Mulligan

Illustrations by Stan Skardinski

Random House · New York

Library of Congress Cataloging-in-Publication Data
Mulligan, Tim, 1938–
Virginia: a history and guide.

Includes index.
1. Virginia—Description and travel—1981–   —Guide-
books. 2. Historic sites—Virginia—Guide-books.
3. Virginia—History, Local. I. Title.
F224.3.M85   1986   917.55'0443   86-6724
ISBN 0-394-74648-1

For Jerry Aiello

CONTENTS

ACKNOWLEDGMENTS

Throughout the time I spent in Virginia researching this book I met with nothing but kindness from everyone with whom I had contact. Three people, though, deserve especial thanks: Linda Royall of the Metropolitan Richmond Convention and Visitors Bureau, and Martha Steger and Pamela Jewell of the Virginia Division of Tourism. Their commitment, professionalism, knowledge, kindness, humor and warmth make them invaluable assets to an already great state.

I would also like to particularly thank the following, all of whom took time from their busy schedules to inform me on their particular part of—and love for—Virginia: Diane Bechtol, Alexandria; Albertine N. Bridges, Accomac; Susan Q. Bruno, Colonial Williamsburg Foundation; Hill and Helle Carter, Shirley Plantation; Ellen Clark, Mount Vernon; Bobbye Cochran, Charlottesville; Martha M. Doss, Lexington; Matthew V. Gaffney, Monticello; John M. Gazzola, Jr., the Homestead; Suzanne Hall, Virginia Museum; Bill Lindley, Norfolk; Agnes Downey Mullins, Arlington House; Paul Perrot, Virginia Museum; Michael L. Ramsey, Roanoke; Turner Reuter, Middleburg; Diann Stutz, Norfolk; Mrs. Harrison Tyler, Sherwood Forest.

Others who offered invaluable help: Margaret D. Austin, Science Museum of Virginia: Rear Admiral Thomas E. Bass III, Stratford Hall; Lynn A. Beebe, the Jefferson Poplar Forest Fund; the Reverend William H. Brake, Jr., Pohick Episcopal Church; Mary M. Calos, Hopewell; Dennis Carter, Shenandoah National Park; Ann R. Childress, Blue Ridge Parkway; Nancy C. Coor, Warm Springs; Patrick Daily, Red Hill Shrine; Mr. and Mrs. Robert W. Daniel, Jr., Brandon Plantation; Barbara Dombrowski, Oatlands Plantation; Carol Dunlap, Valentine Museum; Philip G. Emerson, the Mariners' Museum; Frederick S. Fisher, Westover Plantation; Karen Hedelt, Fredericksburg; Matthew Hessburg, the Wolf Trap Foundation for the Performing Arts; J. Robert Hicks, Jr., Maymont Foundation; Tucker Hill, Museum of the Confederacy / White House of the Confederacy; Kathleen R. Huftanen, Woodlawn Plantation; Malcolm

Jamieson, Berkeley Plantation; Robert K. Krick, Fredericksburg and Spotsylvania National Military Park; Robert S. Myers, New Market Battlefield Park; James P. Oland, Great Dismal Swamp National Wildlife Refuge; Kalyn Rehrig, Lynchburg; Constance H. Rhodes, Isle of Wight / Smithfield; Dot Ritchie, Bacon's Castle; Thomas L. Sherlock, Arlington National Cemetery; Dody Smith, Middleburg; Donald R. Taylor, Gunston Hall; Ronald G. Wilson, Appomattox Court House; John G. Zehmer, Historic Richmond Foundation.

This is only a partial list, for many others throughout the state gave of their knowledge to help make this book an interesting one. I thank them, one and all, for their great help.

And last I would like to thank Becky Saletan, my editor, and Annik LaFarge, also of Random House. What began as a happy professional relationship has now, for me, become two great friendships.

AUTHOR'S NOTE

VIRGINIA, as you will see, falls quite naturally into six distinct divisions, and that is how I have sectioned this book. At the end of each you will find a list of places to stay and to eat that I feel can be recommended. Every once in a while, if a place is truly bad and you might be misled into staying or eating there, I will tell you about that too.

Prices were accurate as the book went into print, and so were the visiting hours and other service information. All, of course, are subject to change, and if you are on a closely structured budget or timetable, you may wish to check these in advance.

I have followed the same procedure in this book as I did in *The Hudson River Valley: A History and Guide,* namely to write as I would to a friend and to include my personal opinions and tastes; this is, I feel, the only honest way. I have not written about every single thing to see and do in the state. As is true anywhere, one finds some things boring, others of little interest; and if I'm bored writing about it, you'll certainly be bored reading about it. On the other hand, I do include some things about which I'm not too wild, because they're well known or heavily promoted. In these instances, you can decide for yourself. And if you come across something you think is wonderful that I haven't included, let me know.

I would suggest that if you can visit Virginia during Historic Garden Week, usually the last week in April, do, by all means. Houses that are closed at other times of the year are open then, it's a perfect time to travel in terms of weather and many of the gardens are then so beautiful that they will become permanent and cherished memories.

One last comment. Many of the treasures of Virginia, and therefore of the nation, beginning with Mount Vernon and including the overwhelming majority of historic sites throughout the state, were first recognized as vital to our heritage and then saved by women. Our debt to them is incalculable; without their foresight, intelligence, determination, courage and taste, we, as a nation, would be much the poorer. And today they continue the work (see my acknowledgments), asking for no recognition and, unfortunately, rarely receiving it. Thank you, I say, and may your work continue to prosper.

INTRODUCTION

$\bigvee$IRGINIA. The very name is soft and sweet and sensuous, just like the state it adorns. Sir Walter Raleigh named it after Elizabeth I the Virgin Queen in 1584, but it was not until May 14, 1607, that three small ships, the *Godspeed,* the *Susan Constant* and *Discovery,* dropped anchor at Jamestown and the small band of men aboard founded the first permanent English settlement in America on the James River, which was, they wrote home, "for breadth, sweetness of water, length navigable into the country, deep and bold channell, so stored with sturgeon and other sweet fish as no man's fortune hath ever possessed the like."

Slowly the colony grew and prospered, and as tobacco became king, plantations along the James, York, Rappahannock and Potomac moved back into the interior and a colonial civilization of ever-increasing sophistication appeared. The capital moved from Jamestown—first to Williamsburg (1699), then to Richmond (1780), where it remains. And as the Tidewater settlers began moving inland to central Virginia, the western part of the state, particularly the Shenandoah Valley (a land of milk and honey if ever there was one), was being colonized primarily by Germans and Scotch-Irish who were coming down from Pennsylvania. They had little in common with the Tidewater aristocracy; exactly how little would become painfully apparent in the Civil War, when the westernmost part of the state would break away to form West Virginia.

Virginia's greatest glory came at the outset of the Revolution and would only fade with the disappearance of her splendid sons, who then included the starry constellation of George Washington, Thomas Jefferson, Patrick Henry, James Madison, James Monroe, George Mason and John Marshall. Intellectually, the country has never again seen an assemblage to match them; it was Virginia's Periclean age.

In the nineteenth century, as if exhausted by this nova of talent, the state quietly faded from the scene as a mover and shaker in the country's destiny. Then came the Civil War. Virginia was reluctant to leave the Union, but leave she did, and as Virginia went, so went the man who would be her greatest hero of the nineteenth century, Robert E. Lee, member of an ancient Virginia family, general—and gentleman—*extraordinaire*. More than half the bloody battles of this war would be fought on Virginia's soil, for the North became obsessed with capturing Richmond, the capital of the Confederacy. It was General Lee who saved the Confederacy again and again, against seemingly overwhelming odds, until President Lincoln discovered Ulysses S. Grant, who would finally triumph at Appomattox and thereby end the holocaust.

From the end of the war almost to the present, Virginia remained much the same. Now it is growing again, a center of the new South. In area it ranks 36 among the states and has a population of more than 5.6 million people. It's a comfortable state, neither too big nor too small, with its own unique aura of continuity and tradition, particularly appealing against the change celebrated by so much of the rest of the country.

Obviously I love Virginia. I love it for its history, its scenery, its civility, its *douceur de vivre*. "Earth's only Paradise," England's poet Michael Drayton wrote. Perhaps not the *only* Paradise, but certainly in the top ten.

NORTHERN VIRGINIA

*From Alexandria
to Fredericksburg
to the Hunt Country*

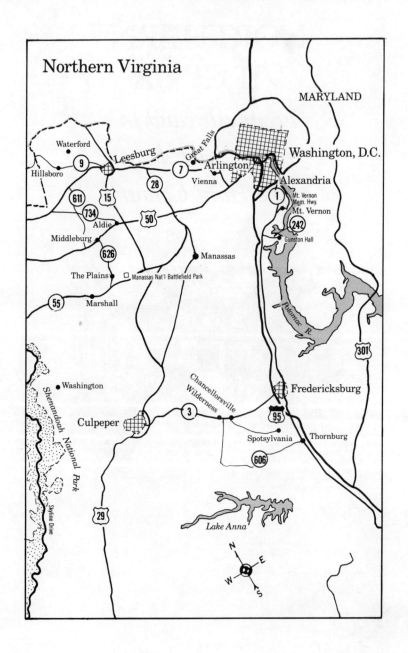

Northern Virginia

THE countryside is so green here, a lush, lush green almost sensual in its variegated intensity. And everything is on a comfortable scale; the towns are small, the landscape more rolling than mountainous. Even the great houses such as Mount Vernon and Arlington have an intimate quality reflective of the gentleman farmers who built them.

Although Washington is never more than an hour and a half away from any of this section of the state, the city's influence is surprisingly modest. One would think, for instance, that Alexandria would be lost in the shadow of its capital-neighbor, but not at all; the town has maintained its own unique flavor. But all the towns and villages here—Middleburg, Leesburg and Fredericksburg being, with Alexandria, my particular favorites—have distinctive qualities that make them a delight to visit.

This is an area for driving on back-country roads, past lovely horse farms and pretty houses, through a gentle countryside of great tranquility and dignity, and then having a delightful dinner before turning in.

ALEXANDRIA

I love color and it often defines my memories. In the case of Alexandria, for instance, I always think of reds, in every shade, variety and even texture. Deep russet. Rose. Pink. Red backgrounds surfaced with silver-green moss. Mottled reds and brick reds and reds flecked with gray . . . It is the secret of the town's great charm, I think, for it gives it a cozy unity, an aura of warmth and welcome that makes you release an unconscious sigh of relief at finding yourself in such a pleasant, civilized spot.

HISTORY

This town of about 106,000 people on the banks of the Potomac is not only among the prettiest in Virginia, but it is also one of the state's best-kept secrets. It is so close to Washington that outsiders expect to find it completely overshadowed by the federal colossus. Don't be fooled. Alexandria has a very impressive history of its own, and although many Washingtonians live here, it is an independent city with a great deal to offer even the casual visitor. I happen to be very fond of it and would highly recommend a weekend visit there.

The town is named after one John Alexander who in 1670 bought six thousand acres of land, including what is today Alexandria, for six hundred pounds of tobacco. From that time nothing much happened until 1732, when several Scottish merchants, including William Ramsay and John Carlyle, established a tobacco warehouse here and the area began to be more heavily settled. Then, in 1749, the Virginia Assembly established the town. This was George Washington's hometown; he was a trustee of it and, tradition says, helped survey it. He definitely bought two lots here in 1763, then built a house that unfortunately was destroyed in 1854.

In 1791, by an act of Congress, Alexandria was included in the District of Columbia. The act's prohibition on construction of public buildings on the Virginia side of the Potomac enhanced the residential character of the town. When the area retroceded to Virginia in 1846, a building boom resulted that lasted to the Civil War.

The city was conservative in its architectural tastes, and many aspects of Georgian and Federal architecture were employed here to a much later date than elsewhere in the country. Perhaps one reason is that it was a planter's city, with its life centered on the docks and wharves along the Potomac. Planter families often maintained homes here and tried as much as possible to replicate the customs, manner and tone of plantation life. Architecture, then, and architectural fashion were not of primary importance; the Georgian style in particular suited plantation living very well. The result is a feeling of homogeneity along the streets that is rare in this country. In addition, Alexandria was untouched by the Civil War—when Virginia seceded on May 23, 1861, Union troops immediately occupied the town—and then was lucky enough to drift sleepily on as a quiet little backwater, stagnation preserving its heritage. This came to an end as Washington began to grow in the twentieth century, and when World War II came along, swelling the federal bureaucracy, Alexandria was rediscovered and the process of restoration and preservation began in earnest.

Today the historic district, which is the Old Town section of Alexandria, is among the most beautiful and extensive in this country—a mix of buildings of national importance, in some instances. They offer a view of our past that is still, unlike Williamsburg, part of a living community. So important is the whole area that the port is a national landmark while the entire district is on the National Register of Historic Places.

WHAT TO SEE AND DO

Alexandria is so rich historically that you could spend several days here and not exhaust its offerings. Planning, then, is important—particularly if you're short on time. Here's what I would suggest. (Keep in mind that for all but a few attractions, what you will see lies between Washington Street and the river, a distance of six blocks, and Oronoco Street [north] and Wolfe Street [south], a distance of seven blocks.)

Begin at the **Ramsay House,** 221 King Street (Open: Daily, 9–5. Closed: January 1, Thanksgiving and December 25. Phone: 703-549-0205), the city's visitors' center, where you can stock up on maps, brochures and so forth. (Also available is a Historic Properties Tour Ticket, which, for $5 [ages 6–17, $3] allows you entrance to the Carlyle House, Gadsby's Tavern Museum, Lee-Fendall House and Lee's boyhood home.) This attractive building is a 1956 reconstruction of the house of William Ramsay, a close friend of Washington and a founding trustee of the city. The original house was built in 1724 in another location and was moved here sometime in the mid-eighteenth century. Ramsay probably lived in it only a short time, as its two rooms on each floor would not have met his needs or his position; when on November 30, 1761, he was elected Lord Mayor for the day, it was noted as "an honour doubly due him, as well for his Virtuous Desserts, as for being first Projector and Founder of this promising city. . . ."

Once you have your material, take a moment to sit in the

secluded little garden above the street to get your bearings.
(King and Fairfax streets were lowered to their present levels
after the Revolution, which explains why the masonry foundations of the house are exposed and the garden is where it is.)
Then walk down King Street to the river. Walking, by the way,
is one of the great joys of Alexandria, the best way to absorb how
much greater is the whole than the sum of its parts.

King is the main shopping and restaurant street in the Old
Town and bustles all day and a good part of the night. It's a
pleasure to stroll here, looking into shop windows and exploring
restaurant menus and generally getting a "fix" on the town.
Certainly the most touristy of the Alexandria streets, it is
nevertheless in no way cheap or tawdry.

When you reach the river, turn right on Union Street for one
block to **Prince Street**, which I have chosen as the block most
representative of the best the town has to offer. The 100 block,
with its wonderfully appealing cobblestone paving, is called
Captain's Row because several of these rather modest brick
shuttered houses used to house ship's captains who sailed from
the nearby docks. Typical of the lot is No. 123, a small, two-story
house with three well-proportioned windows on the second
story, a shuttered door on the first, the whole a cozy arrangement that's most inviting. Again, in this block, it is the overall

*The Potomac at Alexandria still retains a lingering aura of its romantic
past as a port.*

effect that is so pleasant; you would be hard-pressed to find a more charming nineteenth-century street in this country.

The 200 block houses: at 201, the **Athenaeum** (c. 1852) (September–May, Tuesday–Saturday, 10–4; Sunday 1–4. Closed: Holidays and ten days in December, June–August. Admission: Donation. Phone: 703-548-0035). This imposing Greek Revival structure—a rarity in Alexandria—was built as a bank. Today it is the gallery of the Northern Virginia Fine Arts Association and offers challenging exhibits of paintings and sculpture. This block, sometimes called Gentry Row, is much more elegant than the 100 block—as its nickname implies—with three-story houses and much more architectural detail. No. 200, for instance, was built c. 1780 by Colonel Robert Townshend Howe, Alexandria's first mayor, and Washington was a guest here on several occasions. Inside, the house is so handsome that the second-floor parlor was removed and is now installed in the City Art Museum in St. Louis. And 207–215 is considered the finest eighteenth-century street façade in Alexandria.

So it goes as you continue up the street, fascinating house after fascinating house, a visual and historical feast. For instance, in the 400 block—a good example of what the pre–Civil War building boom created—Nos. 413 and 415 served as the headquarters of the Restored Government of Virginia from 1863 to '65, while at 517 is one of the oldest houses (1775) in the city. This single street is a treasure trove of how America lived in the late eighteenth and early nineteenth centuries. You may be interested to know, too, that at 400 Prince is **Cavalier Antiques** (Open: Tuesday–Saturday, 1:00–3:30. Phone: 703-836-2539) which is the finest antique shop in Alexandria. It specializes in eighteenth-century American furniture and "suitable accessories," a suitably vague enough phrase to encompass a wide range of attractive and choice objects. The furniture is very good indeed, and prices high but fair.

You also should plan to see the three finest and most important buildings: **The Carlyle House** (121 N. Fairfax St. Open: Tuesday–Saturday, 10–5; Sunday 12–5. Closed: Thanksgiving, December 24 and 25, January 1. Admission: $2; senior citizens $1.50; children 6–17, $1; under 6, free. Phone: 703-549-2997), **Gadsby's Tavern Museum** (134 N. Royal St. Open: Tuesday–Saturday 10–5; Sunday 1–5. Closed: Thanksgiving, December 25, January 1. Admission: $2; senior citizens $1.75; children 6–17, $1;

under 6, free. Phone: 703-838-4242), and **Christ Church** (118 N. Washington St. Open: March–October, Monday–Saturday, 9–5; Sunday, 2–5. November–February, 9:35–5:00. Closed: Memorial Day, Thanksgiving, December 25 after services, January 1. Phone: 703-549-1450). See page 5 for tour ticket information.

When the **Carlyle House** (1753) was originally built, the Potomac ran through the backyard, the grounds down to the riverbank. It was a real Scottish country house. Today, that situation has to be imagined: The house is hemmed in by other buildings. But even so, it is regally imposing and manages to hold its own very nicely in the company surrounding it. It is the most beautiful house in Alexandria and was built by John Carlyle (1720–1780), one of the original Scottish merchants who founded Alexandria. He was born in Scotland and, as a second son, decided his chances for a bright future looked most promising in the colonies. He emigrated to Virginia in 1744 and soon settled in Dumfries, from which he would move to Alexandria.

His career prospered, and it didn't hurt that he married Sarah Fairfax. The Fairfaxes were among the most important and richest families in Virginia. It was altogether appropriate, then, that he would want to give concrete expression to his eminence. And that he did, by building one of the most beautiful houses of its time in Virginia. The house was probably based on a design in an architectural handbook entitled *Vitruvius Scoticus* that was the creation of William Adam, a leading Scottish architect of country homes. (Adam's more famous son, Robert, created some of the most beautiful buildings in England in the eighteenth century, and, with his brother, introduced the light and decorative Adam style.)

The stone façade is dignified and beautiful, with stone quoins at the corners, around the door, and outlining the central pavilion. All is symmetry: two chimneys, an equal number of windows, equally spaced, to either side of the pavilion. This is a typical Georgian house, serene and assured, almost startling in the middle of contemporary Alexandria. As you walk toward the house from the street, look at the keystone over the doorway and you will see John and Sarah Carlyle's initials and the date of the completion of the building.

The Carlyle House fell into disrepair for many years and was saved only in 1970. It opened to the public in 1976 after extensive restoration. Remarkably, the most beautiful room, the parlor, survived intact, and what you see is pretty much the original room. It is stunning. The two doorways are surmounted by deeply carved broken pediments. The chimneypiece is superb, the fireplace framed in egg-and-dart molding. The chair rail bears the Greek scroll-and-key design. The molding around the room is of carved rosettes between the ornamental brackets. The effect: lavish splendor. The carving in the parlor alone makes this one of the more important eighteenth-century houses in Virginia. And it has been furnished with some first-rate pieces.

I also find the central hall to be special. At the back, halfway up the staircase, is a large Palladian window that offers a wonderful view across the formal garden and floods the space with light. And the hall itself, even in its grandeur, has an overall effect of familial warmth. It's not hard to imagine a party here, and I tend to linger, enjoying its friendliness, until the guide pushes me on.

I should tell you that the house has a certain historical importance aside from its architectural quality. It was here, in 1755, that General Edward Braddock, Commander in Chief of the British forces in America, called a conference of the colonial governors of Virginia, Maryland, Massachusetts, New York and Pennsylvania to consult with him on the upcoming campaign against the French and Indians in the so-called French and Indian Wars and to ask the governors to help defray the costs.

The governors flatly refused to commit any money to the cause, and the campaign itself was a disaster—Braddock stupidly used European fighting methods against the Indians' guerrilla tactics and therefore lost over half his force and his own life when he was shot in the lungs. But something else happened that would bear fruit much later. Before he left on his campaign, Braddock sent a testy dispatch to London in which he came up with a novel idea: "I cannot but take the liberty to represent to you the necessity of laying a tax upon all his Majesty's dominions in America, agreeably to the result of council for reimbursing the great sums that must be advanced for the service and interest of the Colonies in this important crisis."

Nothing came of the suggestion at the time, but it was indirectly to lead to the Stamp Act and other taxes, a series of

events that culminated in the Revolution. The conference, by
the way, was held in the parlor described above, and caused a
proud John Carlyle to write his brother that it "was the Grandest Congress . . . ever known on this continent."

Gadsby's Tavern Museum   The tavern and the museum are
actually two buildings built roughly twenty years apart. The
building on your left as you face them houses the museum, parts
of which go back to 1770. The building on the right was completed in 1792 and contains a restaurant open to the public (more
on that below), and the great ballroom, the original of which is
now in the Metropolitan Museum of Art in New York City.

John Gadsby, whose name is still associated with the buildings, leased the building on the right, the City Hotel, from
1796–1808, and the building on the left, the Coffee House, from
1802–1808. Under his management the hotel came to be considered perhaps the finest inn in America.

George Washington was a patron here as early as 1755 and
was associated with the hotel to the end of his life. Here were
the famous Washington birthnight balls, at least one of which
the general attended in 1798 and which were described by his
step-grandson, George Washington Parke Custis (see page 18) as
"instituted at the close of the Revolutionary War and its first
celebration, we believe, was held in Alexandria. Celebrations of
the birthnight soon became general in all the towns and cities,
the 22nd of February, like the Fourth of July, being considered
a national festival . . ." He also describes a ball: "Among the
brilliant illustrations of a birthnight of five and thirty years
ago, the most unique and imposing was the groups of young and
beautiful ladies, wearing in their hair bandeaux or scrolls, having embroidered thereon, in language both ancient and modern,
the motto of 'Long live the President!' " Shades, in a modest
way, of those French ladies of the court of Louis XVI who incorporated into their hairdos symbols of the issues of the day before
joining their doomed companions in the splendid chambers of
the great palace of Versailles.

In any case, long after Washington's death the tavern remained preeminent; as late as 1824 a dinner was held here for
the Marquis de Lafayette, and other prominent guests over the
years included John Adams and Thomas Jefferson.

From outside, the Georgian buildings are very handsome—

particularly the older one, whose superbly realized doorway, its elegant pediment with a dentiled cornice supported by fluted Doric pilasters, is among the finest eighteenth-century doorways in Virginia.

Gadsby's Tavern Restaurant, three rooms in the newer building, is, bluntly, too cute and touristy for my taste. The costumed waiters and waitresses are attentive, but when I see costumes in a restaurant like this, one of my favorite theories comes to the fore: Costumes mean the food is only fair. I'm not inevitably right, but in this instance I am. Still, it is pretty and can be pleasant enough for a Sunday brunch. But if you decide to pass it by for a meal, you can always walk in and take a peek just to see what it looks like.

The museum is well done, with authentically re-created rooms, but the real reason to see it is the ballroom, duplicated from the original that New York's Metropolitan Museum of Art bought in 1917 to install in its American wing. It is a great room. Extending across the front of the building on the second floor, it is Georgian in its detail: the doors and windows are symmetrically placed, the scrolled pediments over the fireplaces are deeply and exquisitely carved, as is the cornice. The walls are paneled from the chair rail to the floor, and the chair rail itself is banded with a fretwork design. One touch I particularly like is the musicians' balcony, tiny and charming, giving added elegance and sophistication to an already splendid setting. If it all sounds rather imposing, it is. Don't miss it.

One last note: Be sure, as you leave, to stroll around **City Hall** across the way. This is one of my favorite buildings in Alexandria. Why, I can't tell you, except there is a sense of whimsy here; perhaps it is the reconstructed steeple, based on the original 1817 one, looking so out of place atop the 1875 Second Empire building. I don't know. I just like it. It makes me feel good. I also rather like the plaza on the southern end, but not the god-awful Colonial Revival structure plunked down in the early 1960's, which has no relation to anything. The Saturday morning market here, by the way, is claimed to be the oldest in continuous operation in the country.

Christ Church   "Looks just like an English country church," I thought when I first saw this building. Not very astute on my part, but accurate, for that's exactly what it was when it was completed beyond the (then) town limits. It was even called "The Church in the Woods," and only when it was consecrated in 1814 did it receive its present name. The steeple, I might add, dates from 1818. The church's unpretentious country air makes it particularly inviting in its now urban setting; overall, a quiet and cozily intimate place to worship.

This is a pleasurable building constructed of brick with stone trimming from a nearby quarry. The white interior is more urbane, although still warm and personal. The rather modest gallery was added in 1787, the formal chandelier under the organ was bought in London in 1818 for £140. The wineglass pulpit—a lovely name and perfect description of the shape— was installed in the 1890's. Behind the pulpit a large Palladian window allows light to flood in, while the tablets on either side, containing the Lord's Prayer, the Creed and the Ten Commandments, have not been touched since 1773, when they were commissioned. (You will see these three tablets in many eighteenth- and early nineteenth-century churches because books were scarce and expensive.)

Both George Washington and Robert E. Lee worshiped here, and dignified silver plates mark their red-cushioned pews. Lee was also confirmed here, and there is another silver plate on the chancel rail marking the spot. He was last here on April 21, 1861; the next day, he left for Richmond and the command of the armed forces of Virginia.

It's an impressive experience, being here among so much history, all the more so when you visit the churchyard and see the tomb of the Confederate soldiers who died in the city's hospitals during the Civil War. It makes me remember Walt Whitman writing of his hospital experiences in the war, as in his poem "The Wound Dresser":

> On, on I go, (open doors of time! open hospital doors!)
> The crush'd head I dress (poor crazed hand tear not
>   the bandage away,)
> The reek of the cavalry-man with the bullet through
>   and through I examine,
> Hard the breathing rattles, quite glazed already
>   the eye, yet life struggles hard,
> (Come sweet death! be persuaded O beautiful death!
> In mercy come quickly!)

OTHER THINGS TO SEE AND DO

Two houses are closely associated with the Lee family, the **Boy-hood Home of Robert E. Lee** (1795) (607 Oronoco St. Open: February–mid-December, Monday–Saturday, 10–4; Sunday, 12–4. Admission: $2; senior citizens, $1.50; children 6–17, $1. Phone: 703-548-8454), and the **Lee-Fendall House** (c. 1785) (614 Oronoco St. Open: Tuesday–Saturday, 10–4; Sunday 12–4. Closed: Thanksgiving, December 25, January 1. Admission: $2; senior citizens $1.50; children 6–17, $1. Phone: 703-548-1789).

Robert E. Lee's boyhood home was also the home of Colonel William Fitzhugh, whose daughter would become mistress of Arlington (see page 18). Lee himself lived here from 1811–1816, from the ages of 4 to 9, and again from 1820 to 1825, when he left for West Point.

The brick house is basically Federal in style, and solid-look-ing, although the details (windows accented by keystones and lintels of white stone, dentiled cornices and a long gabled roof with two dormers separated by a small pediment that—with the central portion of the façade—projects slightly outward) keep it from being stern.

I like the house on the inside, with its period furnishings and big, handsome central hall. And I like Lee's tiny bedroom, with a few steps leading to his mother's room, which is pretty with bright yellow accents on the furnishings and valanced curtains. The morning room downstairs is pleasant, too, a real family room, with friendly Blue Canton china, a good-looking rug, com-fortable chairs, and family items—a chessboard and pipe, for instance—waiting for someone to take them up. The house is not a must, but it provides an affecting look into Lee's life.

The Lee-Fendall House was built by a man who married, in turn, three Lee women, which I find a bit repetitive. The exte-rior was restyled in 1850, and from 1937 to 1969, John L. Lewis, the famous American labor leader, lived here.

The exterior is very homey—white clapboard with dark shut-ters—suggesting a large, happy family within. There is a main building—I particularly like the diamond-paned windows on the top floor—and several smaller appendages, each with a lower roofline, which gives the house a rambling charm. There is also a nice large garden, with massive old magnolia and chestnut trees, roses and boxwood.

Inside, though, it's a disappointment. The furnishings are a mixture of different periods, as is the interior itself. But there is a rather extraordinary folk-art collection of miniature architecture—a wonderful whirligig, a birdhouse chest—all in the shape of miniature houses.

When you leave, go down to see Nos. 301–307 North Washington Street—the Lee-Fendall House fronts on this street—if you have the time or it's on its way. Built in 1808, then renovated and restyled in 1852, they are an interesting early version of row housing.

The Old Presbyterian Meeting House (1774) (321 S. Fairfax St. Open by appointment only. Phone: 703-549-6670)

There's something about this church that radiates peace. Partly, I think, it lies in how the brick façade and windows, although well-proportioned, are simple to the point of severity. The result is an aura of monumental calm and timelessness that draws you into its spell. In addition, I find this church special in a very personal way. It's not beautiful—the interior is pretty, but almost as plain as the exterior; the tiny graveyard is undistinguished, except for the fact that the Carlyles are buried here (see page 8); and here, too, is the Tomb of the Unknown Soldier of the American Revolution. But there's something very human about it, something that makes you linger.

When you leave, note the choice and delicate iron railings in front of the church and next door at No. 323. The church's was installed in 1853, that of the house somewhat earlier. Both are choice examples of early ironwork.

The Stabler-Leadbeater Apothecary Shop (1792) (105–107 S. Fairfax St. Open: Daily except Sunday 1:00–4:30. Closed: holidays and for lunch. Admission: Donation. Phone: 703-836-3713)

Martha Washington bought castor oil and had her prescriptions filled here. And if she were to walk through the door and into the old pharmacy right now, she would find nothing changed. This apothecary shop, the oldest in the state and the second oldest in the country, still has most of its original eighteenth-century pharmacy items, original prescriptions for the Washingtons and Lees and other noteworthy Alexandrians, nine hundred or so hand-blown apothecary bottles—even dried herbs remain. It's a fascinating place to wander about, trying to figure for what some of the items on display were used. Next door, at 105, is an on-consignment antique shop. You enter the museum through here. The collection can be described as "grandmother's attic treasures" in quality, but the profits help support the museum.

The Torpedo Factory Art Center (1918) (105 N. Union St. Open: Daily 10–5. Closed: Thanksgiving, December 25, January 1. Admission: Free. Phone: 703-838-4565)

This was, indeed, a torpedo shell case factory built for the U.S. Navy. Now it has been converted into studio space for more than one hundred seventy-five professional artists, and is visited by more than three-quarters of a million people each year, making it the city's number-one tourist attraction.

The place is huge—71,318 square feet covering a city block— and to have a studio here, an artist must pass a jury review; once accepted, artists pay a modest rent, and devote part of their time to the year-round art school in the building.

I found the building and renovation interesting and imaginative—you can watch the artists at work—and the variety of media represented is astounding: potters, weavers, glass-makers, jewelers, painters, sculptors, musical instrument makers, ceramicists, and so on. The quality of the art itself ranged from good to fair. Still, it's fun to wander through, if only for the omnium-gatherum of the offerings. A final remark: The Alexandria Archaeology Program is here, too, and displays finds from its digs in the city, which can be both fascinating and instructive.

The Lyceum (1839) (201 S. Washington St. Open: Daily, 10–5. Closed: Thanksgiving, December 25, January 1. Admission: Free. Phone: 703-838-4994. Museum gift shop, 703-548-1812)

The second example of Greek Revival architecture here, this building was restored for the Northern Virginia Bicentennial Center in 1974. In between, it was a hospital during the Civil War and then a private residence. Today it houses a museum and center for the history of Alexandria and has a shop with books, reproductions of drawings and various souvenirs. It's intelligently done, and you can get a good background on Alexandria's history here.

The Lloyd House (c. 1797) (220 N. Washington St. Open: Monday–Friday, 9–5; Saturday, 9–1. Summer hours slightly shorter. Closed: Sunday. Admission: Free. Phone: 703-838-4577)

Built by the same man (John Wise) who built Gadsby's, the interior is now used by the Alexandria Library for books and documents relating to the history of Virginia and Alexandria. The exterior is worth noting as a fine example of Georgian.

There also are two private residences and a firehouse that you should see if you have time . . . or that you should be aware of it if you happen upon them. The **Lord Fairfax House** (1816), 607 Cameron Street, has, I think, an outstanding and unusual façade. It was once the winter residence of Thomas, Lord Fairfax, ninth Baron Cameron and head of the great Virginia family bearing that name. I also greatly admire another 1816 residence, the **Lafayette House** at 301 Saint Asaph Street, so called because Lafayette stayed there during his visit in 1824. Very different from the Fairfax house, this Federal building is perfection in its styling and detail; do, for instance, take time to examine the elegant beauty of the front door. And, finally, there is the **Friendship Fire Engine Company** at 107 South Alfred Street. This 1855 building houses a company established in 1774. George Washington was a member and donated a fire engine he bought in Philadelphia for £80. It is a deliciously giddy, totally endearing Victorian confection. Striving for height and massiveness in a narrow space, the façade manages only to look steep. I love it—and its weathervane. Inside are some of the earliest fire engines in America.

Finally, there are the **George Washington Masonic National Memorial** (1923–32) (King St. and Callahan Dr. Open: Daily, 9–5. Closed: Thanksgiving, December 25, January 1. Admission: Free. Phone: 703-683-2007); and **Fort Ward Museum and Historic Site** (4301 W. Braddock Rd. Museum open: Tuesday–Saturday, 9–5; Sunday, 12–5. Closed: Thanksgiving, December 25, January 1. Park open: Daily, 9–sunset. Admission: Free. Phone: 703-838-4848). The Masonic Memorial can be seen from almost everywhere in Alexandria, particularly at night, when it is floodlit. It is a rather heavy looking, 333-foot-tall structure, but it sits 108 feet above sea level and offers a splendid view of Washington. Founded by contributions from Freemasons around the country, it was built to house the Washington relics in the possession of Alexandria-Washington Lodge No. 22, of which Washington was the first master. Inside it's all very grand, in the twenties' and thirties' spirit of the more marble and granite in (preferably) vast amounts of space, the merrier. The huge Memorial Hall, for instance, has eight 60-ton polished green granite columns, two 46' × 18' murals of Washington, and a bronze statue of Washington as Worshipful Master of his lodge. It is 17' 3" high, weighs almost eight tons, and makes him look like a muscular 1940's movie star in a wig and apron. Nevertheless, there are interesting Washington memorabilia— his family Bible, for one, and his clock, stopped at the moment of his death by his physician. And it is all done with such devoted sincerity that it is hard not to be affected.

Fort Ward is the only Union fort from Washington's Civil War defenses system of 161 forts and batteries to have been developed into a major site. It is owned, with forty acres of woodland, by the City of Alexandria. The reconstructed museum, based on a Matthew Brady photo of Union Army headquarters in Alexandria, displays Civil War objects and material from the extensive permanent collection. There also are an outdoor amphitheater and picnic facilities. It's creatively accomplished, and a pleasant spot to visit.

ARLINGTON

Arlington, a few miles west of Alexandria, is not a city, it's a county. Originally it was a part of the District of Columbia; then, in 1846, it retroceded to Virginia. In 1920 the slightly more than twenty-five square miles was named Arlington to honor Robert E. Lee, whose home had been at Arlington House. At the time, Arlington had a population of only 16,000, but the growth of neighboring Washington, particularly after World War II, changed all that; now Arlington has more than 150,000 people, the majority of whom work for the federal government.

The result of this rapid growth is that the area has no center. Rather, there are several centers, including one called Crystal City, a multi-building development that has all the warmth of Brasilia but does offer a first-rate hotel (the **Marriott Crystal Gateway**) as well as The Underground at Crystal City, four acres of stores, shops and restaurants . . . all, indeed, underground, and covering almost every conceivable interest. For me it doesn't come off; there's no warmth, just a sense of variations on the same theme that ultimately becomes faintly depressing.

What Arlington does have to offer, and what makes it worth a special trip, is Arlington House and Arlington National Cemetery.

Arlington House (1818)   Visiting Arlington House is deeply moving. A magnificent preserve set in the middle of our greatest national cemetery, its view from the portico across to the Lincoln Memorial is so apt and touching as to bring tears to the eyes. And apart from its very real antebellum splendor, this house has a fascinating, sometimes tragic history that makes it worthy of being one of our most famous national monuments.

The land originally entered into the possession of the Custis family in 1778 when John Parke Custis, George Washington's stepson, bought it all for £11 per acre, a price that Washington felt was too high. For once he was wrong. Custis, though, died in 1781 of a fever contracted at the Battle of Yorktown, and the 1,100 acres were inherited by his son, George Washington Parke Custis.

Young Washington, as he was called, was brought up at Mount Vernon by an adoring grandmother and a loving but disapproving step-grandfather who felt that Custis was—a wonderful word—"inert" and eventually gave up trying to run the young man's life, finding his attempts "as idle as the endeavors to stop a rivulet that is constantly running."

I can't help but feel that George was a bit harsh, as Custis turned out to be a relatively interesting and much-beloved man. One of the more endearing stories about him is that every year he would ride the Yule log into the house in his nightcap, and he spent a good part of his life enshrining the memory of his step-grandfather, both at Arlington and in the hearts of his countrymen. He was also a famous orator, a relatively accomplished painter and a playwright; he wrote one play in a nine-hour burst of creativity, and his works—the most famous of which was *Pocahontas* (1830)—were performed in New York, Baltimore and Philadelphia as well as Washington.

In any case, it was Custis who built Arlington House, named after the ancestral Custis estate in Northampton County, Virginia, beginning in 1802 with the north wing. The south wing was added in 1804, and the central section was completed in 1818. (An interesting aside: Roger G. Kennedy, in his fascinating book *Architecture, Men, Women and Money* [Random House], points out that Custis built his house as a memorial to Washington and made sure that it could be seen from almost every part of the capital. He also tells us that he built it in the Greek Revival style to spite his enemy, Thomas Jefferson, who intensely disliked Greek architecture.)

Washington Custis' only surviving child was a daughter, Mary Anna Randolph Custis, called the heiress of Arlington. In 1831 she married her third cousin once-removed, Robert E. Lee. Lee loved the estate and came to consider it his home. "My other place in the world," he wrote—and when his father-in-law died in 1857, he took what became a two-year leave of absence from the army to put the estate in order.

In early 1861, as the Union was disintegrating, Lee came back to Arlington from his command in Texas, where on the night of April 19, he reached his heartrending decision to resign from the U.S. Army. It was, one of his daughters later said, as though there had been a death in the house, and Mrs. Lee wrote to a friend, "My husband has wept tears of blood over this terrible

Arlington House, Robert E. Lee's beloved home. The Greek Revival façade, visible from much of Washington, was put there by Lee's father-in-law to irritate Thomas Jefferson, who loathed this style.

war, but as a man of honor and as a Virginian, he must follow
the destiny of his State." Wrote Lee himself, "I have not been
able to make up my mind to raise my hand against my relatives,
my children, my house." He then left Arlington to report to
Richmond, never again to see the house he loved.

Mrs. Lee and the family soon followed, and in May, federal
troops occupied the house and its grounds as part of the defense
of Washington. Enter the villain of the piece, Edwin M. Stanton,
Secretary of War. Stanton decided to do everything in his power
to see that the Lees would never regain possession of their estate.
In 1863, he created a Freedman's Village at what is now the
southernmost part of the cemetery. The purpose of this village
was to provide ex-slaves with homes and employment. It originally consisted of one hundred frame houses and two churches,
and even had a school. It lasted into the 1890's, by which time one
article called it a slum "of squalid want and destitution."

A tax was also levied on the property—$92.07—which re-
quired payment in person by the owner. Mrs. Lee obviously
couldn't come from Richmond to pay the tax, and sent the
money by a relative. This was not acceptable, and the confis-
cated estate was put up for auction by the government on January 11, 1864. Bidding was less than spirited, as most people felt
that, under the circumstances, the legality of the auction was
suspect. The government itself bought the property for $26,800,
ironically making this the first federal purchase of a historic
property.

Stanton himself may have had some lingering doubts about
the effectiveness of his actions, because he played one more card
—the winning one, as it happened. In May 1864, at the suggestion of Quartermaster General Montgomery C. Meigs, he
created a national cemetery on the grounds, and Meigs made
sure that some graves were located near the house itself.

The Lees were not defeated, though. In 1872 Mrs. Lee peti-
tioned Congress for compensation. She got nowhere, but her
son, General George Washington Custis Lee, went a different
route and took the government to court. In December 1882, the
Supreme Court ruled in his favor and Congress then appro-
priated $150,000 to pay Lee for conveying to it his title to the
estate. But it wasn't until 1925 that Congress authorized the
restoration of the house to its condition during the tenure of the
Lees. Secretary Stanton must have spun in his grave.

The exterior of the house is so handsome as to rank it among this country's greatest. Designed by George Hadfield, who also worked on the Capitol building and designed the old Marine Barracks (1805) in Washington, the portico is a masterpiece of Greek Revival with its eight massive—but not ponderous—marbleized Doric pillars supporting a simple pediment, all painted in graceful shades of ochre and creamy beige. The portico alone is worth the trip, for its symmetry, clarity of design and truly classical sense of repose. The feeling is of an early Greek temple —nothing so elaborate as the Parthenon—man-made perfection that is part of, yet enhances, its natural setting. Its view of Washington is awesome, with the Lincoln Memorial almost dead center in the panorama. The experience is as somber and grand and moving as any this country has to offer. (The view of it *from* Washington is splendid, too—as Custis planned it to be; hence the massive pillars.)

No matter how grand its exterior, though, Arlington was a farmhouse, and the inside of the house is relatively simple. Comfortable is one word for it, hospitable another; one knows he would be well entertained here. No great examples of furniture, and many of the paintings are copies of paintings that once hung in Arlington, albeit good ones; but it's a very friendly place to visit. Perhaps the best example of what I mean is Mr. Custis' study, with his paintings hung about and an overall sense of cozy disarray. It's definitely a family home filled with very personal things—the painting of the Hudson seen from West Point, for instance, reminds one of Lee's superintendency of the academy—and lots of Washington memorabilia. Do note, though, some of the architectural detail, in particular the lovely fanlights with their delicate bowed metal tracery.

Upstairs, the bedrooms are rather uninteresting, as in so many Virginia houses of this and earlier times. Social life, after all, was everything—Virginians did not gain their reputation for hospitality for nothing—so it is the public rooms that always received their most lavish attention.

Another nice thing about the house is that there is no formal tour, although period-costumed hostesses will answer questions.

Arlington House is open daily, April–September, 9:30–6:00; October–March, 9:30–4:30. Closed January 1, December 25. Admission: Free. Phone: 703-557-0613.

Arlington National Cemetery In the years since Arlington
National Cemetery was established, it has become not only our
most famous national cemetery, but its commemoration of the
lives and services of the many who have fought in our armed
forces has also come to symbolize many of the values the nation
holds dear. Every war we have fought is represented here. Two
presidents, William Howard Taft and John F. Kennedy, are
buried here. Four unknown American servicemen, from World
Wars I and II, the Korean conflict and the Vietnam conflict,
receive perpetual homage at the Tomb of the Unknowns. Today
more than 200,000 men and women lie at rest in these 612 acres.

Other famous people are here, too. Pierre Charles L'Enfant,
architect of the Capitol, is entombed in front of Arlington
House, and Oliver Wendell Holmes lies buried not far from the
Kennedy gravesite. But it is, and rightly so, our soldiers and our
heros—Admiral Richard E. Byrd, General George C. Marshall,
Admiral Robert E. Peary, General Philip H. Sheridan, and others—who give the cemetery the aura of a national shrine.

A visit to the cemetery is an intensely personal and moving
experience. Although you can reach the most famous sites by
Tourmobile, I would strongly urge that you walk. The places
you will want to see are not a great distance from the parking
lot, and somehow a bus seems inappropriate. I would also suggest that you get a map of the cemetery at the Visitors' Center.

I have visited the cemetery several times—some of my family
is buried here—and usually follow the same sequence. I go first
to the Kennedy gravesite, for two reasons: because to me it
represents the quintessence of the spirit of Arlington, and because the reactions of other visitors are so impressive.

On the hill above the site looms Arlington House, benign and
protective, a tall flagpole flying the nation's colors in front of it.
In the opposite direction lies the Lincoln Memorial. All around
are the graves with their simple, uniform markers. The site
itself is a gently sloping plaza, its walls engraved with some of
Kennedy's most famous words: "Now the trumpet summons us
again . . ." At the center of the gravesite is the eternal flame;
to each side, the graves of his two infant children. It is done with
the utmost simplicity, and is all the more affecting for that; yet,
it exudes an essential monumentality of the spirit that seems
to embrace the throngs of visitors, and it is not unusual still to
see people moved to tears. The cameras click away, it's true, and

the ubiquitous tour leaders opening their umbrellas to signal straying visitors that it's time to move on sometimes look on the verge of frenzy, but nowhere is there a sign of disrespect, only a desire to somehow retain this moment, and the feeling that for once we are in the presence of something not only bigger than ourselves but even of the man honored. Here is a memorial to move a nation.

As you leave, bear right and you will come upon Robert Kennedy's gravesite. This too is starkly eloquent, particularly the small white cross on the grave and the delicate sound of water falling over the low spillway of the fountain. Through the trees you can still see the flickering flame that marks his brother's grave.

The last time I was there I went to the Memorial Amphitheater, a glistening white marble edifice that is primarily used for services on Memorial Day, Easter sunrise and Veterans Day. As I entered, a small group of young people and nuns were singing the Battle Hymn of the Republic to the accompaniment of two guitars. I stayed until a young priest began the service, then I walked around to a spot behind the Tomb of the Unknown Soldier, where a boy and a girl from a Chicago high school were presenting a wreath to the mournful strains of "Taps." Needless to say, I was transformed into a quivering mass of patriotic emotionalism. And why not? That's the way it should be. But I was brought back to earth by an all-American machine-printed sign as I was leaving the grounds: "Please bare [sic] with us. We have minor water problems to correct."

Arlington National Cemetery is open daily, April–September, 8:00–7:00; October–March, 8:00–5:00. Admission: Free.

The Iwo Jima Statue and the Netherlands Carillon The statue, a Marine Corps war memorial, is based on the famous World War II photograph of Marines raising the flag on Mount Suribachi. Vast in size—it is the largest statue ever cast in bronze—it somehow lacks the splendor of the photograph and is particularly static. Impressive, yes; moving, no. On Tuesday evening throughout the summer, the Marine Corps presents sunset dress parades here. For exact times phone 703-433-6060.

The nearby carillon tower and bells were presented to the people of the United States by the people of the Netherlands in gratitude for our aid during and after World War II. Recitals

are played every Saturday from April to September beginning
at 2:00 P.M.

The statue and bell tower are located near Arlington National Cemetery on Arlington Boulevard.

Sully Plantation (1794)   This interesting and well-restored
house was built by Richard Bland Lee, a younger brother of
"Light Horse Harry" Lee and the uncle of Robert E. Lee. (Harry
Lee, famed for his brilliant military abilities in the Revolutionary War, was also the man who eulogized George Washington
with the famous words "First in war, first in peace, first in the
hearts of his countrymen.")

Although not so well known as others in his family, Richard
was a distinguished man. He served in the first Congress—his
constituents included George Washington—and was instrumental in creating the District of Columbia. While in Philadelphia, he met and married Elizabeth Collins, daughter of a
prominent local family, and brought her to live here. When the
house was completed, a cousin of Mrs. Lee's wrote, rather
chauvinistically, that the house was furnished as well as "the
very best furnished house in Philadelphia."

Today the grounds have two small, attractive gardens. The
house itself, rather small but nicely furnished with some family
pieces as well as other Federal examples, is worth a visit. But
be warned—when I was there the tour took an hour, which was
far too long.

Sully is located in Chantilly on Route 28, ¾ mile north of U.S.
Route 50 and four miles south of the Dulles Airport Access
Road. The house is open daily, mid-March–December except
Tuesdays, Thanksgiving and Christmas, from 11:00–5:00. Admission: $2; senior citizens and children under 15, $1. For the remainder of the year the house is open weekends only, 11–4.
Phone: 703-437-1794. Sully also offers special events throughout
the year, such as Plantation Days in May, Harvest Days in
October, and others.

Wolf Trap Farm Park for the Performing Arts   1624 Trap
Road, Vienna 22180. The Filene Center is open end of May–
August; The Barns, year-round. Phone: 703-255-1900.

The first thing everyone seems to want to know about this,
the nation's only national park for the performing arts, is how

its name came about. In the seventeenth and eighteenth centuries wolves were a serious problem for the colonists, and the Virginia Legislature rewarded those who could prove they had killed one or more of the animals. By 1705, wolves caught or trapped in pits brought a reward of 300 pounds of tobacco; those done in by other means paid only 200 pounds of what James I of England called "this stinking weed." Hence the term "wolf trap." In addition, there's a stream that runs through the park called Trap Run, so when the founder of the Farm Park, Catherine Filene Shouse, first purchased land here in 1930, she decided to call it Wolf Trap Farm.

Mrs. Shouse is a fascinating woman. Born in Boston in 1896, she was heir to the Filene's Department Store fortune, and in her long and rich life she has accomplished a remarkable amount: She was the first woman appointed to the National Democratic Committee, for instance, and the first to receive a degree from Harvard. She has also received six decorations, including the Medal of Freedom, and thirteen honorary degrees. Presidents beginning with Herbert Hoover have sought her advice and aid. But I would suggest that she would say her greatest achievement is this performing arts center, on the land she gave to the nation in 1966 and 1981.

Mrs. Shouse also funded the original Filene Center, a 6,500-seat outdoor theater that burned down in 1981 but has been rebuilt with federal and private funds; and The Barns, two pre–Revolutionary War barns moved from New York State that provide an absolutely delightful setting for chamber opera, dance, music performances, film, conferences and so forth.

The Barns at Wolf Trap, where intimate opera and chamber music performances are offered in two prerevolutionary buildings moved here from New York State.

All kinds of events are held in the Filene Center, from the
National Symphony Orchestra to Harry Belafonte to American
Ballet Theater to Frankie Avalon and the Manhattan Transfer.
Still, my particular fondness for The Barns is for their intimacy
and thoroughly genial atmosphere. A summer evening here or
at the Filene Center, with a picnic before on the invitingly
landscaped grounds, is an especially pleasant event. And if you
have children, you should know that the National Park Service,
which runs Wolf Trap in conjunction with the Wolf Trap Foundation for the Performing Arts, offers free programs for children and adults in the Theater-in-the-Woods, a delightful
open-air theater set right among the trees, during June, July
and August. For information and reservations phone 703-255-
1827/8.

"Wolf Trap no longer belongs to me," says Mrs. Shouse, "it
belongs to the thousands who have attended performances and
the thousands of children who have enjoyed their Theater-in-
the-Woods. These thousands feel they are a part of Wolf Trap."
What more can anyone ask of his gift? And there it is, to be
enjoyed by still more thousands.

What can one really expect of **Mount Vernon,** this symbol of
America that holds for us much of the mystery and wonder that
the Parthenon must have held for the ancient Greeks? Well, for
me at least—perhaps out of a perverse need to bring things
down to earth?—it's the humanizing elements of house and
grounds that make it truly important and moving. George
Washington's great love for it is apparent in the personal, intensely cared-for gardens; in his study, with a view of the Potomac that, more than any other famous view from the house,
suddenly transports you back to the eighteenth century and
gives an intimation of Washington's private sense of his house
and its setting; in the brilliant, recently rediscovered colors of
the paints used throughout the house, almost shockingly
straightforward in their tones; the view of the house from the
Upper Garden, the roof a red jumble of restless lines and angles
and chimneys, the boxwood and trees a contrasting rich green,
the whole creating a sense of personality very different from the
standard views of the house; in the gravesite that so perfectly
expresses the simple republican sentiments of our forefathers.

Anyone seeking a visual expression of what our founders were all about will come away with something that will always remain in his memory—for when all is said and done, it is not for nothing that Mount Vernon strikes such a responsive chord in the American psyche.

HISTORY

The first Washington to arrive in this country was John, in 1657. He married well, prospered greatly (as they used to say) and, in 1674, received a patent with one Nicholas Spencer for five thousand acres of land on the upper part of the Potomac from Thomas, Lord Culpeper, proprietor of the Northern Neck.

In 1690 the tract was divided among John Washington's son, Laurence, and the Spencer heirs. Laurence, in turn, left his 2,500-acre share to his daughter Mildred. In 1726, she sold the land, known as the Little Hunting Creek Plantation, to her brother, Augustine Washington, George's father. He moved his family there in 1735, when George was three years old, and they remained, in a small story-and-a-half house that has been incorporated into the present structure, for four years. Washington would later write: "No estate in United America is more pleasantly situated than this. It lies in a high, dry and healthy country 300 miles by water from the Sea . . . on one of the finest Rivers in the world . . ." In many ways Mount Vernon would be the great abiding passion in his life.

In 1740 Augustine gave Lawrence, his eldest son and George's half-brother, the Little Hunting Creek Plantation and the house, then called Epsewasson. Lawrence settled there in 1743, after serving with the British admiral Edward Vernon in the Caribbean. So admiring was Lawrence of the admiral that he renamed the estate in his honor.

Lawrence died in 1752, and his will provided that if George was to outlive Lawrence's wife, Ann, and if Lawrence's only child died without issue, George would inherit the estate. The child, a daughter named Sarah, died even before the will was probated, and Ann remarried soon after. In 1745, George leased Ann's life interest in Mount Vernon at a yearly rent—of his choice—of either fifteen thousand pounds of tobacco or £100 cash. When Ann died in 1761, it fell to him.

From 1745 to his death in 1799, Washington never ceased expanding and improving his estate, which, when he died, amounted to 7,600 acres—the equivalent of twelve square miles —consisting of four working farms plus the Mansion House Farm, five hundred acres that were made up of the house and the gardens and woods that you see today. This was the soul of the estate.

Washington greatly expanded and enhanced the mansion and its surroundings, and when he died, left this part of his holdings to a nephew, Bushrod. By the 1850's, however, the Washington family heirs could no longer maintain the property, and in 1858 John Washington sold it to the Mount Vernon Ladies' Association of the Union. This private, nonprofit organization was founded by Miss Ann Pamela Cunningham of South Carolina, a remarkable woman who created a national movement to save the estate from exploitation. The Association still operates Mount Vernon, in the spirit of Miss Cunningham's final declaration to them: "Ladies, the home of Washington is in your charge—see to it that you keep it the home of Washington. Let no irreverent hand change it; no vandal hands desecrate it with the fingers of progress. Those who go to the home in which he lived and died wish to see in what he lived and died. Let one spot in this grand country of ours be saved from change. Upon you rests this duty." The nation owes a great debt of gratitude to Miss Cunningham.

The Mansion House As Mount Vernon receives roughly a million visitors each year, a good deal of attention has been paid to getting them through it in a reasonable amount of time without hurrying them. Visitors are asked to line up outside the house and are then sent through in small groups. Inside the house, hostesses succinctly describe what you are seeing and then you move on.

It would be a bore to have me describe everything you will see. Instead, I'll tell you about my two favorite rooms—both downstairs—and give you my impressions and odds and ends of information. But before you enter the banquet hall or large dining room, be sure to notice the weathervane on the cupola, which Washington ordered from Joseph Rakestraw of Philadelphia in 1787: "I should like to have a bird . . . with an olive branch in its mouth. The bird need not be large (for I do not expect that it will traverse with the wind and therefore may receive the real shape of a bird with spread wings), the point of the spire not to appear above the bird." Indeed, the vane is not all that large (42 ¼ inches in length), but it stands out impressively, a wonderful symbol of Washington's hope for his country's future.

Now into the large two-story dining room, the first room you see and far and away the most impressive and splendid in the mansion—also the last to be finished. The first thing you notice is the brilliance of the greens—a shock, given the paler colors long associated with the late eighteenth century. This change in scholarly opinion of what eighteenth-century colors were like has come about as the result of a scientific paint study begun here in 1979 and completed in 1980 under the direction of a specialist in paint colors, Matthew J. Mosca. In his report he notes that he examined samples "microscopically in their natural state" and exposed them "to ultraviolet light for various controlled periods which reduced the yellowing of the paint material caused by the aging of the linseed oil vehicle. Following the ultraviolet treatment, the paint layers were recorded and matched to standards in the Munsell Color System, a universally accepted code of color notation. The assembled complete chromochronologies of the rooms formed the basis for

Beyond the Palladian window is the most imposing room at Mount Vernon, the two-story Adamesque dining room with its beautifully executed plaster ceiling.

determining the finishes used during General Washington's lifetime. The physical examination of the various paints also included chemical testing and spectroscopic examination."

Not everyone is pleased with the results of Mr. Mosca's travails, but I happen to love these rediscovered colors. In comparison to the long-accepted ones, it's like drinking a deep, rich burgundy after a light but somber table wine. You simply cannot ignore them, and I suppose that annoys some people.

The room is Adam in style. A large Palladian window in the north wall adds to its great sense of ceremony. The exquisite plaster decoration employs motifs from the tools of husbandry, Washington's favorite occupation. This is a very beautiful space that would accommodate the most elegant group. (Remember the famous dinner party Mrs. Kennedy gave here during her husband's presidency?) Some details: The paintings are somewhat unusual, in that landscapes were not particularly popular in Washington's time. The two over the doors, supposedly of the Hudson, are definitely Romantic in feeling, interesting precursors in the world of art.

The mantel, a gift from an English admirer named Samuel Vaughan (as were the porcelains on the mantel), seems almost too decorated for the room, which, elegant as it is, has a somewhat simple dignity. And the magnificent Hepplewhite sideboards, custom-made in Philadelphia in 1797 by John Aitken, are a reminder that most of the finer furnishings in the mansion came from the North.

It is not surprising that the dining room is the most magnificent in the mansion, for here is the very focus of the hospitality for which Virginia is famous. It was rare, indeed, for the Washingtons not to have dinner guests—although by no means were they always served here—but this room, because of its function and meaning in the Virginia of its time, could demonstrate ritual and underline Washington's position in a way that no other in the mansion possibly could.

From here you pass out to the portico, the first Southern piazza and Washington's main contribution to American architecture, with its eight plain white squared pillars and the famous view across the Potomac, a mile wide here, to the forested far shore. It is almost exactly what Washington himself saw and very lovely. Then, in the central hall—typical of a Virginia home in that it runs the full depth of the house—please be sure to note the key ring on the left wall. It was sent to Washington by Lafayette and holds the main key to the Bastille. A highly appropriate and moving gift, I think, and one that Washington obviously treasured.

My other favorite room, the last you visit, is the study, another addition made by Washington to the original house. If the large dining room was to fulfill hospitable and ceremonial functions, this was the General's sanctum sanctorum in which only the very privileged were welcome. Here he began his day, and from here he managed his estate and—before assuming the presidency—helped to establish the federal government. When he visited Mount Vernon during the presidency, it was from here that he executed the duties of his office. It is a room of awesome associations, and is also the most intimate in the house and the one that brings you closest to the man as opposed to the legend.

The walls are white, the room bathed in light from its southern exposure, the vista out to the Potomac restful. Graining is employed on the bookpress, the fully paneled mantel wall and elsewhere. (Graining is an involved process of simulating exotic woods with paint and was common in the eighteenth century.) Every object in the room is useful; there are no frills, not even curtains or rugs. There is a portrait of Washington's beloved brother Lawrence, probably the member of his family that he most respected. (Washington rarely mentioned his father, found his mother something of a trial—see page 46—and showed no interest in his ancestry.)

On a bracket over a door is a copy of the great French sculptor Jean Antoine Houdon's bust of Washington—the original is in the Mount Vernon Museum—which many of his family and contemporaries felt was the single best likeness of him.

The Grounds The lawns, trees (some of the larger ones around the great lawn or bowling green were planted by Washington himself), shrubs and gardens combine to make this one of the most beautiful estates in Virginia, and you must allow adequate time—an hour, at the least—to stroll about and enjoy them and the outbuildings.

I like to begin by heading south. You can look at the outbuildings as you go—kitchen, smokehouse, stables and so forth—if the mood moves you. I like best the brick stable with its steeply raked roof, built in 1782 and on two levels. I really prefer, though, to get down to the river and relax a bit in the quiet, to absorb what I've seen. On the way back, I stop at the **Tomb**, where George and Martha are buried, and then go on to the **Lower Garden**—my favorite of the two extensive gardens, I think, although I could easily be swayed. Vegetables are here, and espaliered trees and herbs, all in great profusion; and the handsome brick walls at the edge of the garden are surmounted by lovely white fencing. At one end is an octagonal toolhouse, white with a red conical roof, the perfect touch. (Another, in the Upper Garden, is decorated as a schoolhouse.) Dozens of plants would have been enough to supply the mansion with a delicious variety of foods throughout the growing season. Wandering here is a great pleasure, yet, strangely, the garden seems to draw fewer people than other parts of the grounds.

The **Upper Garden** offers perhaps the most beautiful view of the house and has splendid examples of boxwood hedges (many planted by Washington himself) and an extensive rose garden. In short, you can wander here, absorbed, for some time. Do not miss, though, the **Little Garden** near the museum, which has exotic plants that were of special interest to Washington and with which he experimented in the Virginia climate.

Of all the outbuildings, the one not to miss is the **Museum**, and this I save for last. Here are kept on changing display personal possessions of the Washingtons—clothing, jewelry, china, silver, the Houdon bust I mentioned earlier, Washington's swords, miniatures . . . there was even what must be one of the original pairs of sunglasses the last time I was there. Taken all together it is a unique glimpse at the quality of the Washingtons' lives and so makes a perfect finale to a visit to the nation's most famous and revered home.

Mount Vernon is nine miles south of Alexandria on the Mount Vernon Memorial Highway, a lovely drive that follows the Potomac. There is a trail along the highway for the use of bikers, joggers and hikers, as well as picnic and fishing facilities. Just outside the entrance gate is the Mount Vernon Inn and Gift Shop, which features a restaurant, a snack bar and a large shop. Near the Upper Garden, in the old Slave Quarters building, you will find the Museum Shop. Smoking is prohibited on the entire estate.

Mount Vernon is open every day of the year from 9. From

March 1 to November 1 the entrance gate closes at 5. From November 1 to March 1 at 4. Admission: $4; senior citizens, $3; children 6–11 and students, $2. Phone: 703-780-2000.

Woodlawn Plantation and the Pope-Leighey House I love Woodlawn. I also love its setting and the gardens. It's not pretentious, but it is beautiful and inviting—a home, in short.

Woodlawn was the home of Eleanor Parke Custis, later Lewis, known as Nellie, who was the step-granddaughter of George Washington. Her husband, Lawrence Lewis, was Washington's nephew. (Nellie, from all accounts and from existing pictures, was both pretty and charming.) Wrote Benjamin Henry Latrobe, the great architect, she "has more perfection of form, of expression, of color, of softness, and of firmness of mind than I have ever seen before or conceived as consistent with mortality."

The couple were married at Mount Vernon on February 22, 1799, Washington's last birthday. Washington would later give them one of the Mount Vernon farms, Dogue Run, as well as a gristmill and a distillery, for a total of two thousand acres, a gift that was confirmed in his will. The restored gristmill, originally built in 1772, lies between Mount Vernon and Woodlawn just off Mount Vernon Memorial Highway and is now known as **Grist Mill Historical State Park**. Open: Daily, Memorial Day–Labor

Woodlawn is the homiest of all the plantations, comfortable and cozy; it should be full of children and dogs.

Day, 10–6. Admission: 75¢; children 6–12, 50¢. Other times
phone: 703-780-3383.

Construction began on the house in 1800, based on the plans
of Dr. William Thornton, original architect of the Capitol.
(Thornton, a doctor who did not practice, was an amateur architect with not one iota of training as such. He entered a competi-
tion for the Capitol in 1792 and won. Other of his buildings still
survive in Washington, including the Octagon House, headquarters for the American Institute of Architects.) By 1802 the
wings were completed and the Lewises moved in with their two
children. The center portion was completed in 1805.

The façade of the house was modified in the early part of this
century when the wings and hyphens (the two extensions connecting the wings) were raised to accommodate modern con-
veniences.

This rose-red brick mansion remains a typically Georgian
house with its five-part composition—a central block connecting by the hyphens to two dependencies—but its overall formal-
ity is softened and warmed by the generously proportioned
windows with shutters and the small pediment in the roof with
its *oeil-de-boeuf* window. Further touches—the stone lintels,
the fanlight over the shuttered front door, the delicate tracery
of the second-floor hall window, the dentilation under the eaves
—add to the graciousness of this house. Unlike so many of the
great plantation houses, this is not a grand statement; rather,
it has the feel of a comfortable country house designed for people who love the outdoors and dogs and horses and children and
entertaining. You can imagine yourself living here.

Inside, the house is not grandly impressive, either, although
it has some excellent furnishings and so forth. Again, it looks
lived in; the rooms are bright and airy with high ceilings and
good, solid proportions. From the second floor, looking toward
Mount Vernon, you can see the tops of the trees that Washington planted, a nice reminder of the tie between the two estates.
And there are some endearing family mementos—for instance,
Nellie's irresistible painting of a cedar waxwing perched on a
fruit-laden branch.

The theme of unpretentious welcome is carried throughout.
Downstairs there is a room where children can play with toys
of the period. And the delightful basement shop offers wonderful quilted pillows and other items that are the product of Nellie's Needlers, volunteers for Woodlawn.

The grounds won't let you down, either. The brick walks are especially appealing, while the gardens have a rich informality in a flawless setting that makes them among the most charming in Virginia. I do have one favorite view of the house from the grounds: walk out across the bowling green until all you can see is the central block. From there it looks like a wonderful stage set for a comedy of manners. There also are two nature trails, one featuring bird and plant life, the other wildflowers.

That's not all, though. There is still the Pope-Leighey House to see, only a short walk from the mansion. This house was designed by Frank Lloyd Wright. It is what he calls a Usonian house, a term borrowed from Samuel Butler, who used it in his 1872 novel *Erewhon* to describe the United States. Wright wrote of the purpose of this attempt to create a well-designed house at moderate cost: "To give the little family the benefit of industrial advantages of the era in which they live, something else must be done for them than to plan another little imitation of a mansion." Of the design he wrote: "The Usonian house, then, aims to be a *natural* performance, one that is integral to site; integral to environment; integral to the life of the inhabitants." The first house was built in 1937.

Built in the 40's in Falls Church, Virginia, this particular house was threatened when an interstate highway was planned

This Frank Lloyd Wright house was the result of his attempt to create a well-designed house at a reasonable cost for the average American family.

to go right through the living room. The second owner, Mrs. Marjorie Leighey, decided to do all she could to save it, and she succeeded. It was agreed that the house would be moved to a similar setting—in Wright's planning, the site was very important—and Woodlawn was chosen. By June, 1965, reconstruction was complete.

The house is made of cypress, brick and glass and is quite small. The flat roof and grouped windows emphasize the horizontal line that Wright so admired; it conveyed a sense of unity with the earth, he felt. The living area, typical of Wright, is not one space but a whole series of spaces. Even ceiling height has been used to create certain effects—the low-ceilinged entrance makes the higher-ceilinged living room seem more spacious, for instance. Today the house seems surprisingly contemporary and makes a striking contrast to Woodlawn. The latter is made for children and entertaining; it brings the world inside. Pope-Leighey is more of a retreat, a "natural" house in a natural setting; it very definitely shuts out the world.

Woodlawn Plantation is three miles beyond Mount Vernon at the conjunction of the Mount Vernon Memorial Parkway and U.S. Route 1. Open: Daily 9:30–4:30. Closed: Thanksgiving, December 25, January 1. Admission: $4; senior citizens, $3; students, $3. Phone: 703-557-7881.

The Pope-Leighey House is open March–November, Saturday and Sunday, 9:30–4:30. Admission (tickets are available at Woodlawn mansion): $4; senior citizens, $3; students, $3. Phone: 703-557-7881.

Pohick Church This looks like Christ Church in Alexandria without the steeple. For good reason, too, as it is probable that the plans for these two churches as well as one in nearby Falls Church were conceived in the main by the same man, Colonel James Wren.

Pohick (from an Indian word meaning "hickory") was built between 1769 and 1774. From 1771 on, it came under the supervision of George Mason of Gunston Hall (see below). George Washington served on its building committee and may have had a hand in its design. The church is rectangular, two stories in height; with two tiers of windows, square on the first floor, arches on the second. There is no steeple or belfry—like so many of the churches that served the plantations, no parishioners lived within the sound of bells.

The church is both dignified and elegant, an impression that is further enhanced by the Flemish bond brickwork and stone quoins and the very fine doors, of which there are three: a central door on the south side, and two on the west, one for men and one for women. All are delineated by well-carved Ionic pilasters and topped with a triangular pediment.

The interior, white with red and gold accents, has been much restored since it fell into disuse after the Revolution and was badly damaged during the Civil War. I find it captivating in an intimate, almost vernacular way. The pulpit and canopy, as specified in the Articles of Agreement, are "of pine, wainscotted with proper Cornice, and executed in the Ionic Order." The altarpiece, twenty feet high and fifteen wide, is also wainscotted, with a broken pediment and Ionic pilasters. It contains the Creed, the Lord's Prayer and the Ten Commandments. The cross in the window here is of walnut from Mount Vernon. The box pews have seats on several sides and are arranged according to the tradition in English churches. (Numbers 3 and 4 belonged to George Mason, Number 28 to George Washington.)

I should tell you that Parson Weems was a temporary clergyman here. It was he, you may remember, who did the biography of George Washington that started that dreary old chestnut about the cherry tree. (He also wrote moral tracts with marvelously menacing titles: "God's Revenge Against Adultery" and "The Bad Wife's Looking Glass" are two that come to mind.)

Gunston Hall   At first sight, Gunston Hall can be something of a shock, for it is so plain on the exterior and relatively so small that you may think it can't possibly live up to its reputation as one of the most beautiful houses of the period. But this house is a must. So are the splendid gardens, also among the finest in the country.

George Mason (1725–1792) is one of the most fascinating (yet probably least-known) Americans of the Revolutionary period. Mason, who grew up on this land, began building the house in 1755. His is basically a simple design—a story-and-a-half Georgian brick building in Flemish bond brick with aquiastone quoins. Four chimneys, two at each end, and five dormers, on

Who would imagine that within this unpretentious house are interiors of such exquisite beauty as to rank them among the most important examples of Georgian architecture in the country?

both sides of the roof, complete the façade. But note the land-front porch, the first hint of something special. It is, in fact, Palladian in design, a central arch flanked by two lower rectangular openings. It not only fits beautifully under the gabled roof, it also gives relief and interest to a façade that otherwise would have been too severe. (On the river side is an even more interesting porch, this time an unusual semi-octagonal design with Gothic arches.) These and the interior are the work of one of America's greatest colonial architects, William Buckland.

As Mason began the house in 1755, he took time out to write to his younger brother in London and asked him to bring back to Virginia a master craftsman to take charge. Buckland, the brother's choice, was perfect for the job. He had learned both the joiner's and carpenter's trades and would show real brilliance as both an exterior and interior designer and as a woodcarver. He signed a contract of indenture for four years, and once in Virginia became totally responsible for the house, which was completed in 1759. (Later he would move to Annapolis, Maryland, where he would design a number of houses, including the Hammond-Harwood House [1774], perhaps the finest colonial townhouse in America.)

Inside, the house is divided in half by a wide central hallway.

To the left are the master bedroom and study; to the right, the dining room and parlor, also known as the Palladian Parlor, and the most magnificent room in the house. Upstairs are seven small bedrooms and a storage closet of minor interest.

Let me give you some idea of the splendors of the two most beautiful rooms.

The dining room is the first example in this country of the Chinese style, evident in the frames over the windows and doors, and the fretwork below. The carving is done with a confidence, verve and professionalism that makes it the peer of any similar room of its period. And the furnishings, superior examples of the Chippendale style, perfectly complement the room. (Buckland was strongly influenced by Chippendale's *The Gentleman and Cabinet Maker's Director* [1754], a folio of the furniture he had designed that was also the first important published book of such designs and a landmark as such.)

If the dining room is remarkable, the parlor is resplendent, a masterpiece both of the woodcarver's and designer's arts. Consider the moldings, for example: a basic egg-and-dart design, but so proportioned and carved as to go beyond decoration to give the room a powerful overall definition that organizes the other elements within it, such as the pilastered door, window and niche frames. The latter, in turn, have such style and vitality that they can only be called sumptuous. But enough. You really must see it yourself. It is, indeed, a very great room of its period —or of any period.

Outdoors and on to another renowned pleasure, the formal gardens, which contain only those plants found in the gardens of the period. The most immediately noticeable feature is the English boxwood allée, planted by George Mason himself and now a spectacular twelve feet high. It is, horticulturists say, the finest of the period, and Thomas Jefferson took cuttings from it for his garden at Monticello. "It was here," Mason's son John wrote, "that my Father in good weather would several times a day pass out of his study and walk for a considerable time wrapped in meditation, and return again to his desk, without seeing or speaking to any of his family." It is a delight to wander here and in other parts of the garden, or to take the nearby nature trail down to the Potomac, only a half-mile away.

Finally, a word about George Mason, a close friend of both Washington and Jefferson and of whom Jefferson wrote that he was "a man of the first order of wisdom among those who acted in the theatre of the revolution, of expansive mind, profound judgment, cogent in argument, learned in the lore of our former constitution, and earnest for the republican change on democratic principles." He was both a statesman and a political thinker of depth who wished to avoid the limelight—a prophet in a cave, he's been called, and the pen of the American Revolution. He was so shy of the public arena that he refused to serve as the first U.S. senator from Virginia. To cite only two of his accomplishments, he prepared the Declaration of Rights and most of the Constitution (both 1776) for Virginia; and had, thereby, an enormous and direct influence on the Declaration of Independence and, later, the French Declaration of the Rights of Man. It was he who inspired Thomas Jefferson by first writing "That all men are by nature equally free and independent and have certain inherent rights . . . namely, the enjoyment of life and liberty, with the means of acquiring and possessing property, and pursuing and obtaining happiness and safety." It gives me a great sense both of satisfaction and of decorum that this great spirit was matched with this great home. No wonder he refused to leave it for the political quagmire.

Gunston Hall is about fourteen miles south of Alexandria off Route 1 on Route 242. Open: Every day, 9:30–5. Closed: December 25. Admission: $3; senior citizens, $2.50; children, 6–15, $1. Phone: 703-550-9220.

FREDERICKSBURG

Fredericksburg is one of my favorite places. When I first saw it I thought, "This is the quintessential American town." What I meant was that the town, having so much that is uniquely American as well as so many important relics of our past, still looks more nineteenth than twentieth century. You feel instantly at home here and sense faintly that you've arrived in a vital center of our shared national history.

HISTORY

One of the most engaging towns in Virginia, Fredericksburg should be on your "must see" list. It is only about fifty miles from both Richmond and Washington, an unfortunate proximity during the Civil War, when it changed hands seven times. Four major actions of the war took place here, at the "gateway to Richmond": the Battle of Fredericksburg, December 11–15, 1862; the Chancellorsville Campaign (including the battles of Chancellorsville, Second Fredericksburg and Salem Church), April 27–May 4, 1863; the Battle of the Wilderness, May 5–6, 1864; and the Battle of Spotsylvania Court House, May 8–21, 1864. Today its cemeteries are the final resting places for 17,000 of the soldiers who died in these engagements.

The historical interest of the town, though, is far from being limited to the Civil War. Fredericksburg—it probably was named after Frederick, Prince of Wales and son of George II, and many of its streets still carry the names of members of the Royal Family—was granted a charter in 1727 by the House of Burgesses at Williamsburg. Situated just south of the falls of the Rappahannock, it was an excellent location for a town, as ships could put in here to exchange goods for those brought in from the west. It was here, too, that George Washington spent part of his youth, his father having moved to the town in 1738. And here his mother and sisters lived in houses that are now open to the public.

The town prospered, and by the time of the Revolution it was the tenth-largest shipping center in the colonies. But after the war its development slowed considerably, for two reasons: settlers were moving even farther westward and Fredericksburg was no longer a convenient "gateway" for them, and ships were becoming too large for the capacity of the river. (Steamboats, though, did continue to operate between here and Baltimore until well into the twentieth century.)

Still, it did expand, and by the time of the Civil War had grown to (a still modest) 730 households. After the war the town slowly recovered and even grew. Today it is one of the more rapidly growing towns in Virginia and has a population of about 15,000 people.

Because the town is so alluring and there is so much to see,

Almost every street in Fredericksburg, one of the prettiest towns in Virginia, is worth strolling along.

you will need a minimum of two full days here, one for the town itself and one for the battlefields.

WHAT TO SEE AND DO

Begin at the **Visitor Center** at 706 Caroline Street. Here you will see an excellent orientation film that will help to familiarize you with your surroundings. The Center has a walking-tour brochure, very helpful when there's so much to see, and you can buy combination tickets for six of the sights, thereby gaining a discount.

There are five buildings that you really must see, in order of my preference: **Kenmore** (1201 Washington Avenue. Open daily, April–October, 9–5; November–March, 9–4. Closed Thanksgiving, December 24–25, December 31–January 1. Admission $3.00; children 6–16, $1.50. Phone: 703-373-3381), the **Mary Washington House** (1200 Charles Street. Open: Daily, April–October, 9–5; November, December, March, 9–4; January, February, 10–4. Closed: Thanksgiving, December 24–25, December 31–January 1. Admission: $2; children 6–16, 50¢. Phone: 703-373-1569), the **James Monroe Museum and Memorial Library** (908 Charles Street. Open: Daily 9–5. Closed: Thanksgiving, December 24–25, December 31–January 1. Admission $1.50; children 6–16, 50¢. Phone: 703-373-8426), the **Rising Sun Tav-**

ern (1306 Caroline Street. Open: Daily, April–October, 9–5; rest of year, 9–4. Closed: Thanksgiving, December 24–25, December 31–January 1. Admission $2; children 6–16, 50¢. Phone: 703-371-1494) and the **Hugh Mercer Apothecary Shop** (1020 Caroline Street. Open: Daily April–October, 9–5; March, November, December, 9–4; January–February, 10–4. Closed: Thanksgiving, December 24–25, December 31–January 1. Admission: $1.50, children 6–16, 50¢. Phone: 703-373-3362).

Kenmore   The primary reason to see Kenmore is for its plasterwork, the finest in America and so beautiful as to have one of the rooms in this house included in "The 100 Most Beautiful Rooms in America." In addition, the house has been brilliantly restored, and is considered to be one of the most superbly furnished homes of the Colonial period of this country. (Please note that, before you go into the house, there is an excellent little museum where you pay your admission fee. Put aside fifteen minutes or so to enjoy it.)

The house was built by Fielding Lewis (1725–1781), George Washington's brother-in-law through Lewis' marriage to Betty (1733–1797), George's only sister. In fact, Washington surveyed the original 861-acre estate for Lewis in 1752, the year he began building the house for his new bride.

Lewis was an extremely prosperous merchant who was ruined by the Revolution. During that war he did everything he could to help the American cause, but his ruination would be brought about by the Fredericksburg Arms Manufactory, of which he was the founder and principal backer. The problem: He was never reimbursed for his expenditures, and when Betty died in 1797 the estate had to be sold to cover their debts.

From then until 1922 the house drifted slowly downhill until a developer considered demolishing it. (It was during those years, though, that Kenmore received its name, from the Gordon family that owned it between 1819 and 1859. They named the estate after a Gordon estate in Scotland called Kenmuir.) In that year it was put up for public auction and was bought by a group of women formed for the purpose of preserving and restoring it.

The exterior—a quietly elegant Georgian red brick building flanked by two dependencies—does not prepare you for the dazzling brilliance of the three greatest rooms, all on the ground

In spring, during Historic Garden Week, it seems that every inch of land becomes achingly beautiful.

floor: the dining room, the drawing room and chamber. It is believed that all are the work of an anonymous craftsman whom George Washington referred to as "that Frenchman" and who probably did work at Mount Vernon, as well, after he completed the rooms here about 1775.

My two favorite highlights from these rooms: first, the drawing-room mantel and chimneypiece is as beautiful as any in this country. The overmantel scene, taken from Aesop's fable of "The Fox and the Crow," is said to have been suggested by Washington. It is done with a delicacy and sureness of touch that allow even the smallest detail an almost three-dimensional presence. The scene is encircled by a garland so finely modeled as to seem to float within the overall framework. And then there's the ceiling in the chamber, "The Four Seasons," whose four corners have palms (for spring), grapes (summer), acorns (fall) and mistletoe (winter). The whole design is derived from a book published in London in 1740, Batty Langley's *City and Country Builder's Treasury.* It is an endless delight of form and design.

Some of the furnishings in the house belonged to the Lewises; all are of superior quality. The result is a fascinating museum-quality collection that alone would make the visit worthwhile. There also are two three-quarter-length portraits of Fielding and Betty Lewis by John Wollaston. Wollaston, particularly

well known for his ability to paint drapery, did portraits of
many great families of the South. Not a great painter, but honored, nevertheless, in a curious poem by Francis Hopkinson,
better known as the designer of the American Flag. The poem
begins:

> To you, famed Wollaston, these strains belong,
> And be your praise the subject of my song . . .

From there it goes ever more rapidly downhill.

When you leave, you are offered tea and gingerbread in the
kitchen dependency to the left of the house. The gingerbread
recipe is that of Mary Washington. To the right is the gift shop,
large and attractive. And now, explore **the gardens.**

These gardens, restored under the direction of the Garden
Club of Virginia, are responsible for Historic Garden Week,
that spring festival in Virginia now known countrywide. The
original idea, in 1929, was that owners of various important
homes and estates would, for a fee, open their properties to
visitors, and the proceeds would benefit the restoration of Kenmore. So successful was the plan that Garden Week immediately became an annual event, and the monies raised have gone
to the aid of many Virginia properties.

The boxwood is outstanding, and there is an eighteenth-century herb garden as well as a sweet-smelling cutting garden.
But it is the entire design, vastly appealing in an odd congruity
of intimacy and informality, that is so effective. I also like the
two summer houses, copies of one at Federal Hill, another house
in Fredericksburg. The gardens, in short, are worthy of the
splendor of the house.

Mary Washington House The very first time I visited here,
in the late morning, the furniture had just been freshly waxed
and that lovely, rich, clean smell followed me throughout the
house. Needless to say, it strongly reinforced my sense of overall
domestic coziness. I like this house very much; it brings on
feelings of gentle affection.

George Washington bought this property for his mother,
Mary Ball Washington, in 1772, and she moved here from
nearby Ferry Farm where she had lived for many years. In this
small, but I think rather elegant, house she would spend the

*During the Revolution, Mary Washington told everyone who would
listen that her son was "off doing things that are none of his business."
George was not amused.*

remainder of her days—she died in 1789—within visiting distance of her daughter at Kenmore. (There was, in fact, a path
between the two houses.)

Mother and son did not have the happiest relationship. She
couldn't have been an easy woman to be around; according to
Washington biographer James Thomas Flexner, during the
Revolution she was "so uncomplimentary about Washington's
activities that she had generally been considered a Tory." She
told people who praised him, Flexner writes, "that he was off
doing things that were none of his business and allowing her to
starve." Washington, quite naturally, found this intensely ir-
ritating. Still, she must have loved him above the other siblings,
for when she died she made him her principal heir.

As I said, this house has great charm, the rooms being spacious, comfortable, well planned and beautifully furnished.
They contain many of her private possessions, including her
"best dressing glass" which she left to George but which, over
a year after her death, he had failed to send for. One nice
eccentric touch on someone's part: Why is there a sedan chair
—albeit a very handsome French one—in the dining room?
Don't tell me; I'd rather speculate.

Before you leave, take a look at the nice little garden restored
by the Garden Club of Virginia in their usual impeccable taste.
It would be hard to imagine someone's not having a plesant time
on a visit here.

James Monroe Museum and Memorial Library Before you visit here, take a little walk in the **Masonic Cemetery** (1784) to your left as you face the museum. It is one of the country's oldest Masonic burial grounds and has some wonderful stones to peruse as you wander about.

The museum houses the law offices of James Monroe from 1786–1789. (Also see page 136.) What makes it particularly interesting is that it now contains so much of what he bought in France during his time (1794–1796) as a U.S. minister there, including the Louis XVI desk—a beauty—on which he signed the Monroe Doctrine. There are other handsome examples of French eighteenth-century furniture, which he had with him in the White House. There is, by the way, a recorded narrative in each room. I much prefer this to a guided tour—you get the facts and all you need to know quickly and succinctly.

In any case, the Louis XVI furnishings, pictures (including the Rembrandt Peale portrait of Monroe), china, silver, clothing and so forth are interesting not only because of the Monroe connection but also in their own and historical terms. At first it's a bit curious seeing this rather splendid collection in such a simple setting, but it connects two aspects of his life. The library, housed behind the law offices, has thousands of books and manuscripts related to Monroe. It's a different experience,

A walled garden that is part of the James Monroe Museum and Memorial Library, which contains fascinating Monroe memorabilia.

visiting here, but one I think you'll like. And once again, before you leave, allow yourself a few minutes to enjoy the pleasant walled garden.

Rising Sun Tavern Washington's brother Charles built this as a home in 1760 and it later became a tavern. It has been splendidly restored and furnished, but I have one major complaint—the guided tour. The idea is that your hostess-guide will transport you back in time to the eighteenth century and act as the tavern wench. It's an idea whose cuteness is cloying. It takes away from the very real merits of the tavern and is, I feel, demeaning to the hostesses. Here I am in what is, after all, a fascinating re-creation of the eighteenth century, being treated as an idiot who can only understand a fact if it is presented to him in the simplest and most condescending manner. Well, enough of that. Go despite the tour—there are some truly wonderful things here, and the restoration itself has been done in excellent taste.

Hugh Mercer Apothecary Shop Hugh Mercer was a Fredericksburg doctor and a close friend of George Washington. A supporter of the doomed Stuart cause in Scotland, he had fled to this country after the battle of Culloden (1746) in which Charles Edward Stuart, Bonnie Prince Charlie, was defeated by the English.

He met Washington in Pennsylvania and moved to Fredericksburg on his advice. With the advent of the Revolution he sided with the colonists and became a brigadier general on Washington's staff. It was at the Battle of Princeton (1777) that he received the seven deep wounds from which he died. His most famous descendant: General George S. Patton.

The building was almost destroyed in the 1920's but was saved at the eleventh hour through the efforts of two women, Mrs. Vivian Minor Fleming and her daughter Annie Fleming Smith, who also were central in the effort to rescue Kenmore.

The shop is, of course, historically interesting and is full of pharmaceutical curiosities. It is of particular interest to children because of the peculiar remedies the guide will tell them about, so if you are traveling with children this is a must. But aside from that, it's pretty. In fact, it's very pretty, and a stop here is worth your while. There's also a room here that Washington used as his office when in Fredericksburg, and his accounts are still here.

OTHER THINGS TO SEE AND DO

Several other buildings deserve at least a mention. **St. George's Episcopal Church and its churchyard** (northeast corner of Princess Anne and George streets) was consecrated in 1849 and has three Tiffany windows. Patrick Henry's uncle, also named Patrick, was the first rector. The churchyard has stones going back to 1752. The **Presbyterian Church** (southwest corner of Princess Anne and George streets) is a more handsome building. Greek Revival in style, it was dedicated in 1833. You can still see damage on the exterior from Civil War cannonballs. Pews were torn from the church to make coffins for the soldiers. It is said that Clara Barton nursed here. Today the most interesting aspect of the church is the massive, magnificent nineteenth-century iron lamps on the exterior.

The **Masonic Lodge No.** 4 (Princess Anne and Hanover streets) was where Washington was initiated into the Masons; it has some Washington memorabilia, and the **Court House** (Princess Anne Street near George Street), built in 1852, is a Gothic Revival building designed by James Renwick, whose most famous buildings are St. Patrick's Cathedral in New York City and the original building of the Smithsonian Institution in Washington.

The **St. James House** (1300 Charles Street. Open: Garden Week and first week in October, other times by appointment only. Admission: $2; children 6–16, 50¢. Phone: 703-373-1569) was built in the 1760's, has handsome period furnishings and is an excellent, rare example of what a standard pre-Revolutionary Fredericksburg house must have looked like.

At 813 Sophia Street is the **Silversmith's House**. Open: Daily, except Monday, 9–5. Closed: Thanksgiving, December 25, January 1. Admission: Free. Phone: 703-373-5646. An eighteenth-century building, this was home to the city's first silversmith and now is a center for creative arts and offers the work of local craftsmen, several of whom are quite good. You can get a brochure here and at the Visitor Center giving a brief description.

Belmont, 224 Washington Street, Falmouth. The grounds are open daily. The house is open daily, 9–5. Admission: $2; students, 50¢. Phone: 703-373-3634.

Belmont is an eighteenth-century farmhouse that was enlarged to twenty-two rooms in 1843. It was bought by the American artist Gari Melchers in 1917. Well known for his portraits as well as his later, Impressionist-influenced work, he is perhaps best remembered today for his murals in the Library of Congress.

The house is furnished with pictures, antiques, porcelains and so forth collected by the Melchers, and three galleries in the artist's nearby stone studio display his work.

There is an excellent antique shop, the **Virginians Antiques** (913 Charles Street. By appointment only. Phone: 703-373-8896), with very good examples of eighteenth- and nineteenth-century furniture.

I would urge you to walk and explore in Fredericksburg in order to enjoy its architecture and pleasant ambience that ranges from the eighteenth century through the Victorian period. This is a charming town and you should give yourself the time and opportunity to enjoy it. In particular, visit the 1100–1300 blocks of Charles Street and the 100–600 blocks of Lower Caroline Street, which offer some of the finest residential architecture in the city, and the 400 block of Hanover Street, with its antebellum brick townhouses and where, at 404, Abraham Lincoln and Clara Barton dined together.

The Civil War Battlefields

The four battles fought within a seventeen-mile radius of Fredericksburg from 1862–1864 make this the most heavily fought-over ground in the Civil War. More than 100,000 men were casualties here, 70,000 from the North, 35,000 from the South. And here are found some of the most moving episodes of the entire war. In many ways, these campaigns can serve as a microcosm of the war.

As mentioned earlier, this territory was so important because Fredericksburg was halfway between Richmond and Washington and controlled the main connecting routes; it was therefore believed that the Union had to control this city before it could

launch an attack against Richmond. (The cry "On to Richmond!" preoccupied the North and caused it, some historians
feel, to expend too much energy in this area. It was the Army
of the Potomac versus the Army of Northern Virginia that
caught—and kept—the public's attention.)

A BRIEF INTRODUCTION

The Battle of Fredericksburg (December 11–15, 1862) The
Union army of about 106,000 men under the command of Am-
brose E. Burnside was soundly defeated by Robert E. Lee and
his army of approximately 75,000.

Burnside, one of a series of incompetent generals to command
the Army of the Potomac, planned badly from the beginning.
Said one of his staff on hearing his plans, "If you make the
attack as contemplated, it will be the greatest slaughter of the
war." He did and it was.

The bloodiest fighting was at Lee's strong point on Marye's
Heights, just west of the city. So impregnable was Lee's situation that one of his commanders commented that "not even a
chicken could live" to cross the fields before the Heights. Nothing deterred, wave after wave of Union troops were sent to
storm the position and to make the fruitless sacrifice. To give
you an idea of the slaughter, in one hour two Union divisions
received 3,200 casualties. Wrote one Union man, "It was a great
slaughter . . . they might as well have tried to take Hell." It cost
the Union 12,700 men, killed and wounded—while the Confederates lost 5,200—before Burnside reeled away from this scene of
devastation that solved nothing. Said Lee: "I wish these people
would go away and let us alone."

The Battle of Chancellorsville (May 1–4, 1863) Another
major victory for Lee, this time against the too optimistically
nicknamed "Fighting Joe" Hooker, who announced on his appointment to the top command: "May God have mercy on General Lee, for I will have none." He also made detailed plans for
his arrival in Richmond, about which Lincoln was heard to
remark that "the hen is the wisest of all the animal creation
because she never cackles until the egg is laid."

Chancellorsville had several results. It was during this battle,
Lee's best-fought, that he lost his brilliant lieutenant, "Stone-

wall" Jackson, whose own men mistakenly fired on him. And because of the scope of Lee's victory, it removed any lingering doubts from the minds of the powers in Richmond of allowing Lee to carry the campaign to the north. It thus served as a prelude to the Battle of Gettysburg, the turning point of the war.

It was an extremely bloody event. The Federals had 17,287 men killed, wounded or missing in action, while the Confederates had estimated casualties of 12,821. In fact, so great were the casualties that the wounded were still being returned to field hospitals more than a week after the battle. Wrote Walt Whitman, who was there, "Then the camps of the wounded—O heavens, what scene is this?—is this indeed *humanity*—these butcher's shambles? There are several of them. There they lie, in the largest, in an open space in the woods, from 200 to 300 poor fellows—the groans and screams—the odor of blood, mixed with the fresh scent of the night, the grass the trees—that slaughter house! . . . One man is shot by a shell, both in the arm and the leg—both are amputated—there lie the rejected members. Some have their legs blown off—some bullets through the breast—some indescribably horrid wounds in the face or head, all mutilated, sickening, torn, gouged out—some in the abdomen—some mere boys—many rebels, badly hurt . . . Such is the camp of the wounded. . . ."

The Battle of the Wilderness (May 5–6, 1864) Here, for the first time, Lee and Grant met as opposing heads of their armies. Again it was a nightmare scene, for the Wilderness was a gloomy, almost jungle-like tangle of pine and underbrush, with visibility limited to extremely short distances. In this hellish environment Grant and Lee fought to a draw, the bullets of their soldiers setting the wood afire and either burning to death or suffocating many of the wounded.

This time, though, it was not a victory for Lee but rather a draw. And this time Grant, instead of retreating, as had the earlier generals, headed south. His men, when they realized they would not be turning back, cheered their new, more audacious commander. It was a bad sign for the South.

The Battle of Spotsylvania Court House (May 8–21, 1864)
The most famous—or infamous—part of this battle occurred on

May 12, one of the bloodiest days of the war, and is known as the fight for the Bloody Angle, during which some of the most savage fighting in Army history took place. It was, wrote one Union man, "a boiling, bubbling and hissing cauldron of death." On this day the Union suffered 6,800 casualties, the South 5,000. So many bullets were fired that they literally severed an oak tree 63 inches in girth. (The stump is now in the Museum of American History in Washington, D.C.) So many dead soldiers were there that the bodies were piled in heaps.

And when it was all over, what had been achieved? The tenor of the war had finally changed. The North was, at last, on the way to Richmond, and the unrelenting and massive pounding of the South by Grant had begun. "It is," said Lincoln, "the dogged pertinacity of Grant that wins."

VISITING THE BATTLEFIELDS

The men dropped here and there like bundles. The captain of the youth's company had been killed in an early part of the action. His body lay stretched out in the position of a tired man resting, but upon his face there was an astonished and sorrowful look, as if he thought some friend had done him an ill turn. The babbling man was grazed by a shot that made the blood stream down his face. He clapped both hands to his head. "Oh!" he said, and ran. Another grunted suddenly as if he had been struck by a club in the stomach. He sat down and gazed ruefully. In his eyes there was mute, indefinite reproach. Farther up the line a man, standing behind a tree, had had his knee joint splintered by a ball. Immediately he dropped his rifle and gripped the tree with both arms. And there he remained, clinging desperately and crying for assistance that he might withdraw his hold upon the tree.

———*The Red Badge of Courage*

The casualties of the Civil War were so monumental that the individual disappears in the horror of the overall carnage. A bundle. Many of these deaths were useless, often due to the ineptitude of the commanding officers. So, for me, the contrast from what I have read of the scenes of horror and butchery and, today, the trenches filled with graceful blue and yellow wildflowers bending in the breeze is, at first, almost obscene. In truth, a day visiting these sites is both a fascinating and beautiful experience, a strange, at times macabre, combination of the horrors of some of the bloodiest battles we've ever fought in a silent and sylvan setting that in itself now serves as a lovely memorial.

Some general pointers. You will need a full day to tour the area leisurely. You can take a picnic; there are plenty of facilities, and this would be the most practical way to use your time. On the other hand, if you wish to have a more formal lunch, you could plan to visit the **Olde Mudd Tavern** (see page 73). (If you only have a few hours to spend, I'd suggest Fredericksburg and Chancellorsville as the most interesting. And both also have visitors' centers with excellent slide programs and exhibits.) I would also consider seeing **Chatham Manor** and the **Stonewall Jackson Memorial Shrine**, about both of which I'll tell you a little.

Chatham is an eighteenth-century Georgian brick mansion of serene beauty that now serves as the headquarters of the Fredericksburg and Spotsylvania National Military Park. It lies just across the Rappahannock from Fredericksburg and offers a wonderful view of this still nineteenth-century-looking town. A great many famous people have visited here, including Washington, Lafayette and Lee. (Mrs. Lee's grandfather, William Fitzhugh, built the house.) During the Civil War it became the headquarters for several Federal generals, and the Union soldiers ripped out the paneling to serve as firewood. More honorably, both Clara Barton and Walt Whitman nursed the wounded here. Today the ground floor is used to show the development and history of the estate, but the real interest lies in the gardens and grounds, particularly the richly planted rose beds.

Fifteen miles south of Fredericksburg is the Jackson shrine, a small, lone office building on the former plantation of Mr. and Mrs. Thomas Coleman Chandler, who had shown Jackson several kindnesses in the past and where Jackson chose to go to begin his recovery from the wounds received at Chancellorsville. I find this a particularly moving site. Simple, set deep in the countryside, it has an unpretentious quality perfectly suited to the man it honors. Even the fact that none of the other plantation buildings survive seems right, as if they had given way to his greatness.

Chancellorsville was where Jackson had his most dramatic success on May 2, 1863, when he made a brilliant flank march

The Stonewall Jackson Shrine. "Let us cross over the river and rest under the shade of the trees."

that literally fractured the Union XI Corps. Later, though, coming back to his lines in the darkness, his men mistakenly fired on him and hit him with three bullets, one shattering his left arm near the shoulder. It became necessary to amputate, and recovery went well enough to move him back to the Chandlers' for his further recovery. Here, though, he developed pneumonia, and on May 10, shortly after three on a magnificent spring Sunday afternoon, he spoke those famous words—"Let us cross over the river and rest under the shade of the trees"—and died. The South had lost one of its most brilliant generals. As the Richmond *Examiner* had earlier pointed out, "His extraordinary ability and the astonishing prestige which attends him everywhere, is a power of the republic, and the loss . . . would be ill replaced by the accession of 50,000 troops to our present force." It was an ill omen for the future success of the Confederacy.

MIDDLEBURG, LEESBURG AND THE SURROUNDING COUNTRYSIDE

In a state famous for its natural beauty, this area must rank as one of the most breathtaking. You are in hunt country, and to me there is nothing more splendid to the eye than an elegant horse farm, its brown or white or stone fences languidly stretching out over a rolling, rich green countryside, shaping the landscape in graceful arc patterns.

Fox-hunting and steeplechasing were first established in America in Virginia, both being introduced by George Washington's mentor, Lord Fairfax, in the mid-eighteenth century. Today there are more than twenty hunt clubs throughout the hunt country, making it the center for hunting in this country. Steeplechasing in Washington's time was a horse race through the countryside, over such natural obstacles as streams, hedges and fences. It usually ended at a steeple, as this was generally the tallest object on the landscape and therefore the easiest to follow. Today it is a race over a course with artificial obstacles over which the horse must jump.

Plan to spend a long weekend here, drinking in the luminous scenery, walking about the towns and generally enjoying as relaxed and civilized a setting as can be found.

It is almost too perfect in its appeal, this mill, as if it were a stage set. But it's real, all right, and it's placed in one of the most delightful settings imaginable.

Middleburg

Only about forty miles west of Washington, Middleburg, the lovely, sophisticated unofficial capital of the hunt country, primarily consists of one main street bordered by chic shops, a first-rate inn and an excellent bed & breakfast. Because of the last two, I would suggest that you stay here. Even though the town is small—it would take you a minute or two to drive through, depending on whether you hit a red light—the weekend I suggest is barely enough to explore it and the surrounding area.

I would stay at the **Red Fox** (see page 70), one of the best-known inns in Virginia, dead center in the town at 2 East Washington Street. It has been in operation since 1728. George Washington and Thomas Jefferson both supped here, and during the Civil War John Mosby is said to have planned many of the guerrilla raids here that were so devastating to Federal supply routes. (A typical story about Mosby, one of the South's most colorful generals, has it that he once captured a Union general, asleep in his bed at the time, after pulling down the covers and waking him with a slap on the backside.)

The inn today is divided into four sections. The Red Fox Inn and Tavern has six bedrooms; five have canopied beds, fireplaces, and period wallpapers. The principal dining room is here, on the first floor—there's another upstairs—and is a fine-looking country restaurant with low, beamed ceilings, stone walls and a fireplace. As for the food, it's of good quality and well prepared, while the wine list offers some excellent selections from the immediate area. It is the best restaurant in town.

Behind the Red Fox is a large, separate building known as Mosby's Tavern. The bar is the local hangout, and here you will catch all the local news and gossip. The restaurant offers a light menu—excellent charcoal-broiled hamburgers, for example—and its informality is infectious.

The third section is the Stray Fox Inn, with eight additional guest rooms furnished with period fabrics and wallpapers and housing four-poster beds and, in some cases, fireplaces, and the fourth, McConnell House, has five rooms, all with fireplaces.

All inn "sections" offer pleasant extra amenities—terrycloth bathrobes, fresh flowers, cookies, chocolates and fruit at bedside

in the evening, the Washington *Post* at your door in the morning. The last time I was there, on a radiant October weekend,
wood smoke filled the air and I could hear, just outside my room,
water splashing into a basin from a pretty lion's-head fountain.
It is a delightful place both for food and for a relaxed stay.

One serious drawback; because there are so few rooms, reservations can be a problem and you should reserve well in advance. But if you can't get a reservation, I would strongly
recommend the **Luck House** (see page 70), just down the street
at 205 East Washington, and a satisfying cross between an inn
and a bed & breakfast. The innkeeper, a pleasant woman named
Stephanie Hartman, offers several large rooms with fireplaces
and canopy beds as well as a suite on the top floor. Best of all,
each bedroom has a private bath.

Exploring this well-restored colonial town can make for a
very pleasant afternoon—and an expensive one, for there is a
shop suited to nearly every taste; and inevitably, you will be
sorely tempted. In fact, were I to have a complaint about Middleburg, it would be that it teeters on the edge of being touristy
and is only just maintaining its balancing act. And you should
take a peek through the doors of Emmanuel Episcopal Church
on East Washington to look at the needlepoint kneeling cush-
ions the parishioners have made and placed throughout the
church. Do note the generally pleasing architecture of this village of roughly 650 people.

Two Drives

One of the great joys of this area is driving the many back roads,
both dirt and paved. Whole days can be spent exploring without
exhausting your options. The two drives I am suggesting, then,
are to give you a taste of what the region has to offer. Each
should take about a half day at a leisurely pace. Go in the
morning, then, early, and be back for lunch.

DRIVE I: A VISIT TO A VINEYARD

This drive will take you to two excellent vineyards, Meredyth
and Piedmont. Nearby are Naked Mountain Vineyards and

An old Lutheran church by the roadside; nothing special architecturally, and yet it and the tiny cemetery speak so quietly but movingly of our past.

Oasis Vineyard. It will also give you an idea of the magnificence of the horse farms.

From the Red Fox, go west on Route 50 and then turn left at Route 626, a few blocks beyond the inn. Almost immediately you are in lush Virginia countryside, the little road twisting and turning through trees and fences and fields of beguiling charm. Soon, on your right, serene on its hill, you'll see Waverly, the dignified yellow antebellum mansion with white columns that is headquarters for Piedmont Vineyards. (For tour schedule phone: 703-687-5134.) This vineyard was founded by Mrs. Thomas F. Furness at the age of seventy-five; she is still the only woman to start a winery. Thirty acres are currently under cultivation and produce white wine varieties. (As a rule of thumb, one acre produces about four tons of grapes, or about six hundred gallons of wine, or about three thousand bottles.)

Continue on Route 626 to Route 628, and turn left. Watch for signs for Meredyth Vineyards, and soon you will turn left on a dirt road that will take you past the romantic stone ruins of a house built in the 1770's and up to the vineyards buildings. (For tour schedule phone: 703-687-6277.)

This award-winning vineyard, now consisting of fifty-five acres of vines set on silt-loam hillsides, was founded in 1972 by Archie Smith, Jr. and his wife, Dody. The wine-maker now is their son Archie III; their daughter Susan is the marketing director. (Another son, Robbie, is an architect.) They produce red, white, and rosé varieties. The site, redolent of wood and wine, offers wonderful views of the Bull Run Mountains, and the enjoyable tour, relaxed and informal, takes perhaps thirty minutes.

"We produce more than thirty thousand gallons of wine a year and sell it in about eleven states," says Dody Smith. "This makes us one of the biggest wineries in the state. Wine-making is a real industry in Virginia now. When Archie started the Virginia Wineries Association back in 1977 there were only two of us. Today there are more than two dozen—and growing."

When you are through here, go back the way you came and, when you reach 626, turn left and continue to The Plains. Here you will turn right on Main Street, which is also Route 55. Now let me get the directions for the rest of the drive out of the way. Go about two miles to the first numbered road on the right. Turn right and continue to next intersection. Then take any side roads to east or west to get back on 709. Turn right on 709. When you come to a stop sign, you'll be back in Middleburg.

The purpose of all this is to allow you to see some lovely horse farms with their formal entrances, handsome signs and gateposts and, often, heavy tubs filled with flowers running riot. In fact, I would suggest that you confuse matters even more and get off onto the unmarked dirt roads to enjoy an even better

This is hunt country, a sophisticated, almost lavishly beautiful area filled with intriguingly grand houses.

sense of the countryside, the wonderful houses set back from the roads and proudly dominating their gentle, genteel surroundings. There is, in short, nothing to do on this drive but enjoy yourself.

DRIVE II: A VISIT TO OATLANDS PLANTATION

This drive, though not as consistently beautiful as the other, is in some ways more interesting.

When you leave the inn, again go west on Route 50, this time to Route 611 and turn right here. This will take you to 734 and, once again, turn right. This landscape is, to me, different enough from the earlier drive as to be surprising. First, it's more hilly, but—perhaps because of the placement of the farms and buildings—it also seems older and more settled, the buildings more a part of the setting than lordly surveyors of all they possess. I like it very much.

Eventually you will come back to Route 50. Turn left, and soon you will arrive at the little town (about 100 persons) of Aldie, whose stone bridge worried John Mosby during the Civil War because it would "allow the enemy to cross four abreast." The wonderful old grain mill on your right is one of the last tandem-wheel-powered mills in the country. Right now, area residents are trying to raise funds to restore it. Continue on 50, east, until you come to 15, where you will go north to **Oatlands**. (Open: mid-March–late December, Monday–Saturday, 10–5; Sunday 1–5. Admission: $4; senior citizens and youth, $3; under 7, free. Phone: 703-777-3174.)

There are three distinct elements of Oatlands that are of interest: the façade, the interior and the gardens.

The Façade I feel that this house has one of the most distinquished façades in Virginia. In 1798 George Carter, a descendant of the famous Robert "King" Carter of Corotoman (see page 260) and a member of one of Virginia's most distinguished families, became the owner of 3,500 acres of land in Loudoun and Fairfax counties through a lottery set up by his father to divide the property among his ten children. He began building the house himself in 1804, moved in before 1810, and sometime between 1825 and 1830 added the two stair wings and the Corin-

Oatlands has as lovely gardens as you could wish for, full of what the last owner called "mystery, variety and the unexpected."

thian portico. During this period, too, the original brick, made right here on the estate, was stuccoed and painted the creamy buff color you see today. Although no architectural plans have ever been found for the house, it is known that he based his plans on Sir William Chambers' *Treatise on Civil Architecture* (1759) and that Henry Farnham of New York City carved the flawless Corinthian capitals.

The portico is my favorite part of the house; what a splendid entrance with its exquisitely graceful columns that draw the eye up their seemingly weightless shafts to the explosion at the top of those superlative Corinthian capitals. But the whole "feel" of the building is extremely pleasing to me—even though individual elements, the end bays, for instance, may initially seem clumsy—particularly when seen from the garden side with all its angles and forms and additions clearly exposed.

The Interior The interior is distinguished by two features. The first: When Carter did the exterior work mentioned above, he also improved the interior with elegant Adam-inspired cast plaster that is flawlessly crafted. It shows to particular advantage in the entrance hall. The second: The octagonal drawing room is as pleasing as any room can be with its absolutely just proportions.

The furnishings are from the collection of the last owners,

Mr. and Mrs. William Corcoran Eustis. (His grandfather founded the Corcoran Gallery in Washington. Their daughters gave the plantation house and 261 acres of land to the National Trust in 1965.) So what you see is not a period re-creation but how a family lived here in the first half of the twentieth century. The result is a cross-section of French and American styles that give a pleasant feeling to the house of being lived in, a feeling reinforced by the family photographs and the fresh, fragrant flowers from the garden.

The Gardens I saved the best to the last. By all means plan to spend time in these lovely gardens, as charming as almost any I can think of in the state. Mrs. Eustis wrote that in a garden one should always strive for "mystery, variety and the unexpected." I happen to agree with her, and it is a pleasure to tell you that she achieved all of her goals while at the same time restoring the terraced formal gardens designed by George Carter.

Walk down a seemingly simple path, turn a corner, and bang, you're in a rose garden. The terraces, which unfold before you as you pass, offer an infinite variety of flowering color and texture, brick, stone, marble, wood. Come upon a shady little spot so cunningly planned it seems forgotten. And finally, enter the boxwood gardens, some of which go back to Carter, and see how they make a formal coda that is exactly appropriate. Mrs. Eustis sums up the results perfectly: "It was a thankful task to restore the old beauty, although the thoughts and conceptions were new, they fitted it, and every stone or bench, every box-hedge planted, seemed to fall into its rightful place and become part of the whole."

Leesburg

When I first saw Leesburg, I fell in love with it. Totally without pretension, this town, the county seat, has a wonderful feeling of "rightness" and balance. The buildings, early and late, make a harmonious whole that can only come about naturally. And, because the Union controlled the town during the Civil War, very little damage was sustained. Plan to spend some time walking the streets; it's an impossibility that you wouldn't enjoy it.

Leesburg, thank God, is little changed from the nineteenth century, so it has a settled and natural charm that invites you to walk about and explore its delights in detail.

The first thing to do in Leesburg is head directly for the **Loudoun Museum** (16 West Loudoun Street. Open: Monday–Saturday, 10–5; Sunday, 1–5. Closed: Thanksgiving, December 25, January 1. Phone: 703-777-7427, 0519). This pleasantly restored nineteenth-century building has exhibits and memorabilia of Loudoun County, but more important, it offers an excellent audiovisual presentation, "A Special Look at Loudoun," that will give you good background material on the town and county. Be sure, too, to pick up "A Walk Around Leesburg," a complete, free, walking-tour booklet listing the important and historic buildings—written by a resident who has included anecdotes and details only a native could know. This is available at the **Information Center** at Market Station at the corner of Harrison and Loudoun streets. (This complex was created from an old loading wharf, train depot, dairy barn, feed mill and log house. All have been moved here to form an unusual shopping complex.) Open: Monday–Saturday, 10–5; Sunday, 1–5. Closed: Thanksgiving, December 25, January 1. Phone: 703-777-7427.

With all this information in your pocket and mind, there's no need for me to add more specifics, but I would like to make a general comment or two. King Street, the main street though Leesburg, could serve as an almost pure example of a mid-Atlantic American village of the nineteenth century. It has charm without cuteness, and I fervently hope that it can stay that way. And do be on the lookout for individual buildings like

Even with the front stoop missing, this doorway exudes dignity.

the old red brick Baptist Church (1884) at 7 South Wirt Street with its eccentrically placed Palladian window and rather jaunty air. This town is a treasure trove of fine eighteenth- and nineteenth-century domestic architecture, and I never tire of its delights.

Morven Park One mile north of Leesburg on Route 7 on Old Waterford Road. Open: Weekends from May 1–October 17. From Memorial Day weekend–Labor Day weekend, Tuesday–Saturday, 10–5; Sunday, 1–5. Admission: $3; senior citizens discount; children, $1.50. Phone: 703-777-2414.

This 1,200-acre estate has three sections open to the public: sixteen rooms in the mansion, which has developed from a 1781 farmhouse to its present late-nineteenth-century pillared splendor and includes a Jacobean dining room, Renaissance hall and French drawing room; the Morven Park Carriage Museum, a collection of over a hundred vehicles ranging from coaches to gigs, surreys, carts and sleighs; and the boxwood gardens and the self-interpretive nature trails. It is a very engaging spot, and although the house is not one of the great examples of Virginia architecture, you should consider a visit here.

This old red brick Baptist church has something of a rakish air; it is a building with a sense of humor.

A DRIVE FROM LEESBURG

The primary purpose of this drive is to get you to **Waterford**, an enchanting hamlet of about three hundred people that was originally settled by Pennsylvania Quakers in 1733. The whole drive can be accomplished in an hour or two, but I feel certain you will want to take your time in order to soak it all in.

Waterford, a one-time Quaker village, reminds me of a friendly country dog of indeterminate heritage but splendid character.

Leave Leesburg going west on Route 7, then turn right on Route 9 and go to 622, which you will follow into Waterford. Park your car and walk around this distinctive—even quirky—National Historic Site. The Waterford Mill, built in 1830, is the most obvious landmark, its rosy pink brick and white-paned windows a gentle reminder of a far simpler industrial time. Along the main street, I particularly like an arched entrance-way; look through and you see a flight of stairs disappearing upward, some flowers here and there giving it color and vibrancy and helping to define its space. It's strangely reminiscent of Seville—rather startling in northern Virginia. There are other nice touches almost everywhere you look. The town reminds me of a friendly country dog of indeterminate heritage but splendid character.

When you leave, go back to Route 9, turn right and go to 671, a right from 9. The countryside is pleasing to the eye here, relaxing and gentle with its rolling hills and scenic vistas. The village of Hillsboro makes an interesting contrast to the generally rural environment. Be sure to stop at the old stone Lutheran Church (1835)—it will be on your left—and explore the country graveyard and simple, dignified building. If you go to the end of 671 you will come to Route 340, and if you turn left here you will, in a few minutes, arrive at Harper's Ferry, West Virginia, now a National Historic Park.

NEARBY

Manassas/Bull Run National Battlefield Park In the North this site became known as that of the First and Second Bull Run; in the South, First and Second Manassas. In fact, Bull Run is a creek that runs by the town of Manassas. Today the battlefields are commemorated at this 4,500-acre park that offers exhibits, a slide program explaining the battle in lucid detail, and a scale model of the battlefield as well as marked tours of the battlefields.

Manassas was important because it was a major road and railroad junction which, among other things, controlled communications with the Shenandoah Valley, the breadbasket of Virginia. And Bull Run, a narrow stream with deeply sloping banks, seemed to the Southern commanders an excellent choice for their line of defense.

When the battle opened on Sunday, July 21, 1861, the first major battle of the Civil War, each side was convinced it would achieve immediate and total defeat of the enemy. In fact, confidence was at such a peak on the Union side that parties of men and women rode out from Washington, a mere 26 miles away, bringing picnics and planning to watch the rout. At first it looked as if there might, indeed, be a show, when the Confederate forces fell back to Henry House Hill where Thomas Jonathan Jackson, like some Old Testament prophet, stood his ground and rallied his men. "Look!" someone is said to have cried. "There stands Jackson like a stone wall! Rally behind the Virginians!" Thus are legends born and battles turned. The South began to gain the upper hand; the Union retreat soon became a chaotic disaster, with whole units disintegrating before their officers' eyes and passing, on the way back to Washington, the detritus of picnickers' baskets and shawls and bonnets and top hats. Fortunately for the Union, the Confederates were too exhausted to pursue. The war, both sides now knew, would not be over for some time and would have to be taken very seriously indeed.

The second campaign, August 26–September 1, 1862, was once again a disaster for the North. The immediate result, aside from increasing the fame and seeming invulnerability of Robert E. Lee and "Stonewall" Jackson, was to enable Lee to prepare for his first invasion of the North, the Antietam campaign.

A few statistics and facts from the two battles:

• In the second battle, within 15 minutes, the 5th New York suffered 124 killed and 223 wounded out of 490 present. This was the highest percentage of men killed outright in a single Civil War battle.
• Major Wilmer McLean, a Confederate, evacuated his farm here to take his family farther south to safety. He chose Appomattox, and in his house there Lee surrendered to Grant on April 9, 1865. (See page 145.)
• In the two battles the Union lost 17,170 men, the Confederacy 11,456. In the first campaign there were more killed and wounded in the seven-hour battle (3,553) than at Tarawa in four days (3,178). At Iwo Jima, over 36 days, 20,326 lives were lost.
• In the second campaign, one eyewitness watched two men

carrying a wounded comrade in a blanket. Suddenly a shell exploded near them. The two men dropped their burden and ran off. The "burden" rose from the blanket and quickly overtook them on the way to safety.

• In the first battle, Adelbert Ames of Maine refused to leave the field though wounded and no longer able to even sit upright. For his courage he was awarded the Medal of Honor in 1894—the medal was established during this war—and he lived until 1933, the oldest living graduate of the U.S. Military Academy.

WHERE TO STAY AND EAT

Area Code: 703

WHERE TO STAY

Alexandria

Princely Bed & Breakfast, 819 Prince Street, Alexandria 22314. Phone: 683-2159. Rates: From about $65 for a double with private bath. Includes Continental breakfast. No credit cards.

Virginia has several first-rate bed and breakfast organizations. Alexandria has one of them, Princely Bed & Breakfast, run by E. J. Mansmann. Call him, describe exactly what you want, and chances are he will be able to place you comfortably in any one of his thirty-three historic houses. I think it is the nicest way to stay in Alexandria.

Old Town Holiday Inn, 480 King Street, Alexandria 22314. Phone: 549-6080. Rates: For a single, from about $85; for a double, slightly higher. Credit cards accepted.

The rooms here are comfortable in that anonymous Holiday Inn kind of way. The reason I recommend it, though, is that it's so conveniently located in the heart of Old Town. This would be my second choice.

Fredericksburg

The Kenmore Inn, 1200 Princess Anne Street, Fredericksburg 22401. Phone: 371-7622. Rates: From about $65 for a single; for a double, slightly higher. MasterCard and Visa accepted.

I find this a very pleasant spot to stay in. It also is centrally located and has a good dining room (see page 73). Because it's small—there are only ten rooms—the atmosphere is friendly. In addition, four rooms have working fireplaces, and at night, at least when I have stayed there, there is that most romantic and sad of all sounds, a far-off train whistle.

Middleburg

The Red Fox Inn, P.O. Box 385, Middleburg 22117. Phone: 687-6301. Rates: From about $65 for a double. Credit cards accepted. (See page 57.)

Luck House Inn, P.O. Box 919, Middleburg 22117. Phone: 687-5387. Rates: From about $75. Includes breakfast. No credit cards. (See page 58.)

Little River Inn, P.O. Box 116, Aldie 22001. Phone: 327-6742. Rates: From about $65. Breakfast included. MasterCard and Visa accepted.

A pretty, restored nineteenth-century house with five guest rooms, only a few miles from Middleburg. There also is an adjoining log cabin and another early nineteenth-century outbuilding for overnight accommodations.

Washington

The Inn at Little Washington, P.O. Box 300, Washington 22747. Phone: 675-3800. Rates: From about $115, higher Saturday night. Closed Monday and Tuesday. Breakfast included. Credit cards accepted.

Here it is, folks, the most beautiful inn in Virginia—and the best restaurant, too (see page 75). It's expensive, but beg, borrow or steal to stay in this small country inn with eight guest rooms and two penthouse suites. It's only sixty-seven miles southwest of Washington, D.C., while the Skyline Drive (see page 84) is only minutes away.

Each room in the inn is furnished in the style of a grand Victorian English country house. Cookies, fruit and a bucket of ice greet each guest; in the morning the Washington *Post* is outside your door; marble bathrooms have heated towel racks . . . and on and on, for no detail has been overlooked. Please be sure to notice the two-story staircase ceiling, which is decorated so cunningly with wallpaper cutouts so as to look like stained glass.

As for Washington itself, it's a delightful little hamlet with several attractive shops—in particular the **Rush River Co.** on Gay Street, an artisans' cooperative where you will see unusually handsome furniture by master cabinetmaker Peter Kramer as well as first-rate paintings, porcelains, stoneware, clothing and so forth. The shop is open: Daily, 10–4. Phone: 675-3410. Nearby, in Sperryville, there are some antique shops for pleasant browsing.

Two attractive guest houses are available here if the inn is booked, the **Mayes House** and the **Gay Street Inn.** The Mayes House is available for about $110 for one couple, $145 for two couples. Accommodations at the Gay Street Inn are about $55 for a shared bath, $70 for a private bath. Breakfast is not included at either house, and both are under the same management. Phone: 675-3410.

WHERE TO EAT

Alexandria

One can eat very well in Alexandria, very well indeed. I've listed the four restaurants I like best in no particular order— they're all too different to say one is clearly superior over the others. I also have listed L'Auberge Chez François in nearby Great Falls as one of the four; it's worth the extra effort to eat there. The remaining restaurants are listed in order of preference.

The Wayfarer's Pub, 110 South Pitt Street. Phone: 836-2749. Credit cards accepted.

A large, handsome restaurant filled with antiques and pictures and reached through an unpretentious, almost hidden doorway. The emphasis is on English cooking but there also is an excellent selection of other foods. Their salmon pâté with horseradish is first-rate, as are their deviled crab cakes and steak and oyster pie, to mention a few dishes. One complaint: the coffee is awful. Expensive. Lunch: Tuesday–Saturday, 11:45 –2:00. Dinner: 6–10, to 10:30 Friday and Saturday. Closed Sunday. Reservations suggested, especially on weekends.

219, 219 King Street. Phone: 549-1141. Credit cards accepted.

Creole cooking in a heavily Victorian setting in three formal dining rooms on two floors. The food is accompanied by excellent service and a good wine list, including top-quality Virginia wines. Like fried catfish? It's done to perfection here. So is all

their seafood. And their praline cake and praline sundaes are
not to be sneezed at, either. Downstairs, in the Bayou Room, you
can have good soups, salads, sandwiches, barbecued shrimp,
catfish nuggets and so forth. Good for a quick lunch. Expensive
upstairs, moderate downstairs. The 219 is open, Monday–Saturday, from 11:30–10:30; Sunday brunch, 11–4. Reservations suggested.

East Wind, 809 King Street. Phone: 836-1515. Credit cards accepted.

A Vietnamese restaurant that is memorable. Small, tastefully decorated; the food is delicious. If you've never tried Vietnamese cuisine, put yourself in the hands of the capable
waiters. If you have, discover one of the best Vietnamese restaurants in the East. Expensive. Lunch: Monday–Friday, 11:30–
2:30. Dinner: Open 7 days, 6–10 every night except Friday and
Saturday, from 6–11. Reservations suggested.

L'Auberge Chez François, 332 Springvale Road, Great Falls.
Phone: 759-3800. Credit cards accepted.

One of the best-known and most chic restaurants in Virginia,
this specializes in Alsatian food—a cuisine I like a lot, by the
way—and traditional French food. It's pretty, with a fireplace,
highly polished copperware and so forth, and the service is tops,
with a maître d' constantly on the prowl to make sure everything is just right. But is it worth reserving two weeks in advance for? Not really. It's very good, no doubt about it, but it's
not a great restaurant. At least not when I've been there. Expensive. Dinner: Tuesday–Saturday, 5:00–9:30. Sunday, 2:30–
8:00. Closed Monday. Reserve two weeks in advance.

La Bergerie, 218 North Lee Street. Phone: 683-1007. Credit
cards accepted.

This seems to be the spot long-time Alexandrians favor; it has
that feeling of waiters and customers at least knowing each
other by sight. It's not very attractive, but it's not bad, either,
and it's comfortable. The food is standard French with Basque
overtones and is prepared and served in a highly professional
manner. Overall it's good; it's just not very exciting. Expensive.
Lunch: Monday–Saturday, 11:30–2:30. Dinner: 6:00–10:30. Closed
Sunday. Reservations suggested.

Gadsby's Tavern, 138 North Royal Street. Phone: 548-1288. Credit cards accepted. Moderately expensive. Lunch: Monday–Saturday, 11:30–3:00; Sunday brunch, 11–3. Dinner: Monday–Sunday, 5:30–10:00. Reservations requested. (See page 11.)

Fredericksburg
(In order of preference.)

Kenmore Inn, 1200 Princess Anne Street. Phone: 371-7622. Credit cards accepted.

The small dining room is divided by a handsome arch, and there are two working fireplaces. It is a most attractive setting. The food is good; in fact, it's the best in Fredericksburg, with a comfortably broad selection and a pleasant, moderately priced wine list. Moderate. Lunch: Tuesday–Sunday, 11:30–2:30. Dinner: Tuesday–Sunday, 5:30–9:30. Closed Monday. Reservations suggested on weekends.

Olde Mudd Tavern, U.S. Route 1 and Route 606 at Thornburg, twelve miles south of Fredericksburg, a quarter mile west of I-95. Phone: 582-5250. Credit cards accepted.

Remember Dr. Samuel Mudd? It was he who set John Wilkes Booth's broken leg, and this tavern is on the site of a building owned by his family. Pleasant inside and the food is good. I particularly appreciate the basket of delicious and varied breads that they serve. Moderate. Open: Wednesday–Saturday, 4–9; Sunday, 12–9. Closed Monday and Tuesday. Reservations required for dinner.

La Petite Auberge, 311 William Street. Phone: 371-2727. Credit cards accepted.

The only French restaurant in Fredericksburg, it is decorated to look like a French sidewalk café. A curious conceit to begin with, and one well beyond the powers of the decorator. For instance, the brick walls have an inlaid lattice fence, and lamp-posts serve as sconces. Ah well . . . it certainly gets conversation off to a rapid start, and it has a sort of innocent charm. As for the food, it's pretty good, and the service is warm and friendly. I rather like eating here, and it's very moderately priced. Lunch: Monday–Friday, 11:30–2:30. Dinner: Monday–Saturday, 5:30–10:00. Closed Sunday and the first Monday of the month. Reservations required for dinner.

Ramparts, 816 Caroline Street. Phone: 373-5526. Credit cards accepted.

There's a bullet hole in the brick wall opposite the bar, a legacy of the Civil War. And the pressed tin ceiling is spectacular. Over and above these attractions, the food at lunch isn't bad and it makes a nice and convenient break from sightseeing. The menu is broad, with everything from omelets and hamburgers on up. I'd skip it for dinner, though. Very moderate prices. Lunch: 11:30–5:00. Dinner: Monday–Thursday, 5–10; Friday and Saturday, 5–11; light fare from 10:30–12:00. Reservations unnecessary.

Middleburg—Leesburg
(In order of preference. Also see L'Auberge Chez François, listed under Alexandria, and The Inn at Little Washington, listed under Washington.)

The Red Fox Tavern, 2 East Washington Street, Middleburg. Phone: 687-6301. Credit cards accepted. Moderately expensive. Lunch: Monday–Saturday, 11:30–2:30. Dinner: Monday–Friday, 6–9; Saturday, 5:00–9:30. Sunday, 12–8. Reservations suggested. (See page 57.)

Mosby's Tavern, Marshall Street, Middleburg. Phone: 687-5282. Credit cards accepted. Moderate. Lunch: Monday–Friday, 11:30–3:30; Saturday and Sunday, 11–3. Dinner: 5–11. Reservations unnecessary. (See page 57.)

Green Tree Restaurant, 15 South King Street, Leesburg. Phone: 777-7246. Credit cards accepted.

This restaurant serves authentic colonial recipes which are changed with the seasons. I have found that the quality ranges from good to only fair, for unfathomable reasons, so I'd say it's worth a try and hope you hit on a good day. Moderately expensive. Lunch: 11:30–3:00. Dinner: 5:00–9:30. Reservations suggested for dinner.

The Laurel Brigade Inn, 20 West Market Street, Leesburg. Phone: 777-1010. No credit cards.

Housed in one of the most handsome buildings in Leesburg, it has a reputation for serving quite good food, but I'm sorry to report that the times I've eaten there I've found the food to be mediocre, with overcooked vegetables and lackluster entrées. I list it here only because it is so well known. Moderate. Lunch: Tuesday–Saturday, 12–2. Dinner: Tuesday–Saturday, 5–8. Sunday, 12–7, brunch to 2. Closed Monday and January–mid-February.

Washington

The Inn at Little Washington, Washington. Phone: 675-3800. Credit cards accepted.

The best inn in Virginia (see page 70) also offers the best restaurant. If you're staying here, hope that at breakfast they will have their superb panbroiled local trout along with the freshly squeezed juices and delicious rolls.

The owners are Patrick O'Connell and Reinhardt Lynch. Mr. O'Connell is the brilliant chef. (Interestingly enough, both worked at L'Auberge Chez François. See page 72.) Local produce is used extensively and all ingredients are of the highest quality. The menu notes that the food pays homage "to the lawmakers of Classical French Cuisine," and indeed it does, but innovation is also a part of Mr. O'Connell's style; shad roe accompanied by grapefruit sections or bananas, for instance. (Both were delicious.) This is an innovative American restaurant with roots deeply entrenched in the French countryside. But who cares. It's enough that the food is superb.

In summer there is a terrace with a reflecting pool where you can enjoy a cocktail before your dinner. Expensive. Dinner: Wednesday–Friday, 6:00–9:30; Saturday, 5:30–10:30; Sunday, 4:00–9:30. Closed: Monday and Tuesday. Reservations must be made three weeks in advance for Saturday and Sunday, two for Friday. Other evenings, reservations are suggested.

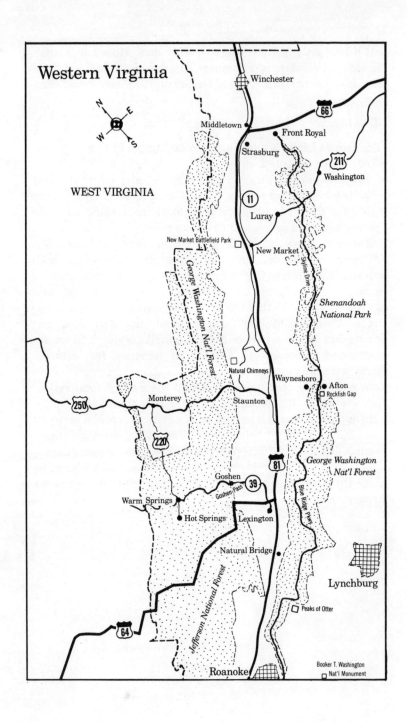

WESTERN VIRGINIA

*The Skyline Drive,
the Blue Ridge Parkway,
the Shenandoah Valley
and the Highlands*

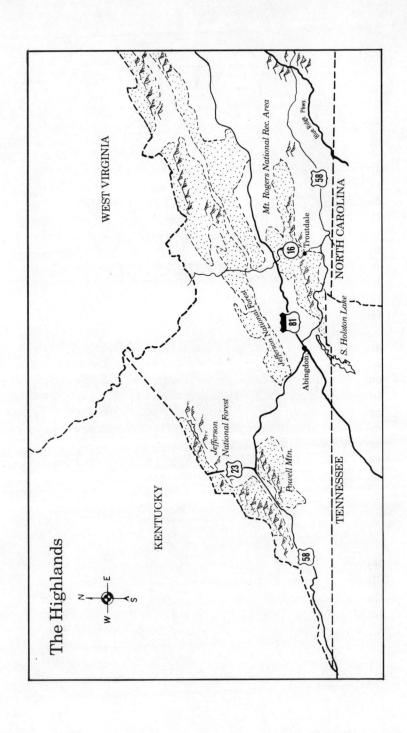

The Highlands

N
W E
S

KENTUCKY

WEST VIRGINIA

Jefferson National Forest

58

23

Powell Mtn.

Jefferson National Forest

Abingdon

81

16

Troutdale

Mt. Rogers National Rec. Area

Blue Ridge Pkwy.

58

S. Holston Lake

TENNESSEE

NORTH CAROLINA

PROBABLY the least visited area of Virginia, except for the Blue Ridge Parkway and the Drive, yet here is found the greatest natural beauty in the state. The famous drives along the Skyline and Blue Ridge defy description and are so stunning that the latter has become one of the most visited of our National Parks. As for the Valley, serenely lovely and an overflowing cornucopia of luscious farm produce, it is different from the rest of the state both in its landscape and in the people who live here. Whereas the predominant settlers of the eastern part of the state were English, the stock here is more Scotch-Irish and German.

You will find hospitality in abundance. Natural beauty is endless. Outdoor activities—hiking, boating, camping, fishing, hunting—are here in enough variety to satisfy the most avid outdoorsman. Here, too, is found the greatest and most sophisticated resort in the state (The Homestead) and one of the two or three prettiest towns (Lexington). There's something for almost every taste in surroundings so generally unspoiled that it's easy to forget this is the end of the twentieth century. I love to visit here; it's rejuvenating for the body, exquisitely relaxing for the mind, balm for the soul.

MIDDLETOWN

Belle Grove (1794) Belle Grove is only one mile south of Middletown on Route 11, and what a lovely setting it graces. From the road you look down to it in its valley, assured and elegant in its quietly rural setting, a miraculously preserved remnant of the eighteenth century and one of the finest houses in this part of the state. Then, as you approach it, you see more clearly its four tall chimneys (they give the whole a certain grandeur) and that the house is made of stone—local limestone, in fact.

The two Tuscan porticoes, front and back, are prominent but also exquisitely refined.

This last feature is one that Thomas Jefferson much admired, and it is known that he did, in fact, advise on the plans and design of the house. Belle Grove was built by Isaac Hite who married Eleanor Conway Madison, sister of James Madison, in 1783. James Madison wrote Jefferson in 1794 asking that the bearer of the letter, a Mr. Bond who was building the house, be given "the favor of your advice on the plan of the house." Madison continues, "Mr. Hite particularly wishes it in what relates to the (Bow?) room and the portico . . . In general, any hints which may occur to you for improving the place will be thankfully accepted."

The interior is relatively modest but has fine woodwork and a wonderful sense of openness and welcome. I particularly like the parlor, whose pilasters have capitals decorated with rams' heads at the ends of the finely modeled swags, and the doorways, with their Jeffersonian fanlights of balanced delicacy.

Belle Grove suffered a great deal of damage during the Civil War. The walls and ceiling of the north portico still have the names of Union soldiers scratched into them, and family papers were stolen—including letters from Jefferson and Washington —that would be priceless today. The house served as General Philip Sheridan's headquarters during the Battle of Cedar Creek (October 19, 1864). Illustrations for the newspapers and magazines of the time depicting the battle show Union and Confederate forces fighting almost at the steps of the house. (It was this battle that, once and for all, destroyed the power of the South in the Valley of Virginia, often called the granary of the Confederacy.)

Today the mansion is part of a working farm owned by the National Trust but run by a local community group; the house often serves for community affairs—a quilt exhibition, for instance, and other programs that emphasize local crafts. It gives a used, lived-in feeling that is most appealing. But whether you see the interior or not, don't miss walking around the exterior of the house and note what, in the eighteenth century, could be done with a farmhouse.

Belle Grove is open from April–October, Monday–Saturday, 10–4; Sunday, 1–5. Admission: $2.50; senior citizens, $2; students, $1.25; under 6, free. Phone: 703-869-2028.

The main section of Belle Grove was influenced by Thomas Jefferson. It is a wonderful, light-filled and refined house. Around it swirled the Battle of Cedar Creek in 1864.

WINCHESTER

"The Apple Capital of the World," that's Winchester's proud boast, and the Shenandoah Apple Blossom Festival takes place here each spring. Essentially, though, this town of slightly more than 20,000 people is pleasant to visit because of its historical associations and interesting older buildings; but to me the most astounding single fact about Winchester is that it changed hands seventy-two times during the Civil War. Its importance was its strategic location at the intersection of east-west and north-south routes. That meant possession of the town meant control both of approaches to Washington from the west and Confederate supply lines down through the Shenandoah Valley.

Winchester lends itself very nicely to a walking tour and, fortunately, there is an excellent little booklet, "A Walking Tour of Historic Winchester," that is widely available in the town. I would suggest that you start at Washington's Office Museum and that you buy a combination ticket there that costs $4.50 and also includes Jackson's Headquarters and Abram's Delight.

Washington's Office Museum   This was Washington's headquarters in 1755 and 1756 when he was in charge of defending
Virginia's frontier. The tiny building now houses relics from the
French and Indian, Revolutionary and Civil wars, some of
which are rather interesting. Worth a short visit. The office is
on the corner of Braddock and Cork streets. Open: April–October, daily, 10–5. Admission: Combination (see above) or $1; chil-
dren under 13, 50¢. Phone: 703-662-4412.

Stonewall Jackson's Headquarters   You can walk here
from Washington's headquarters, and I would strongly advise
that you do so. On the way, note **Sheridan's Headquarters**
(the southwest corner of Braddock and Piccadilly streets), a
Greek Revival building with a large red apple in front of it.
From here Sheridan made his famous ride that turned the tide
at Cedar Grove and gained the Union an overwhelming victory.
And you can't miss the **Handley Library** (northwest corner of
Braddock and Piccadilly Streets), a wonderful Beaux Arts building finished in 1913; it has every extravagance (almost) that you
can think of—allegorical figures, a dome, pillars everywhere.
It's great fun.

Jackson's Headquarters, a handsome Gothic Revival house
(1854), is at 415 North Braddock Street, and it was here that he
stayed from November 1861–March of 1862. The building contains artifacts of Jackson and other Confederates. If you're at
all interested in Jackson, a trip here is worth your while.

The headquarters is open from April–October; daily, 10–5.
Admission: Combination ticket (see above) or $2; children under
12, $1. Phone: 703-667-3242.

Abram's Delight Museum (1754)   This small but well-proportioned stone house is the oldest in Winchester. It is the most
interesting to visit because it is both charming and has some
good antiques given by local people, in particular three first-
rate folk art portraits by Charles Peale Polk of a Judge Robert
White, his wife, Arabella, and probably his daughter, all natives
of Winchester. The daughter is particularly charming, with
pearls in her hair and sky-blue eyes that are matched by her
dress.

Polk was a member of the famous Peale family of painters
and was trained by his uncle, Charles Willson Peale. Among

other portraits of his is one of Mrs. Isaac Hite, mistress of Belle Grove, and her son, James Madison Hite, Jr., that now belongs to the Maryland Historical Society. For Mr. Hite, too, he painted a wonderful portrait of Thomas Jefferson based on his visit to Monticello in 1799 and which is now in a private collection. I like his pictures; he has the ability to draw out his sitters' inner characters. These three portraits are no exception and, in themselves alone, reward a visit here.

The name of the house, by the way, supposedly came about when Abraham Hollingsworth, father of the builder, first saw the site early in the eighteenth century and pronounced it a delight to behold.

The house is located at 1340 South Pleasant Valley Road. You'll need to drive there. Open: April–October, daily, 10–5. Admission: Combination ticket (see above) or $2; children under 12, $1. Phone: 703-662-6519.

NEARBY

Strasburg has two attractions. The first is the **Strasburg Inn**. The restoration is Victorian, but only mediocre Victorian, and I find the rooms on the dreary side, but many people enjoy it and the management is extremely pleasant.

The other attraction is the **Strasburg Antiques Emporium**, a vast barn of a place filled to the rafters with mostly second-rate stuff that can be easily missed.

Front Royal and the Skyline Caverns   Front Royal, right at the entrance to the Shenandoah National Park and the Skyline Drive, can be bypassed; it is a tourist town of the most boring sort, full of fleabag motels and fast-food restaurants. But there are two things of interest here, the Skyline Caverns and the National Zoo's Conservation and Research Center.

Skyline Caverns   From here south, the state is riddled with caverns, the most famous of which are in Luray (see page 88). Perversely enough, I like these in Front Royal the best of the caverns I've seen. They were discovered fairly recently, in 1937, by a man named Walter Amos after extensive probes of the earth's surface. In fact, these are the only caverns to have been discovered in this way.

The atmosphere is slightly less hokey than at the other caverns, and I had a very good guide who gave a witty and intelligent commentary on what we were seeing. There's a pretty falls, and the temperature year-round is a cool 54°, as it is in all the caverns. I liked best the stunning mineral formations called anthodites, which are found nowhere else in the world. In some places they look like sea anemones; in others, like a burst of tiny white fireworks. Fragile and very beautiful, they alone make a visit satisfying.

The caverns are open Saturdays before Memorial Day–Labor Day, 8:30–6:30; Tuesday after Labor Day to the last weekend in October, and Friday before Easter to Friday before Memorial Day, 9:00–5:30; Monday following the last weekend in October to Thursday before Easter, 9:00–4:30. Admission: $6; senior citizens, $5; children 7–13, $3; under 8, free. Phone: 703-635-4545.

The Conservation and Research Center of the National Zoo This cannot be visited by the public, but I mention it because the work the Center does is both important and fascinating. The purpose is to help exotic but endangered species to reproduce. Here are found tree kangaroos and golden lion tamarins (monkeys), rare kingfishers and the clouded leopard, the last true wild horses and the sable antelope. The Center is a refuge for 700 mammals representing 20 species, and 500 birds representing 37 species. Operating for ten years now on their 3,150-acre "spread," which is protected by miles of fencing and shielded and electrified pens, the Center's mission is to reintroduce its species into their former habitats. It is a noble program, and it's nice to think about as you pass through the touristy tawdriness of central Front Royal.

SHENANDOAH NATIONAL PARK AND THE SKYLINE DRIVE

(For complete information and pamphlets write: Superintendent, Shenandoah National Park, Rt. 4, Box 292, Luray, Va. 22835. Phone: 703-999-2266. Admission: $2.)

This, with the Blue Ridge Parkway (see page 91), is one of the most beautiful drives in the country. Mile after mile of forest, spectacular views out over the glorious Shenandoah Valley, the unparalleled peace of the forest . . . that is only a hint of what you can expect. But it wasn't always that way.

The park, all 302 square miles of it, encompasses the ridge and slopes of the Blue Ridge Mountains. These are the eastern ramparts of the Appalachian mountain system and run between Pennsylvania and Georgia. To the west of the park is the Shenandoah Valley, to the east the gently rolling Piedmont section of Virginia. The oldest outcropping of rock, granites and gneisses go back more than one billion years. Man's history in the area is a mere whisper of this at nine thousand years.

The first settlers appeared in the wonderfully fertile Shenandoah Valley in the eighteenth century. By 1840 the Valley was settled, and new arrivals and even some Valley people began to move into the mountains. It was a hard life, for the mountain soil is thin and farming is risky at best. But still they came until, at the turn of the twentieth century, the population reached its peak.

But the soil couldn't sustain the people who were here. The game animals were disappearing, and the once endless forests were, after all, only too finite. People began to leave, and by the 1920's, the population had fallen by half. In 1926, Congress authorized the creation of the present park, and the Commonwealth of Virginia purchased almost 280 square miles of land from the remaining residents, which it then donated to the federal government. The park was dedicated in 1936 by President Franklin Delano Roosevelt, and the Skyline Drive was completed in 1939.

Today the park is eighty miles long and from two to thirteen miles wide. Within its boundaries are 95 miles of the 2,000-mile Appalachian Trail, which stretches from Maine to Georgia. All told, there are about 500 miles of trails in the park. The Drive, which runs the full length of the park, is 105 miles, has more than seventy (!) overlooks and ends at the Blue Ridge Parkway. So successful has been the program to return the park to its natural state, that 95 percent of it now is wooded, with about 100 species of different trees scattered here and there—including hickory, beech, oak, birch, maple and tulip poplar. Two hundred species of birds are here, some as permanent dwellers (ruffed grouse, barred owl and woodpeckers, among others); some, like warblers, thrushes and vireos, as migrants or sum-

mer residents. Animals abound, and it is not at all rare to see
white-tailed deer, woodchuck and the ubiquitous gray squirrel.
There, too, are black bear and gray fox and the magnificent
bobcat. You may even be lucky enough to see a special salaman-
der that is found nowhere else in the world.

And the flowers . . . seventeen kinds of wild orchid alone, not
to mention—such wonderful names—ladyslipper and mustard
and trillium and mountain laurel, Turk's cap lily and gentian
and columbine and touch-me-not and ladies' tresses and I could
go on all day. April and May is the best time to see the wildflowers, October 10 to about October 25 to see the fall coloring.

There are two visitor centers here, the Dickey Ridge Visitor
Center, open daily from about April–November and located at
4.6 miles from the northern entrance to the drive, and the Byrd
Visitor Center at Big Meadows, open daily from early March–
December at Milepost 51. (Concrete milepost markers, both here
and on the Blue Ridge Parkway, go from the northern entrances
—Milepost 1—on to the terminus.) I would urge you to stop at
both of them. The former has excellent exhibits and programs,
and a free movie tells you what you can see and do in the park.
The latter has a museum with interesting exhibits on the people

*"My apple trees will never get across / And eat the cones under his pines,
I tell him / He only says, 'Good fences make good neighbors.'" Robert
Frost, "Mending Wall."*

and natural history of the park, and the movie here, on the establishment of the park, is absorbing.

There also are two lodges at which you can stay, but be sure to reserve well in advance.

Skyland Lodge   At 3,680 feet above sea level, this is located at the highest point on the Drive and is 41.7 miles from the northern entrance. Accommodations are simple but comfortable, and the views from many of the rooms are mind-boggling; there you are, looking out for miles over the Shenandoah Valley, cloud shadows like black puppies chasing each other across the valley floor.

The resort was built in the 1890's by a naturalist, George Freeman Pollack, who also was a leader in establishing the park. There are several trails nearby. One, Limberlost Trail (1.2 miles round-trip), I particularly like because it takes you through several aspects of the park, including remnants of former settlements (old, gnarled apple trees mark an abandoned orchard) and, best of all, a grove of hemlocks, some of which are three hundred years old and which also has white oak that are four hundred years old. This is one of the only places in the park that has always been left undisturbed, and these particular trees came under the protection of Mr. Pollack. An engrossing walk.

Big Meadows Lodge   This lodge, at Milepost 51, is set in one of the more unique areas of the park, for the meadows area is 150 acres and is controlled by burning and mowing the area to prevent trees from growing here. How the site originally was cleared is not known, but it is thought the Indians burned it over regularly because that allowed for thicker growth of the berry bushes so loved by deer and elk. It's maintained that way today because some wildlife is dependent on the open space— white-tailed deer, for instance, goldfinches and groundhogs. It is very pleasing.

Two fine-looking waterfalls are near here: Lewis and Dark Hollow Falls. In spring, I am especially fond of the following walk. Take the "Story of the Forest" nature trail from the northeast end of the parking lot at the Byrd Visitor Center to the swamp, about half a mile. Go past the horse trail but take the next trail on your right. You are in a paradise of wildflowers, one of the prettiest parts of the park.

The entire park is full of these wonderful surprises. Days can be spent here enjoying its splendors. So many people simply drive down the Skyline and let it go at that. Don't you do that. Instead, spend at least one day in the park. You'll be grateful you did.

Off the Drive

Luray The reason people come to Luray, and thousands do each year, is to visit the caverns, the most popular in the East. Since their discovery in 1898, a whole industry has grown up around them to further entertain the tourists. There is, for instance, the Historic Car and Carriage Caravan, a transportation museum one of whose highlights is Rudolph Valentino's 1925 Rolls-Royce. And nearby is the Luray Singing Tower, with a 47-bell carillon that is played each Tuesday, Thursday, Saturday and Sunday from early spring through late fall. (Phone: 703-743-5062.)

Still, it's the caverns that are—and rightly so—the real attraction, and they are indeed worth a visit. One room, for instance, is 300 feet wide, 500 feet long and 140 feet high. Stalactites and stalagmites are of a size and in such abundance as to be truly impressive. The rock formations range from delicate lacy patterns to immense columns. It is fascinating. But, as unfortunately can happen at a popular spot, the tours are perfunctory, the information and anecdotes repeated almost by rote. And sometimes the truly hokey makes a cameo but rich appearance. Here, two things get my vote: the first is the petrified fried egg. Don't ask me to explain, just look for it. The second is "The Great Stalacpipe Organ," which, to quote from a brochure, "provides music of concert quality from solid rock by striking stalactites with rubber-tipped hammers." And, for me, the *pièce de résistance*: "This is the world's largest musical instrument, covering 64 acres." Last time I was there it played (what else?) "O Shenandoah." I would love to have met the man who thought this one up.

The caverns are open: Daily, March 15–June 14, 9–6; June 15–Labor Day, 9–7; day after Labor Day–November 14, 9–6; November 15–March 14, 9–4, Saturday and Sunday, 9–5. The Car and Carriage Caravan is open: 10–½ hour after last cavern tour.

Admission: $8; children 7–13, $4; under 7, free; senior citizens, $7. Fee includes the Caravan. Phone: 703-743-6551.

New Market The points of interest are the **New Market Battlefield Park** and the **Hall of Valor** museum. The latter offers the finest presentation on the Civil War in Virginia.

The Park now consists of about 260 acres and includes overlooks 200 feet above the Shenandoah River that offer sweeping views of the Valley. Both park and museum are operated by Virginia Military Institute (see page 103), and it was the VMI cadets who covered themselves in glory here on May 15, 1864.

The Confederate troops were commanded by Major General John C. Breckinridge, a former vice president of the United States under James Buchanan and, at thirty-five, the youngest man in our history to hold that position. He also was an able commander; so impressed was one Union officer by the way Breckinridge led his forces that day, that he became a Confederate sympathizer on the spot and resigned his federal commission as soon as he could.

The Union general was Franz Sigel, a German immigrant often found at the head of German-American troops, the reason for the slogan current at the time of "I fights mit Sigel," I suppose.

Breckinridge was much the better general, and although heavily outnumbered, would carry the day. But the drama came from a group of 247 VMI cadets, some as young as fifteen and sixteen. Held in reserve until Breckinridge absolutely had to use them, when they did enter the battle—in the last charge on Sigel's center—they fought brilliantly, captured prisoners and a cannon and helped to ensure the final victory. They lost ten of their fellows that day, including Thomas Garland Jefferson, a kinsman of the late president.

The Hall of Valor consists of three connected buildings, a circular central portion flanked by two wings. As I mentioned, what they have to offer on the Civil War is extraordinarily good.

First of all, there are two films. The first, "New Market—A Field of Honor" (12 minutes), details the cadets' role in the battle. The second, "Stonewall's Valley" (16 minutes), is an account of Jackson's brilliant Shenandoah campaign in 1862. You should see both.

Then there is a special wing that, with great imagination,

presents a concise, graphic and chronological survey of the entire Civil War, while on the lower level special exhibits cover diverse subjects related to the war. Other exhibits are scattered along the corridors. If you have any interest at all in the war and are in the neighborhood, I urge you to make a visit here.

The park and Hall of Valor are open daily, 9–5, except on Christmas. Admission: $3; children 7–13, 75¢; under 7, free. Phone: 703-740-3101.

Staunton Sections of the city are very pretty, and you may wish to use the carefully prepared "Walking Tours" brochure available locally, but the main attraction is to see the house in which Woodrow Wilson was born. (The town is pronounced STAN-ton, by the way.) Still, I would suggest that you take some time to at least see the handsome buildings of Mary Baldwin College (Frederick and New streets) and Trinity Episcopal Church (214 West Beverly Street) with its Tiffany windows, as well as Augusta Stone Church (seven miles north of the town on Route 11), the oldest Presbyterian church in the state (1747) and Chimneys Regional Park (eleven miles north on Route 11, then go west on 646 and 747) with its seven natural rock towers that rise 120 feet above the plains. There's also an imposing mountain drive, on Route 250 W to Monterey, of about 45 miles.

This house witnessed the birth of Woodrow Wilson, last—so far—in the long line of Virginia presidents.

Woodrow Wilson's Birthplace Before you enter the house there is a half-hour film on Wilson's life narrated by E. G. Marshall. The house itself contains some of Wilson's family's possessions, but in all truth, the Wilsons were not here very long, and the associations with the house itself are minimal. There's a pretty garden behind the building, and one of his cars, a very grand Pierce Arrow limousine, is here, too.

The house is open daily, 9–5, summer to 6. Closed: Thanksgiving, Christmas and January 1, and Sundays in December, January, February. Admission: $2.50; senior citizens and groups, $2; children 6–16, $1; under 6, free. Phone: 703-885-0897.

THE BLUE RIDGE PARKWAY

(For complete information and pamphlets, write: Superintendent, 700 Northwestern Plaza, Asheville, N.C. 28801. Phone: 704-258-2850, extension 779 or 760. The Parkway is free.)

I suppose it's inevitable to compare the Skyline Drive and Blue Ridge Parkway. After all, the Blue Ridge picks up immediately at the end of the Skyline and then continues for 469 miles to end in North Carolina at the Great Smoky Mountains National Park. So, which do I prefer? I really can't say. The Skyline Drive is through wilderness. The Blue Ridge, on the other hand, has, for much of its length, adjoining farms planted with hay or corn or tobacco. This landscape is therefore very different. (To leave the farms in place was a decision that the National Park Service officials made; they wanted to preserve what remained of the mountain culture.)

In addition, the Parkway, from its beginning—at Rockfish Gap near Waynesboro—to Roanoke, is quite different from the section between Roanoke and the North Carolina border. The reason is simple enough: The Parkway to Roanoke lies on a ridge with usually parallel spurs. To the east is the Piedmont area, to the west the Roanoke Valley and, beyond, the Alleghenies. South of Roanoke, a plateau extends westward from the Parkway and the terrain is more rolling, while to the east, an escarpment plunges sharply down, with ridges that reach more than a mile into the Piedmont. An interesting note: South of Roanoke also is where the Blue Ridge becomes the water divide;

west of the Ridge, water will find its way to the Gulf of Mexico, east of the Ridge, water will flow to the Atlantic.

The Parkway's inception came about in 1933 when President Roosevelt visited Shenandoah National Park. He was most impressed by the scenery, and when Senator Harry Byrd of Virginia suggested that a scenic mountain route be constructed that would connect Shenandoah and Great Smoky Mountains National Parks and that such a route would also be an appropriate part of the public works program (it was the Depression, remember), Roosevelt agreed that this was, as another member of the Roosevelt family would have put it, a bully idea. (It was Byrd's ancestor William, writing in 1728, who was one of the first to note that these mountains "lookt like Ranges of Blue clouds rising one above another.")

For many, many reasons, though, construction did not begin until 1935, and for many, many other reasons, the last section of the Parkway, a 7.7-mile gap in North Carolina, was scheduled for completion in 1987. (Just locating the road was a major undertaking; the landscape architects and surveyors would go through the woods and ask the local people to tell them where the best views were located. They would work from one side of the Ridge to the other this way, and then make their decisions.)

All the trouble has been handsomely repaid, for this is now one of the most popular parks in the nation—the three hundred *millionth* visitor entered the park in 1981—and for good reason; it is, indeed, so very, very beautiful. My favorite single fact about the Parkway: more varieties of wildflowers can be found here than on the entire European continent. You should also be aware that there are six self-guiding nature trails here in the Virginia segment and that they range from visits to a reconstructed pioneer homestead or Mabry Mill to one of the most diverse forests along the Parkway.

I have three favorite stops along the Parkway which I list below, going north to south. (For an explanation of Mileposts see page 86.)

James River Wayside (63.6 miles) The James, one of the country's most famous and romantic rivers, originates in the Alleghenies, cuts through the Blue Ridge and then flows to the Atlantic Ocean. At this particular spot it is captivatingly tranquil, and there is a self-guiding trail, a wonderful footbridge

Mabry Mill, one of the most famous sights in the Virginia section of the Blue Ridge Parkway.

across the river, and a trail to the Kanawha Canal Lock exhibit. (The lock, now restored, was part of a 200-mile canal system that ran from Richmond across the Blue Ridge to Buchanan. It was completed in 1851, and the original plan was to then go on and connect it with the Ohio River system. Railroads killed that idea.) This is a particularly pleasant spot and different from anything else on the Parkway.

Peaks of Otter (85.9 miles)   If the James River site is soft and romantic, this is the quintessential diamondlike mountain lake setting. The lake, a 24-acre glassy blue to silver beauty, is the focal point for the **Peaks of Otter Lodge,** where you might well consider staying for at least one night. As I've suggested, the natural beauty of this small valley between the peaks of Sharp Top and Flat Top would be hard to surpass, and there is a great deal to do in the immediate area. For instance, an information center–museum is there, conducted walks are frequent, and a self-guided trail, Elk Run, explores the forest community from the perspective of the things that live there. It takes about 45 minutes to cover.

Mabry Mill (176.2 miles)   This is the most popular site on the Parkway. Once the property of a blacksmith and miller named Ed Mabry, this grist and sawmill, unbelievably romantic in its —to repeat—unbelievably romantic setting, has been photographed so many times that you may well feel the shock of unexpected recognition when you see it.

Because the mill is so famous, it can be very crowded here, but there's good news too, which is that the exhibits, based on such mountain industries as a blacksmith and wheelwright shop, tanning and distilling, and special seasonal exhibits such as the making of molasses and apple butter are genuinely appealing.

Hot Springs and Nearby

The Homestead The Homestead *is* Hot Springs; it is the sole reason this hamlet exists. And The Homestead is not only the greatest resort in Virginia, it is one of the greatest in this country, offering its guests every amenity they could wish for.

The resort has a long and distinguished history that goes back to 1766 when the first lodge was built on the site of the present hotel. By the mid-nineteenth century, the reputation of the springs both here and in Warm Springs (see page 96) was national. Then, in the 1890's, a syndicate headed by Mr. M. E. Ingalls bought the resort. Eventually the Ingalls family bought out the other syndicate members, and they own The Homestead to this day.

The 15,000-acre resort is in the Allegheny Mountains in Bath County—an area so rural that, it is said, there is not one traffic light to be found in the entire county. The property, like Gaul, is divided into three parts: the Hot Springs area, where the hotel itself is situated; Warm Springs, where the resort owns and runs the baths; and Healing Springs, where they own and operate the Cascades Inn and three 18-hole golf courses. It is the Hot Springs area, of course, with The Homestead itself, that is the most famous.

As soon as you enter Hot Springs, you see *it*, the famous tower that was completed in 1929. Soon you enter the grounds and drive down a longish drive to sweep up before the portico and the splendid veranda with its comfortable rocking chairs.

Once inside you are momentarily bedazzled, for here is one of the great interior spaces of any hotel in America, the Great Hall. This magnificent lobby, with white Corinthian columns elegantly lining the 211-foot length, and suitably rich-looking chandeliers to illuminate the scene, is the heart of the whole operation. It is here that one of The Homestead's most treasured traditions, 4:00 afternoon tea, takes place, with waitresses in black uniforms and white aprons and starched white caps serving tea and pastries while a pianist or chamber-music group noodle away in the background. Be there, for you will see the entire life of the hotel unfold in front of you.

Down the great expanse comes an elegantly dressed woman with a pair of Scotties on a double lead, one with a red bow around its neck, the other sporting a white one. Behind her—and catching up fast—come a couple rushing in from tennis, late for something or other. Across the way is a family—grandmother, son and daughter-in-law (or is it daughter and son-in-law?), and three restless children trying to cop as many extra pastries as they can get away with. Two women are playing checkers at the end of the hall; and there, looking for two free chairs, is that rather eager couple, as someone described them last night. They were dancing, then, an elaborate—and recently learned—rhumba during dinner, and then, without a pause, swept soulfully into "Tonight We Love," a song I hadn't heard in years and which has probably done more to destroy Tchaikovsky's reputation than any other single thing. (Remember those awful lyrics? "And where is bliss? In your kiss" . . . is all I can recollect.)

It's all great fun, and then you go up to your room—which may have a working fireplace—to prepare for cocktails and dinner. The dining room is another splendid creation, with Ionic columns ringing the dance floor and helping to break up the vast size of the room. But why so flatly lit? That's my one complaint.

The executive chef, Albert Schnarwyler, is a Swiss who has been with The Homestead since 1962. Under him are 65 cooks, bakers, pastry men and on into the distance. It is amazing to me that Chef Schnarwyler can serve such consistently good food when so many people are involved and when it must be prepared in such volume. So much for the old saw about too many chefs spoiling the broth. (He seems to be particularly adept with crabmeat, one of my favorite things in the world, and you can't go wrong ordering it.) Even more amazing, the menu changes daily at both lunch and dinner. No chance to grow bored with the selections in this dining room. As for the wines, the list is relatively small, but the selection is nice enough. And the service is considerate and efficient.

When staying there, I prefer to have a room in the tower; and the higher the better, because the view is so pretty. Many of the floors have been redecorated here, and the rooms are pleasing to the eye and extremely comfortable, while the maid service is impeccable.

During your visit the choice of things to do is awesome. Here's a quick list of some of the attractions offered during the year: golf, tennis, skiing, ice-skating, riding, dancing, carriage-riding, swimming (year-round), walking, hiking, bowling, lawn bowling, fishing, skeet- and trap-shooting. And then, of course, there are the springs, which started the whole thing in the first place.

I have a routine that I particularly enjoy when taking the baths. First is a half-hour massage. Then you are taken to a room with a huge tub where the 104° mineral water comes up through the bottom as you soak, every ounce of tension draining away with the overflowing water. Next is the steam room, and then a routine called Salt Glo and Scotch Douche. In this, you are rubbed with salt and then placed in an area with multiple shower heads while an attendant "shoots" you with two hoses, one hot, one cold. Sounds awful, feels great. And when it's all over and you're back in your room, you will feel like the proverbial million dollars.

Please be sure to leave some time just for wandering about; it is so very pleasant to do here. There is, for instance, Cottage Row, a group of eleven cottages built in the nineteenth century and now reincarnated as attractive shops, including the inevitable gift shop, an art gallery, and others. The Café Albert is here, too, a nicely informal spot that serves sandwiches and light food.

See the little village, too. Part of the old railroad station, long since abandoned by the last train, has been converted into a shop, and this and several others are worth browsing in. In any case, whatever you do, you can be sure you will enjoy doing it. This is one place that is designed solely with your comfort and wishes in mind.

The Inn at Gristmill Square and Warm Springs Bath County, for such a small population, has an embarrassment of riches, for not only does it contain the vast and extraordinary Homestead, but it also has the delightful Inn at Gristmill Square whose restaurant, The Waterwheel, is worth a trip in itself.

The inn is actually a small group of five restored nineteenth-century buildings grouped around a little square and with, to the left, a wonderful-looking eighteenth-century mill where The Waterwheel is housed. The Warm Springs Run flows by it, which Thomas Jefferson described as "a very bold stream, sufficient to work a gristmill." It is a superb setting. At the back of the square is a welcoming gift shop, while the other buildings house the twelve guest rooms. (There are additional rooms across the street.) Most have fireplaces and refrigerators, and all are comfortable.

Now for the restaurant. Particularly good is the way they prepare trout, and there also was a very nice chicken roasted with herbs, garlic and white wine. As for their breads, they're home-baked and delicious. So are their desserts.

Warm Springs is not much bigger than Hot Springs, yet it's more interesting to walk through because it is the county seat and therefore has more interesting buildings, including a dignified courthouse and one particularly gracious white-and-pink brick church on the side of a hill, its long windows framed by green shutters and steps, outlined by a white railing, leading up to the rather impressive door.

The baths are divided into two parts: The Men's Pool and Bathhouse was built in 1761 and is now one of the oldest spa structures in this country. The Women's Pool and Bathhouse was built in 1836 and has a curious lowering device that may have been installed for Mrs. Robert E. Lee, who was badly crippled with arthritis. As you might expect from the name, the water here is slightly cooler, at 98°, than in Hot Springs.

A DRIVE

You can go in almost any direction from The Homestead or The Inn at Gristmill Square and be assured that you will enjoy captivating scenery. But one drive, which will take you to Lexington, is ravishing, one of my favorite in Virginia. I've done it several times now, at different times of the day and in different seasons. Each time it has been perfection, and if you can approach The Homestead this way, do. The route number is 39, and from just outside Lexington to the West Virginia border it is achingly alluring.

If I had to choose only one section as my favorite, it would be Goshen Pass, a five-mile gap that the Maury River has cut through the mountains. Through meadows, over rocks and into canyons, the river and its accompanying landscape is constantly changing. Along the hillsides are veritable walls of laurel and rhododendron, a glorious sight. It's an exhilarating experience to drive here, one you should not miss.

LEXINGTON

Lexington is one of the prettiest and most interesting towns in Virginia. Although small—there are about 7,300 people—it has two of the finest architectural complexes in the state (Washington and Lee University and Virginia Military Institute), a natural setting between the Blue Ridge and Allegheny Mountains that is almost unrivaled in Virginia, appealing museums and important historical associations, and a restored downtown

Lexington is among my favorite towns in Virginia, both for its natural setting and for the delights of its vernacular architecture, which can be seen on any number of its streets.

area with such amenities as brick sidewalks and imposing commercial and residential buildings. Restoration has been done with care and taste. No matter what your pleasure may be, you'll find it fulfilled here.

Begin your tour of the town at the Lexington Visitor Center (107 East Washington Street. Phone: 703-463-3777). They offer brochures on all the sights and can answer any questions you may have. From there your first stop will be Stonewall Jackson's house.

Stonewall Jackson House (1801) The most striking aspect of this rather simple house is its façade, which is brick for the top two floors, the living and bedroom area, and stone on the bottom floor, which is the kitchen and storage space. Steps lead up from the street to, curiously enough, two entrances, because, after the house was built, the street was lowered in 1851, by about eight feet.

To enter the house, go around to the back, through the door, and you are in a well-stocked but small gift shop where you can buy your ticket for the thirty-minute tour. Next to the shop is a little museum with Jackson memorabilia, and there is a slide show on his life that takes him to 1861 and his final departure for war.

Jackson came to Lexington in 1851 as Professor of Natural Philosophy (physics) and Instructor of Artillery Tactics at Virginia Military Institute. A deeply religious man, he joined the Lexington Presbyterian Church (see page 105) and even founded a Colored Sunday School that would continue throughout the war. (Typically, immediately after the First Battle of Bull Run [see page 67], where he gained his best-known nickname and laid the foundations for his enduring fame, he sent his minister money for the school and never mentioned his role in the battle.)

In 1853 he married Elinor Junkin, daughter of the president of (then) Washington College, and they lived in a house on that campus (see below) until she died a year later in childbirth. In 1857 he married again, to Mary Anna Morrison, the daughter of a Presbyterian minister in North Carolina, and in 1859 they moved to this house, the only home he would ever own.

The tour is of the second floor and first, and the thoughtful restoration has been based on the years of Jackson's occupancy

and contains objects that did indeed belong to Jackson. For the
remainder, the restorers have relied in particular on the estate
inventory taken only two weeks after his funeral. The period
was not one of our greatest, stylistically, and you will not see
much in the way of choice furnishings. But as a memorial to a
great man and his way of life, it is very moving. Finally, when
you leave, take a moment or two to stroll in the inviting garden,
also restored to the period.

The Stonewall Jackson House is open Monday–Saturday,
9:00–4:30; Sunday, 1:00–4:30. Closed: Thanksgiving, Christmas,
January 1, Easter. Admission: $2.50; children under 12, $1.
Phone: 703-463-2552.

Washington and Lee University   This, one of our oldest college campuses, is, beyond question, one of the prettiest in the
country, and mostly because of its front campus buildings, now
a national landmark, which the Department of the Interior
described as "this splendid succession of columned and pilastered buildings." The oldest of the group of red brick buildings
with their white-washed wood and stucco, Washington Hall,
was built in 1824 based on the designs of Colonel John Jordan,
a Lexington citizen who had worked both at Monticello and the
University of Virginia; Jefferson's influence is readily apparent

*This house was built for Robert E. Lee as president of Washington and
Lee and now forms a harmonious part of the campus, one of the prettiest
in the country.*

in the rectangular temple-form façade. My favorite aspect of Washington Hall, by the way, is the resplendent statue of George Washington now on the top of the building, a first-rate example of American folk art. It was carved in the 1840's by a local cabinetmaker, Captain Matthew S. Kahle, and makes the perfect finishing touch.

When you face these buildings you will note that, to the left, there are three houses. Two are almost-identical Greek Revival structures from the 1840's; the third—and farthest away—is a larger, later house from 1869. The latter was built for Robert E. Lee to use during his presidency of the college (1865–1870) and is still the president's house. (It was Lee who planted many of the glorious trees that add so much to the beauty of the campus.) Next to it is the Lee-Jackson House. This, the first president's house, was where Jackson lived with his first wife and where Lee lived until the newer house could be built. The third house, and two very similar ones to the right of the Washington College group, were built to house faculty.

Washington and Lee is the sixth oldest college in the country and traces its origins back to 1749. First called Augusta Academy, then in 1776, Liberty Hall, it became Washington Academy in 1796 after George Washington, hearing of the severe financial problems faced by the school, endowed it with a gift of $50,000 in stock of the James River Canal Company. (His gift is still part of the endowment and has brought in as much as $400,000 in annual income.) Its present name, Washington and Lee University, came shortly after Robert E. Lee's death, when the trustees decided to honor his immense contribution to the well-being of the institution.

If you face the other direction, with your back to Washington Hall, you will be directly in front of the Lee Chapel (1867), surely one of the more endearing Victorian chapels in this country and designed by Lee, his son General George Washington Custis Lee, an engineering professor at Virginia Military Institute at the time, and (the most important contributor) Colonel Thomas Williamson, also of the Institute.

At first it might seem that this intensely picturesque Romanesque chapel would clash with its grandly classical neighbor, but it doesn't, and I think the reason is its close relationship to its basically rural setting: It looks like part of the landscape and maintains its dignity quite separately from that grand colon-

Robert E. Lee's remains are in this little chapel, which also contains Washington and Lee family memorabilia of great interest.

nade on the crest of the hill. And though its wonderfully flared tower and white diamond-paned windows make the building look snug, the overall design has an integrity and dignity well suited to its surroundings.

The interior, on the entrance level, is in two parts. First is the original chapel, simple in the extreme, with rectangular box pews and a gallery. Then, at the end where originally a three-part central window was placed, an addition (1883) has been made to accommodate Edward V. Valentine's moving memorial sculpture of the recumbent Lee. The general's remains, and those of many members of his family, are in a crypt below this part of the chapel.

Valentine was a well-known Richmond sculptor who had done a bust of what he called, in a letter to his wife before Lee's death, "this grand idol of the South." (He also wrote: "An artist, above all other men, is quick to observe the faintest suggestion of posing; the slightest indication of a movement or expression that smacks of vanity he is sure to detect. Such weaknesses . . . were totally lacking in General Lee.") He was, then, a natural choice to do this moving memorial of a recumbent Lee asleep on the battlefield. It is, I think, the exactly right tribute; Lee was totally devoid of pretension, and a statue of him in a heroic pose would have struck a jarring note, particularly in this place.

There are two other items of great interest on this level; to the left of the statue is a wonderful portrait—the first—of Washington by Charles Willson Peale painted in 1772. In it, Washington wears the uniform of a colonel in the British army. The painting is hugely appealing, perhaps my favorite of the many painted of Washington.

To the right of the statue is a portrait of Lee in his Confederate uniform, painted by Theodore Pine. These two portraits and others downstairs, including the Peale portrait of Lafayette that Washington hung next to his own at Mount Vernon and portraits by John Wollaston (see page 44), are in the Lee Museum and are part of the Washington-Custis-Lee Collection. The collection also includes my favorite painting of Lee, by William Edward West, one of the finest nineteenth-century American portraits. (There is a companion portrait of Mrs. Lee, also excellent, even though she, always of independent mind, had said she "would prefer Sully.")

The Lee portrait, painted in 1838 in Baltimore, shows him in full-dress uniform and clearly demonstrates why he was known not only as the handsomest man in the army but also as "the model of a soldier and the beau-ideal of a Christian man." Young and vital he is indeed in this superb portrait that also shows us eyes expressing intense intelligence and dignity and even a certain wry humor. A revealing and discerning depiction of one of our country's greatest heroes.

The Lee Chapel is open: Mid-April–mid-October, Monday–Saturday, 9–5; rest of year, 9–4; Sunday (all year), 2–5. Closed: Thanksgiving and following Friday, December 24, 25, 26, 31. Admission: Free. Phone: 703-463-8768.

Virginia Military Institute (VMI) Another National Historic District, this school, established in 1839 on the site of a state arsenal, is now the most famous military school in the South. Its most famous graduate: General George C. Marshall. Its most famous faculty member: General Stonewall Jackson.

This "West Point of the South" has been primarily influenced architecturally by two men, Alexander Jackson Davis and Bertram Grosvenor Goodhue.

Davis's masterpiece is Lyndhurst (completed 1866), a house in the Gothic Revival style on the Hudson River in Tarrytown, New York, that has been called "the most profoundly intelli-

VMI is a treasure trove of American Gothic Revival architecture. General George C. Marshall was an alumnus, and an excellent museum on campus is dedicated to his career.

gent and provocative house . . . since Thomas Jefferson's Monticello." Davis was a master of the Gothic Revival; he designed five buildings for VMI in this style, and it has remained the favored style for the campus to this day.

Bertram Goodhue was involved in designing several buildings for West Point, the most famous of which is the Cadet Chapel (1910), as well as several other well-known buildings around the country. He too had a great fondness for the Gothic.

Their combined influence has ensured a Gothic campus with gray, crenellated buildings, some of which are striking, if austere and rather static. But it all comes to life every Friday at 4:00, weather permitting, when there is a parade on the vast VMI parade ground. If you're in Lexington, see it. Stirring in itself, it brings an animation to the campus that otherwise can be lacking. For further information, phone: 703-463-6201.

George C. Marshall Research Library and Museum   At the far end of the parade ground, this 1964 building designed by Alonzo H. Gentry, a VMI graduate and the architect of the Harry S Truman Library in Independence, Missouri, is a major tourist attraction at VMI. The museum traces Marshall's long and brilliantly distinguished career with care, intelligence and originality, creating an absorbing experience for even the casual visitor. (One of the best presentations is, I think, the electric map that details World War II in twenty-seven minutes.) The Library contains the personal and public papers of Marshall, as well as those of some of his friends and colleagues. It is open weekdays to scholars and students of twentieth-century military and diplomatic history. By the way, Marshall was a descendant of Chief Justice John Marshall (see page 168).

The Marshall Museum is open: March–November, Monday–Saturday, 9–5; rest of year, 9–4; Sunday (all year), 2–5. Closed: Thanksgiving, Christmas, January 1. Admission: Free. Phone: 703-463-7103.

The VMI Museum I find small museums like this one fascinating because they preserve things that often are of a very personal nature in local terms and that, therefore, can give great insight into the place they are in and the periods they cover. This museum is no exception. Here you will find, for instance, not only Stonewall Jackson's raincoat, worn when he was wounded at Chancellorsville (the bullet hole is below the left shoulder), but also, rather startlingly, his horse, Little Sorrel, stuffed and outfitted and, unsurprisingly, small, while opposite there is a print of Jackson on the horse. There are also exhibits on past and present cadet life, artifacts such as a finely crafted early nineteenth-century chest of eating, writing and toilet utensils taken from a captured Mexican general in the Mexican War, and so forth. A pleasant half hour or so can be spent here.

The VMI Museum is open: Monday–Friday, 9:00–4:30; Saturday, 9–12 and 2–5; Sunday, 2–5. Closed: Thanksgiving, Christmas, January 1. Admission: Free. Phone: 703-463-6232.

Those are the highlights of Lexington, but there is much more to see here, and I would strongly urge that you pick up the "Residential Walking Tour" brochure at the Visitor Center and follow their suggested tour of the town. Some favorites: The **Alexander-Withrow House** (1789), now an inn (see page 116), with four corner chimneys, unusually interesting corbels, and patterned brick in what is called diapering; the **Presbyterian Church** (1843), where Jackson worshiped, a fine example of Greek Revival; **Jackson Avenue** from 301–311, six excellent examples of Victorian architecture (1884); **Lawyer's Row,** the

A splendid building, one of the handsomest in the town, is the Alexander-Withrow House. It has wonderful features, such as its distinguishing corbels and patterned brick.

mid-1840's and '80's buildings in Courthouse Square; and **Stonewall Jackson Cemetery** (1789) where the great man is buried. The statue of him sculpted by Edward Valentine (see page 102) faces south.

NEARBY

Natural Bridge Once owned by Thomas Jefferson (he bought it, the gorge and 157 surrounding acres, for twenty shillings in 1774), visited and surveyed by George Washington (he carved his initials in its limestone rock), painted by many famous artists, photographed to extinction and long known as one of the seven natural wonders of the world—this was a sight I had long waited to see.

The arch itself, a soaring 215 feet high, 90 feet long and from 50 to 150 feet wide, is as exciting as I had hoped. But what surrounds it and is near it is tawdry. To underline the solemnity of the formation and its creation, canned electric organ and church-bell music sag leadenly between the walls of the gorge. And by the entrance is a gift shop that finally answers the age-old question, "Where on earth do you suppose they got *that*?"

Across the street is another horror, the Natural Bridge Wax Museum, where, on the porch, a little wax boy swings overhead and a wax figure in the corner invites you to "Come set yourself for a spell." I should have done that and skipped the exhibit, for inside . . . well, my favorite exhibits were the Garden of Eden, depicted at the moment Eve handed the apple to Adam; Eve's expression is worth the price of admission. The other exhibit and the ultimate of something but not taste, is a Last Supper based on the Da Vinci painting as seemingly interpreted by the Three Stooges and friends. It could set back our relations with Italy to World War II. Oh—I forgot to tell you—the exhibits, including the Last Supper, move and talk.

Fleeing from there, I went to the third "attraction," the Caverns of Natural Bridge. Uninteresting. As you can see, this was not one of my better days in Virginia.

Natural Bridge is open: Daily, 7:00–dusk. In spring and fall at 8:00, summer at 9:00 and winter at 7:00 there is a 45-minute presentation called the Drama of Creation with narration, music and special lighting. Admission: Day, or Drama of Creation, $3.50; children 6–12, $2; under 6, free. Phone: 703-291-2121 for all attractions.

The Wax Museum is open: March–November, daily, 10–9; summer, 9–10. Admission: $3; children 6–12, $1.50; under 6, free.

Natural Bridge is one of the seven natural wonders of the world, but sadly, it has been tritely commercialized.

ROANOKE

Incorporated only in 1882, Roanoke, once known as Big Lick, came into being as a city because it was a junction and headquarters of the Norfolk & Western Railway, now part of Norfolk Southern Corp. Today, with a population of about 100,000, it is the largest city along the Blue Ridge Parkway. Its location, in a bowl-like valley extension of the Shenandoah called the Roanoke Valley, and between the Blue Ridge and Appalachian Mountains, is a delightful one, and the city offers enough to see and do to make it a surprisingly rewarding stopping-off point— particularly if you're traveling with children, as you'll see.

Center in the Square This center for the arts and sciences opened in 1983 in the renovated McGuire Building, the first concrete and steel building to be built in Roanoke (1914). At that time it was built to house activities in the surrounding farmer's market, still there and going back to 1874. Either before or after visiting the Center, take some time to explore this revitalized market filled with spectacular produce, and particularly the City Market Building, which, with its shops and restaurants, has become a hub of activity for the downtown.

As for the Center itself, it is an ingenious solution to one city's problem of how to attractively house and present, to the widest possible audience, many of its cultural offerings. (Another center, the Roanoke Valley Civic Center, houses the Roanoke Symphony and Youth Symphony and has both a coliseum and an auditorium.)

The interior space is divided into four levels. Level 4 and part of Level 3 is devoted to the **Roanoke Valley Science Museum and Hopkins Planetarium**. (The museum is open: Tuesday–Thursday, 10–5; Friday and Saturday, 10–8; Sunday, 1–5. Closed: Monday, March 31, and holidays. Admission for the museum and planetarium: $2.75; senior citizens and children 6–12, $2. Phone: 703-342-7827.) Part of the remainder of Level 3 contains the **Roanoke Historical Society**. (Open: Tuesday–Saturday, 10–5; Sunday, 1–5. Closed: Monday and holidays. Admission: Free. Phone: 703-342-5770.) Level 2 and part of Level 1 has the **Mill Mountain Theater** (Phone: 703-342-5730 for information on current offerings), while the **Roanoke Museum of Fine Arts** operates on all but Level 4. (Open: Tuesday, Wednesday, Saturday, 10–5; Thursday and Friday, 10–8; Sunday, 1–5. Closed: Monday and holidays. Admission: Free. Phone: 703-342-5760.)

Hands down, the Science Museum is the winner. If it had been in my town when I was growing up, I would have done much better in my science courses; and I can say without hesitation that there isn't a child in the world who won't have a good time here. Or an adult, either. Some of the exhibits include a meteorology area where you—or rather your children—can see themselves as TV "weathercasters" on closed-circuit TV; a short (two-minute) but catchy three-projector audio-visual program outlining Virginia's geological origins and relationship to the rest of the country; a varied assortment of frogs, snakes, lizards and toads; a doctor's office—brilliant, this idea—where you can find out in a highly imaginative way what the doctor is looking for when he gives various tests. There even are computer games that rather mystified me but delighted a neighboring eight-year-old who watched my humiliation with total contempt. But I didn't care. I had a good time no matter what that kid thought.

The Historical Society is also refreshing in its original presentation and teaches you about Roanoke and its history in a painless way. As for the Fine Arts Museum, there are some nice pictures here, particularly some nineteenth-century American ones, and there are an excellent Japanese Gallery, Decorative Arts Gallery, Print Gallery and Regional Arts Gallery. Space has been set aside for area beginners and craftsmen to show their wares. This is not a first-rate regional museum; it doesn't pretend to be. But it does give you a good idea of art life in the region.

Mill Mountain Park and Zoo   Roanoke brings out the kid in me, for this is my second-favorite place to visit. In truth, this may be the prettiest location in the country for a zoo, just off the Blue Ridge Parkway and offering views of the city from two thousand feet up. As for the zoo, it's really quite small but has a jolly innocence. I enjoyed the miniature train that takes you around the exhibits. If you are traveling with a child, take this in. If you're not, go for the view. The park is open year-round. The zoo is open: Daily, May–October, 10–6.

Admission: $1.50; children under 12, 75¢. Phone: 703-343-3241.

Virginia Museum of Transportation   And again, wonderful to see with kids, but also of interest to adults. This museum was extablished in 1963 and now is the largest railroad museum in the Southeast . . . appropriately enough, as Norfolk & Western has its headquarters here. Although the museum covers all modes of transportation from wagons through the space age, the emphasis is clearly on railroads. The old steam engines are particularly interesting.

The museum is open: Daily, May–Labor Day, 9–5; September–April, Wednesday–Sunday, 10–4. Admission, $2; children under 12, 75¢. Phone: 703-342-5670.

Hollins College   This women's college on the outskirts of Roanoke, founded in 1842, has such an agreeable campus—particularly the front quadrangle—that if you have some extra time you would enjoy the short trip here to see it.

NEARBY

Booker T. Washington National Monument   In all honesty, I was looking forward to this with minimal enthusiasm: The day I had chosen was overcast and dull; the drive seemed too long (it's not—the distance is about twenty miles); no one seemed to know much about it or to have been there. Nor did it look terribly interesting when I drove up to the Visitor Center, and it didn't help that I was the only visitor. Well, everyone is missing an absorbing experience.

First, be sure to see the audiovisual presentation on Washington's life and career. He was born here, on the Burroughs plantation, in 1856. In 1861 a property inventory listed, among the farm implements, "1 Negro boy (Booker)-$400." His mother was the cook, and when they were freed in 1865, Booker—he didn't have a surname until he chose Washington several years later —and his mother, along with a brother and sister, joined his stepfather in West Virginia.

By 1872, after incredible difficulties, he entered Hampton Institute, a school for blacks, and was graduated with honors in only three years. In 1881 he was chosen as president of Tuskegee Institute in Alabama, which he developed from thirty pupils, a state grant of $2000 for salaries, and two run-down buildings into a campus that, at his death in 1915, housed 1,500 students, contained over a hundred buildings, had a faculty of about two-hundred and was endowed with $2 million. His autobiography, *Up From Slavery*, became a nineteenth-century classic. When he died—a famous and nationally respected figure—Theodore Roosevelt, who often had sought his advice, said Washington was "one of the most useful, as well as one of the most distinguished, of American citizens of any race." I think Washington would have been pleased with that—for useful, both to his race and country, was what he most wanted to be.

After you have seen the audiovisual presentation, go out the rear door and take the quarter-mile Plantation Trail through a reconstructed small (a plantation doesn't always mean columned porticoes, house slaves by the dozen and mint juleps) tobacco farm of 207 acres from the mid-nineteenth century. I can think of no other place that can give you such a real sense of what life for most farmers of the period in Virginia was like.

A few buildings have been reconstructed—the kitchen cabin, the smokehouse, the birthplace site, the blacksmith shed and so forth—and there are audio presentations at several of the sites to bring the period to life. Best of all, because it really is a working nineteenth-century farm, meat is hanging in the smokehouse and tobacco leaves in the barn, while the chicken house fairly explodes with Buff Orpingtons, Silver-Pensilled Wyandottes, Dominickers—no Rhode Island Reds on this farm. European boar are in the hog lot, while Belgian workhorses, cows, turkeys, ducks and sheep fill out the landscape, just as they would have in Booker's time.

Primarily, of course, the presentation is educational, but it's so well done that it exceeds itself to make you think you really are wandering through a nineteenth-century Virginia farm.

Booker T. Washington National Monument is open: Daily 8:30–5:00. Closed: Thanksgiving, Christmas and January 1. Phone: 703-721-2094.

ABINGDON

Deep in the heart of the Virginia Highlands, that lost-in-time-and-space area far in the southwest of the state, lies the village of Abingdon, county seat of Washington County and, surprisingly enough, one of the oldest towns in Virginia, dating back to the mid-eighteenth century. Since then nothing much has happened here—that is the very good news—so this wonderful little town with its fine-looking brick and wooden houses and courthouse hasn't changed much, and a good part of what was built in the last century still remains.

The surrounding countryside, as exciting as any in Virginia, also is different from what you see in the rest of the state, for here, because of geological folding and lifting millions of years ago, the hilly landscape sometimes looks as if the earth had furrowed its brow. The results are breathtaking, and a stay here while enjoying the simple pleasures (so-called) of swimming, boating, hiking and fishing in this often majestic landscape will add ten years to your life.

The drives, then, can border on the spectacular, and I would strongly suggest that you at least travel on Route 58 through Mount Rogers National Recreation Area. This is one of the most awesome drives in the state and well worth the time you give to exploring it. But no matter where you go, you'll enjoy the scenery.

In Abingdon itself, stroll on West and East Main Street as well as the side streets, absorbing the charms of the village, and then enjoy Abingdon's other offerings.

The village is a delight and has many good examples from different periods of American architecture.

The oldest building in Abingdon, itself a deliciously lost little village in the spectacular Virginia Highlands.

Barter Theater This, the State Theater of Virginia, has a history so unique that it bears repeating.

In the 1930's, during the Great Depression, a young actor named Robert Porterfield, like so many others, found himself out of work. A native of southwest Virginia, Porterfield one day was thinking of the great abundance of produce that the area grew. He also thought of the abundance of acting talent surrounding him in New York City, all of it unemployed. And then his great idea struck: Move to Abingdon with his actor friends (22 of them, as it turned out) and start a theater there. For pay, the troupe would barter their talents for the patrons' farm produce. They opened in June, 1933, and now this is the longest-running professional repertory theater in the country and has "graduated" such stars as Patricia Neal, Gregory Peck, Gary Collins, Rosemary Murphy, Ernest Borgnine and Frank Lovejoy, to name just a few. And playwrights as famous as Noel Coward, Thornton Wilder and Maxwell Anderson have been willing to barter their royalties for a succulent Virginia ham. Except for vegetarian George Bernard Shaw, who demanded spinach.

If the theater is open, go, by all means. You'll thoroughly enjoy it. The interior, by the way, is from New York's Empire Theater. Barter Theater is open: Tuesday–Sunday, April–October. Diagonally across Main Street from the theater is the Play-

This cottage, tiny but definitely assertive, is snugly placed in Abingdon.

house, a smaller theater presenting works in progress, new plays and other productions. Open: June–August. For information, phone: 703-628-3991.

The Cave House Craft Shop, 279 East Main Street. This nonprofit cooperative for local craftsmen offers good-looking wares at fair prices. The building, gabled Victorian and rather pretty, is set against a hill, and a long flight of steps leads up to the front door. Its rather peculiar name goes back to the origins of Abingdon, which was first known as Wolf Hills. One night Daniel Boone camped here, at a site near the present county jail, while marking the Wilderness Road Trail that came from Kentucky and ran through Abingdon. During the night his dogs were attacked by a pack of wolves. The next day he discovered that the wolves were living in a cave where Cave House is today.

Cave House is open: Monday–Saturday, 10–5; Sunday, 1–5. Credit cards accepted.

White's Mill   About five miles north of Abingdon on Route 692, which becomes White's Mill Road, this mill is 150 years old and is still in operation; if you wish, you can buy some cornmeal here. You also can fish for trout, and the miller, named Guy Miller, aptly enough, is always ready for a visit.

White's Mill is open daily, 9–5. Admission: Free. Phone: 703-628-5383.

WHERE TO STAY AND EAT
Area Code: 703

WHERE TO STAY
(Also see The Inn at Little Washington, page 70).

Middletown

The Wayside Inn, Middletown 22645. Phone: 869-1797. Rates: From about $50. Credit cards accepted. This, once one of the best inns in Virginia, is now struggling back from a devastating fire.

Strasburg

Hotel Strasburg, 201 Holliday Street, Strasburg 22657. Phone: 465-9191. Rates: From about $35 for a double. Credit cards accepted. (See page 83.)

A wing of the Martha Washington Inn, a handsome nineteenth-century pile that has now been tastefully restored.

Shenandoah National Park and the Skyline Drive

Skyland Lodge, P.O. Box 727, Luray 22835. Phone: 999-2211.
Rates: From about $30. Credit cards accepted. Skyland Lodge is
open: April–November; December–March, phone for information. Reserve well in advance. (See page 87.)

Big Meadows Lodge, P.O. Box 727, Luray 22835. Phone: 999-
2221. Rates: From about $30. Credit cards accepted. Big Meadow
is open: April–November; December–March, phone for information. Reserve well in advance. (See page 87.)

Blue Ridge Parkway

Peaks of Otter Lodge, Box 489, Bedford 24523. Phone: 586-
1081. Rates: From about $42 for a single, $54 for a double. Credit
cards accepted. Peaks of Otter is open all year. Reserve well in
advance. (See page 93.)

Off the Parkway

Hot Springs

The Homestead, Hot Springs 24445. Phone: 839-5500. Rates:
Modified American plan, from about $190 for a single, $120 for
a double per person. Credit cards accepted. (See page 94.)

Cascades Inn, Hot Springs 24445. Phone: 839-5355. Rates:
Modified American plan, from about $94 for a single, $82 (per
person) for a double. Credit cards accepted.

Owned and operated by The Homestead, all facilities of that
resort are also available to people staying at the Cascades. The
inn consists of a hotel, motel and cottages, and although it isn't
as splendidly luxurious as The Homestead, it is certainly not to
be sneezed at.

Warm Springs

The Inn at Gristmill Square, P.O. Box 359, Warm Springs
24484. Phone: 839-2231. Rates: From about $55 for a single, $60
for a double. Credit cards accepted. (See page 96.)

Lexington

Historic Country Inns, 11 North Main Street, Lexington
24450. Phone: 463-2044. Rates: From about $55 for a single, $60
for a double. Credit cards accepted.

This grouping includes three small inns, the **Alexander-Withrow House,** 3 West Washington Street; **Maple Hall,** I-81 and Route 11 (Exit 53); and the **McCampbell Inn,** 11 North Main Street. Only the McCampbell Inn, a historic building in downtown Lexington, has served as an inn in the past. The Alexander-Withrow house is a stone's throw away and also is one of Lexington's better buildings. Maple Hall is about ten to fifteen minutes from the downtown.

Of the three, the palm must go to Maple Hall (c. 1850), a wonderful porticoed plantation house with graceful steps going up to the main entrance on the second floor. There are sixteen rooms available, thirteen in the main and three in the guest house, and trails through the woods and a trout stream are a few extra amenities. The rooms are well furnished with country antiques. My one objection is the proximity to I-81, but you can't have everything. Stay here, by all means.

The two inns in town are satisfactory and make acceptable alternatives to Maple Hall. The Withrow House has six suites and one room. The McCampbell Inn is larger.

Roanoke

Hotel Roanoke, P.O. Box 12508, Roanoke 24026. Phone: 1-800-336-9684; in Virginia, 1-800-542-5898; 343-6992. Rates: From about $60 for single, $66 for a double. Credit cards accepted. (See page 121.)

The best in town, this hotel goes back to 1882. The rooms are only fair, but the dining room is quite good.

Roanoke Airport Marriott, 2801 Hershberger Rd., Roanoke 24018. Phone: 563-9300. Rates: From about $85 for a single, $95 for a double. Credit cards accepted. (See page 121.)

For a motel this is surprisingly well designed and offers comfortable rooms and efficient service. A nice surprise.

Abingdon

The Martha Washington Inn, 150 West Main Street, Abingdon 24210. Phone: 628-3161. Rates: From about $55 for a single, $65 for a double. Credit cards accepted.

Recently restored and refurbished, this wonderful Greek Revival pile has been reborn—with the aid of a ton of money—as an appealing and luxurious country inn-hotel. Rooms vary widely in size and luxury—some have fireplaces, for instance—

and the furnishings are a happy blend of antiques and reproductions. It's good to have the old girl back, and in such fine fettle, too.

WHERE TO EAT

(Also see The Inn at Little Washington, page 75.)

Strasburg

Hotel Strasburg, 201 Holliday Street, Strasburg. Phone: 465-9191. Credit cards accepted. Moderate. Lunch: Daily, 11:00–2:30. Dinner: Daily, 5:30–9:00.
Lunch here is cheap and good, and the dinner is first-rate, too.

Shenandoah National Park and the Skyline Drive

Skyland Lodge, 41.7 miles. Phone: 999-2211. Credit cards accepted. Inexpensive. Lunch: 12–3. Dinner: 5:30–8:30. Open: April–October; November–March. Phone for information.
The view is special from here, but the room is barnlike, with all the charm of a cafeteria. As for the food, its only so-so.

Big Meadows Lodge, 51.2 miles. Phone: 999-2211. Credit cards accepted. Inexpensive. Lunch: 12–2:30. Dinner: 5:30–8:30. Open: Mid-May–October; November–mid-May. Phone for information.
What I said about Skyland is true here too, although the dining room here is more appealing.

Off the Drive

New Market

The Southern Kitchen, South Main Street, New Market. Phone: 740-3514. Visa and MasterCard accepted. Inexpensive. Open: October–March, Monday–Friday, 7:00–9:30; Saturday, 7:00–11:00; Sunday, 7:00–10:30. April–September, Sunday–Thursday, 6:30–10:00; Friday and Saturday, 6:30–11:00.
This really is only a diner—don't expect fancy fixins—but there's some pretty good food here. Try the peanut soup, for instance. The fried chicken will leave you more than satisfied, too.

Staunton

Rowe's Family Restaurant, on Route 4 about 2½ miles east of Staunton. Phone: 886-1833. No credit cards. Inexpensive. Open: Monday–Saturday, 6:30–9:00. Closed: Sunday.

This roadhouse has stick-to-your-ribs food that is surprisingly good. Basics such as pork chops and mashed potatoes are served, and both are perfectly prepared. Desserts are nice too, particularly a wonderful banana pudding and a great mince pie.

McCormick's Pub & Restaurant, 41 North Augusta Street, Staunton. Phone: 885-3111. Credit cards accepted. Moderate. Lunch: Monday–Friday, 11:30–4:00. Dinner: Monday–Saturday, 5:30–9:30, pub food to midnight.

I prefer Rowe's, but if you want to stay in town and have a little more atmosphere than Rowe's can provide, this is for you. As for the food, it's standard fare.

Blue Ridge Parkway

Peaks of Otter Lodge, 86 miles. Phone: 586-1081. Credit cards accepted. Inexpensive. Lunch: Monday–Saturday, 11:30–2:30; Sunday, 12:00–8:30. Dinner: Monday–Saturday, 5:00–8:30.

Let's face it, neither the Drive nor the Parkway is noted for its gourmet restaurants, but if you're hungry or staying here, it's adequate.

Off the Parkway

Hot Springs

The Homestead, Hot Springs. Phone: 839-5500. Credit cards accepted. Expensive. Lunch: Daily, 12:30–2:00. Dinner: Daily, 7:00–8:30. Reservations advisable. (See page 94.)

Sam Snead's Tavern, 1 Main Street, Hot Springs. Phone: 839-2828. Credit cards accepted. Moderate–Expensive. Open: Monday–Thursday, 11:30–11:00; Friday and Saturday, 11:30–1:00; Sunday, 11:30–9:30. Reservations suggested for dinner, Friday and Saturday.

If you want a break from the grandeur of The Homestead's dining room or some simpler food, this is the place to go. The food is good—ribs and steaks and trout and such—the service low-key and friendly.

Warm Springs

Waterwheel Restaurant at the Inn at Gristmill Square,

Warm Springs. Phone: 839-2311. Credit cards accepted. Moderate–Expensive. Lunch: April–November, 12:00–2:30; Sunday year-round, 11–2. Dinner: Tuesday–Saturday, 6:30–9:00. (See page 96.)

In a word, excellent.

Lexington

Maple Hall, Route 11 at Exit 53 from I-81, about six miles north of Lexington. Phone: 463-2044. Credit cards accepted. Moderate. Dinner: 6:30–9:00. Reservations required.

This restaurant, small and ingratiating, serves absolutely first-class food. Each evening's meal consists of a single choice five-course affair. The ingredients are the freshest available, and because of the small number of guests that can be served and the limitation of the menu, great care can be given to each selection. I can recommend this without reservation. In fact, don't miss it if you're in Lexington or nearby.

Willson-Walker House Restaurant, 30 North Main Street, Lexington. Phone: 463-3020. Credit cards accepted. Moderate. Lunch: Tuesday–Saturday, 11:30–2:30; Sunday, 12:00–2:30. Dinner: Tuesday–Saturday, 5:30–10:00. Reservations suggested for dinner.

Housed in one of Lexington's more handsome Greek Revival buildings (1820), eating here can be very pleasurable. Two dining rooms are open on the first floor, and seat—combined— slightly more than fifty people. The decorations are appropriate to the period of the house, and the food preparation is original in concept without being cute. This is the best in-town restaurant and worth a visit.

The Palms, 101 West Nelson Street, Lexington. Phone: 463-7911. Credit cards accepted. Moderate. Open: Sunday–Thursday, 11–midnight; Friday and Saturday, 11–1.

A typical college-town restaurant offering very good soups and burgers and huge sandwiches through full dinners and lush desserts. It's fun to watch the kids, and the atmosphere of this pub is relaxed and friendly.

Roanoke

The Library, 3117 Franklin Road (S.W.), Roanoke. Phone: 985-

0811. Credit cards accepted. Expensive. Dinner: Monday–Saturday, 6:15–11:00. Closed: Sunday.

The food here is very, very good. The menu is fairly standard, but great attention is paid to the preparation of everything—the vegetables are particularly outstanding. It is one of the best restaurants in the state, in fact. The setting: You're surrounded by books, an interesting idea not pushed too far. The service: The cliché "killing with kindness" must have originated here. Frankly, it's a bit overdone, but in this case too overdone is better than too rare. Reservations recommended. By the way, this can be hard to find; look for a small shopping center called Piccadilly Center and turn in there. The Center will be on your right if you're coming from downtown.

Regency Room of the Hotel Roanoke, 19 North Jefferson Street, Roanoke. Phone: 343-6992. Credit cards accepted. Expensive. Lunch: Monday–Saturday, 11:30–2:30; Sunday brunch, 11–3. Dinner: Daily, 5–11.

I have a prejudice that hotel restaurants are usually poor and overpriced. Here, I am pleased to say, the food is quite good, and I can easily recommend it. A slight word of warning: Their Virginia specialites, such as peanut soup (which they claim to have invented) and spoonbread, are only fair.

Remington's of the Roanoke Airport Marriott, 2801 Hershberger Road, Roanoke. Phone: 563-9300. Credit cards accepted. Expensive. Dinner: Sunday–Thursday, 5:00–10:00; Friday and Saturday, 5:00–11:00.

The food here is good and is prepared with some care—rare enough to find in most motels. It's a bit on the bland side in terms of seasonings, but the service is courteous, efficient and professional, and the setting agreeable.

Abingdon

The Martha Washington Inn, 150 West Main Street, Abingdon. Phone: 628-3161. Credit cards accepted. Expensive. Lunch: Monday–Saturday, 11:30–2:00; Sunday brunch, 9–3. Dinner: Monday–Thursday, 5:30–10:00; Friday and Saturday, 5–10; Sunday, 5:30–9:00.

Under the old management, I ate what could certainly qualify as some of the worst meals of my life. The dining room is much improved now, quite decent in fact, but it's outrageously expensive for Abingdon and the area, and teeters on being too pretentious.

The Tavern, 222 East Main Street, Abingdon. Phone: 628-1118. Credit cards accepted. Very moderate. Open: Monday–Saturday, 11–11; Sunday brunch, 11:00–3:00.

Located in Abingdon's oldest building, there's a cozy bar downstairs, dining rooms with fireplace upstairs. The food is simple and standard but good—sandwiches, burgers, soups and salads at lunch; chicken, steak and seafood at dinner.

Nearby

The Troutdale Dining Room, Route 16, Troutdale. Phone: 677-3671. No credit cards. Moderate–Expensive. Open: May–October. Dinner: Tuesday–Saturday, 5:00–9:30; Sunday, 1:00–9:30. Closed: Monday. About 45 minutes to one hour from Abingdon.

A refurbished former small hotel offering well-prepared standard food—scallops, steak, chicken—with one or two surprises . . . quail, for instance. The setting is rural and homey, the trout from local streams. A good place to consider; even though the drive is somewhat long, the scenery makes it worthwhile.

THE PIEDMONT
From Charlottesville to Lynchburg, Richmond and Petersburg

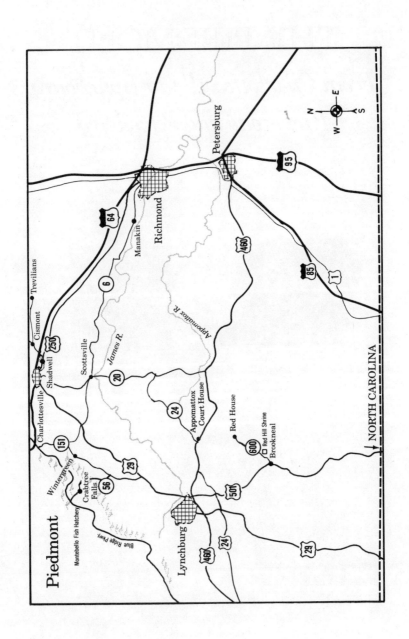

Piedmont

THIS central plateau area of Virginia, between Tidewater and the Blue Ridge Mountains, is not, generally, as naturally beautiful as the rest of the state, but historically it is immensely rich. Here is the home of the nation's most intellectual president and civilized man, Thomas Jefferson, and in many ways he still bestrides the area, a dominant, benign colossus whose architectural contributions and home bring people from all over the world.

Another major force shaping the history of the Piedmont—as of all Virginia—was the Civil War. Richmond and Petersburg suffered dreadfully, and Petersburg never really recovered, while tiny Appomattox Court House, not far from Lynchburg, witnessed the death of the Confederate hopes and the rebirth of a country united once again.

From our beginnings, then, crowned by the burning laser of Jefferson's intelligence, through the deeply tragic dark days of our division, the Piedmont has been at the eye of our history.

CHARLOTTESVILLE

A smallish town with a permanent population of only about 40,000, Charlottesville nevertheless offers more sights of great quality, both natural and man-made, than several major cities I could mention. You really need three or four days here, but I would grudgingly say that you could take in the highlights in two days.

Let me whet your appetite a little with what it has to offer: America's greatest architectural complex; the homes of three of our presidents, one a house that is among the country's most beautiful; a restaurant in an old and dilapidated building that serves some of the best meals in the state; and one of the prettiest drives in Virginia.

I would suggest that you start your visit by going to the

Thomas Jefferson Visitors Bureau, just outside the city on 20-S. (Open: Daily, 9–5. Phone: 804-293-6789.) The extremely capable staff can answer any questions you may have.

The town itself is appealing, and you should drive about its streets exploring its charms. You might also take a walk in the small historic downtown area that is bordered by High Street (north), Market Street (south), Second Street (east) and Seventh Street (west). Within this little district, Court Square is the most interesting. Even though it is in need of some expert restoration, it is a charming, rather typical southern county seat. The Albemarle County Courthouse, built between 1803 (north wing) and 1859 (south wing), with the portico added in 1867, is on the site of an older (1762) courthouse that also served as a meeting place for all the religious denominations in the area. Thomas Jefferson referred to it as the "Common Temple" and worshiped here. So did James Madison and James Monroe.

There's also an interesting story connected with the present site of The Red Land Club on Park Street, which is where the Old Swan Tavern stood during the Revolution. The Jouetts were the tavern-keepers in those days; and son Jack, in 1781, saved Jefferson, Patrick Henry, John Tyler, Richard Henry Lee and almost the entire Virginia legislature from capture by the British under Colonel Sir Banastre Tarleton—who acquired a reputation for barbaric cruelty in this war—by riding over forty miles cross-country from Louisa to the Old Swan to spread the alarm. I also would suggest that you take a look at Jackson Park, with its imposing equestrian statue of the Confederate general.

Finally, you should know that there are two excellent antique shops here that are definitely worth a visit. The first is Ann Woods Ltd. (1211–1215 West Main Street. Open: Monday–Saturday, 10–5. Phone: 804-295-6108), particularly good for silver and porcelain. The other is the 1740 House, which has nice examples of eighteenth- and nineteenth-century American furniture. (Route 250-W, 1½ miles from Boar's Head Inn. Open: Monday–Saturday, 10–5. Phone: 804-977-1740.)

But the real pleasures of Charlottesville are still to come.

Monticello

And our own dear Monticello, where has nature spread so
rich a mantle under the eye? mountains, forests, rocks, rivers.
With what majesty do we there ride above the storms! How
sublime to look down into the workhouse of nature, to see her
clouds, hail, snow, rain, thunder, all fabricated at our feet!
and the glorious Sun when rising as if out of a distant water,
just gilding the tops of the mountains, & giving life to all
nature!
> —Jefferson to Maria Cosway, Paris (1786)

Mr. Jefferson is the first American who has consulted the
fine arts to know how he should shelter himself from the
weather.
. . .
It seemed as if from his youth he had placed his mind, as
he has done his house, on an elevated situation, from which
he might contemplate the universe.
> —Marquis François Jean de Chastellux,
> *Travels in North America* (1782)

"I don't see how he could do and be so many things."
> —Harry Truman after seeing Monticello (1960)

Frank Lloyd Wright once said that designing a home is like
painting a portrait. An interesting and, I think, penetrating
observation. It is particularly applicable at Monticello, a self-
portrait if ever there was one, and among the most fascinating
in the history of architecture. A good part of Jefferson's life was
spent building his home—"They was forty years at work upon
that house before Mr. Jefferson stopped building," recalled his
servant Isaac Jackson in his memoirs—and his very essence is
evident in every centimeter. Certainly one of America's greatest and most beautiful houses, it also is one of the most intelligently conceived—and it has the added attraction of a
breathtaking setting.

History The house was built in two parts. The first, begun in
1769, was a Palladian villa. Andrea Palladio (1508–1580) was the
most influential and among the greatest of Italian architects.

What particularly appealed to Jefferson was his revival of Roman planning values and his system of harmonic proportions. Jefferson felt that colonial architecture, in particular English Georgian, was outmoded; political feelings, it has been pointed out, influenced his architecture away from English models, but not, I might add, his landscape design. He felt that the republican Romans exemplified qualities he wished to see evidenced in his own countrymen's public buildings. Antique architecture had, he said, "the approbation of thousands of years" and might cast, by association, some of its glories on this country. In addition, the Palladian villa was ideally suited to the house of a Virginia gentleman of the eighteenth century because it was designed for a similar way of life based on agricultural pursuits. Very broadly speaking, the philosophy behind the villas was that a dignified rural home was meant to be the center of an estate where affairs of business could be transacted, of course, but also a setting conducive to artistic and intellectual endeavors shared with friends and family. Following this philosophy, the first version of Monticello was completed in 1779.

Jefferson's stay in Paris from August 1784 to September 1789 exposed him to the best of eighteenth-century architecture, particularly as exemplified by such architects as Pierre Rousseau, creator of that lovely French Palladian palace the Hôtel de Salm (1785), now the Palace of the Legion of Honor and by which Jefferson said he was "violently smitten," and the more avant-garde Étienne-Louis Boulée and Claude-Nicolas Ledoux. The latter were French Romantic Classicists who stressed geometrical shapes—the sphere, cylinder and Jefferson's beloved octagon—and an international style that departed from regional forms in a highly imaginative and original way.

When, therefore, Jefferson returned to America with his vastly expanded knowledge of contemporary architecture and its treatments, he set to work in 1796 to re-create Monticello into the building that we see today. It was finally completed in 1809.

The Exterior   You arrive at the east portico of the house. (The more famous portico, surmounted by the dome, is on the west.) Although there actually are two floors on this side, they are designed to look like one, with the small second-floor window-frames touching those of the first.

On the west—the garden—side is one of Jefferson's most original ideas. Normally a house such as this would have its dependencies flanking the house on the entrance (east) side. But
Jefferson moved them to the back, forming an angled U, and
tucked them away under the ground so that all you see from the
house, to the north and south, are their roofs, which also serve
as terrace walks. Each walk extends out from the house for 100
feet and then turns at a right angle for another 100 feet to the
two end pavilions, the one on the south being the first building
on the site, the one on the north the last. Underneath these
roofs are storage cellars, the kitchen, wine cellar, laundry, servants' rooms, offices, all the chambers necessary for conducting
the business of the household and estate.

What you are looking at as you approach the east portico,
then, is the family section of the 35-room house. This building
contains, on the first floor, the entrance hall and, to the south,
Jefferson's bedroom, cabinet, a greenhouse, a guest room and a
library; to the west, the parlor; to the north, the dining room,
the tea room, the north piazza and two guest rooms.

When I first saw the house, I had several immediate impressions. First of all, it looked much smaller, somehow, than I had
expected; yet it moved me with its monumental presence

*"Mr. Jefferson is the first American who has consulted the fine arts to
know how he should shelter himself from the weather." Marquis François Jean de Chastellux,* Travels in North America.

and the flow of its general design. To explain: It looks small because of its disguised second floor and because so much of it is concealed, while its monumental presence comes from the simple yet very handsome portico, whose buff-colored Doric columns contrast impressively with the red brick, white wood and dark green shutters of the rest of the building. The sense of flow is brought about in two ways. First, the house, seen dead-on, is defined by mysterious, half-revealed angled forms; your eye wanders over them trying to get an idea of the interior, while they invite you to walk around them in order to discover how the whole defines itself and to enter to see what they contain. The second reason is that you look directly through the house and out the glass doors of the west portico, which has the delightful effect of helping to dissolve the solidity of the building and making it an integral part of a setting that changes in mood with the light. It is a house of seeming contradictions that, though they eventually sort themselves out brilliantly, have the immediate effect of drawing you inside to discover the building's secrets and keeping you slightly off balance.

The west side offers the most famous view of the house, in large part because of the extraordinary octagonal dome—the first over an American house—that dominates and defines, the building, giving it a strong vertical accent very different in feeling from the eastern entrance. And the terraces with their charming end pavilions provide a romantic, even theatrical, setting for the lawn and gardens. Here, once again, is that Jeffersonian attention to design detail that turns the distinguished into brilliant perfection: the benches along the terraces designed in the Chinese style to complement the Chinese-inspired balustrade—both work beautifully with the classical style of the house—or the chimneys on the terraces, whose slightly curved bases and tops are also reminiscent of Chinese forms.

The exterior, in short, gives endless pleasure, whatever your approach. As with all great buildings, the more attention you pay to it, the more you will be fascinated and rewarded.

The Interior   Dazzling. That is the only word to describe the result of the long concentration of Jefferson's brilliant mind. Dazzling in its intellectual detail—almost every room, for example, has an entablature or frieze based on one from a Greek or Roman temple, and he used different classical orders in different rooms (Ionic in the entrance hall, Doric in the dining room, Corinthian in the parlor). Dazzling in its practical yet almost playful inventiveness—his ingenious dumbwaiter in the dining room, the parlor doors that open together, the folding ladder in the entrance hall . . . on and on it goes. Dazzling in its overall conception and decoration, whose sum effect makes it one of the most beautiful interiors in the United States.

This is a house that must be seen, and I therefore won't describe it room by room. Instead I'll pass on some observations intended to give you a feel for the genius of the house.

There is a wonderful overall sense of lightness, partly because doors, windows and skylights—fourteen of the latter alone— seem to be everywhere, creating an openness that is downright exhilarating. An endearing eccentricity also shows through from time to time; in the entrance hall, for instance, with its extraordinary calendar clock whose weights go through the floor thanks to a small misjudgment by Mr. Jefferson. Constant reminders of his design ability are everywhere; the clock and the coffee urn, the Windsor chairs in the hall, the delicate cherry-and-beech parquet floor. The solutions to practical problems are of a pragmatic ingenuity that still startles; the placement of his bed in an alcove between his study and the bedroom itself, giving a wonderful sense of person; intimacy and unity sheltered from a prying world. This is a house to savor, like a fine, complex wine whose components only sort themselves out in your mind if you come to it open and curious. It can be visited over and over again, for it never tires, never palls.

The Grounds The setting for Monticello, on a leveled mountaintop, is nothing short of spectacular, and Jefferson took great pains to make it as beautiful as he possibly could. "No occupation is so delightful to me as the culture of the earth," he wrote to the painter Charles Willson Peale in 1811, "and no culture comparable to that of the garden . . . But though an old man, I am but a young gardener."

The gardens, both flower and vegetable, have been extensively restored, as have the orchard, the vineyard and the general landscaping. The roundabout walk and flower border on the west front of the house is of the greatest and most immediate interest, and this garden is strongly influenced by what

Jefferson had seen of English gardens. ("The gardening in that country," he wrote in 1786, "is the article in which it surpasses all the earth.") The flower border is divided into 105 compartments, each ten feet in length and planted with single clumps of flowers. It is a glorious sight. But remember that Jefferson never "fixed" his gardens. Rather, he constantly experimented with color combinations and unusual and rare plants as well as the more familiar flowers. So extensive was his interest in gardening, that he brought about what has been called "a living horticultural encyclopedia." This interest extended to trees, as well, and Jefferson was known to take favored visitors to see his pet ones, a few of which survive to this day. But then, what wasn't this man accomplished in? As Harry Truman said, "I don't see how he could do and be so many things." But thank God he did, and was.

Do take time to visit his grave before leaving. Once I was at Monticello on Jefferson's birthday, April 13. Each year at that time wreaths are placed on his grave during a very simple, dignified and quintessentially American ceremony; one, I suspect, that would have pleased him mightily and is suited to the magnificently simple epitaph that he instructed be placed on his marker . . . which he, of course, designed himself: "Here was buried Thomas Jefferson Author of the Declaration of Independence Of the Statute of Virginia for Religious Freedom And Father of the University of Virginia."

Monticello is open daily, except Christmas Day. From March 1–October 31, the hours are 8–5. From November–February, the hours are 9:00–4:30. Admission: $5; senior citizens, $4; children 6–11, $1. Phone: 804-295-8181. You should put aside time to visit the gift shop, too, for it is one of the most attractive I have seen at a historic site. And try to arrive early for your visit, before the long lines develop.

The University of Virginia

I consider the common plan followed in this country, but not in others, of making one large and expensive building, as unfortunately erroneous. It is infinitely better to erect a small and separate lodge for each separate professorship with only a hall below for his class, and two chambers above for himself; joining these lodges by barracks for a certain portion of the students, opening into a covered way to give a dry communication between all the schools. The whole of these arranged around an open square of grass and trees, would make it, what it should be in fact, an academical village, instead of a large and common den of noise, of filth and of fetid air. It would afford that quiet retirement so friendly to study, and lessen the dangers of fire, infection and tumult. Every professor would be the police officer of the students adjacent to his own lodge, which should include those of his own class of preference, and might be at the head of their table, if, as I suppose, it can be reconciled with the necessary economy to dine them in smaller and separate parties, rather than in a large and common mess. These separate buildings, too, might be erected successively and occasionally as the number of professorships and students should be increased, or the funds become competent.

—Thomas Jefferson to Hugh White and others (1810)

In 1976, in a Bicentennial poll conducted by the *Journal of the American Institute of Architects,* of 46 noted architectural practitioners, historians and critics to nominate "the proudest achievement of American architecture in the past 200 years," "far and away in first place was Mr. Jefferson's University of Virginia campus."

A revolutionary idea, this academical village, as Mr. Jefferson (he is still referred to in this way by Virginians) called his most magnificent architectural legacy, which dignifies and graces the large university. It is an extraordinary achievement by any standards, but even more so considering that Jefferson began it at the age of seventy-four. It would remain his heart's project until his death.

His 1810 description of the purpose and use of such a village began to be realized in 1817 with the construction of the first pavilion. He did not mention in that letter what today is at the center of it all, the **Rotunda,** the model for which is Hadrian's Pantheon in Rome but which here has been reduced by exactly half. It was Benjamin Latrobe, architect of the Capitol in Washington, who suggested a domed building on this site. Jefferson enthusiastically adopted his suggestion and wrote that it was to be "accommodated to the purposes of a Library for the University with rooms for drawing, music, examinations and other

The great rotunda, a half-size replica of Rome's Pantheon, is the center-piece of Mr. Jefferson's magnificent campus at the University of Virginia.

accessory purposes." During the nineteenth century it underwent several modifications, including an Annex (1853) on the north side that, in 1895, was destroyed by a fire that severely damaged the Rotunda as well. (Mr. Jefferson's statue by Alexander Galt in the Rotunda was saved from the fire by students—they got it outside by dragging it on a mattress—and if you look carefully you will see signs of the resulting damage.)

The rebuilding was undertaken by Stanford White of the famous New York architectural firm of McKim, Mead and White. One of White's masterpieces was the old Madison Square Garden (1890) in New York City, now destroyed. And it was here, in the Roof Garden, that he was murdered by an unbalanced millionaire named Harry K. Thaw who accused White —correctly—of having an affair with his wife. White considerably altered the interior of the Rotunda; but finally, in 1974, a true restoration to Jefferson's original plan was undertaken, and all that is left of White's changes is the north portico, the north wings and the east and west wings.

The interior now consists of three floors, the top—and most beautiful—being the Dome or Library Room. This, with its alcoves, paired columns and serenely classic open space at the center, is one of the most elegant yet intimate public rooms in this country, a fact not wasted on the university, which commandeers it for its most prestigious entertaining. It is more than worthwhile to spend time exploring this building, enjoying its inherent beauties and also the furnishings and exhibits.

From the south portico steps of the Rotunda you look out over the **academical village.** To your left and right are ranged the pavilions, or lodges as Jefferson called them, each row consisting of five two-story pavilions where the professors both lived and taught, with interconnecting single-story dormitory rooms, all joined by a covered, columned passageway. Each pavilion served as the center for subject studies, with the students clustered around it; each is also unique in design, being either in the style of Palladio or based on one of the great buildings of antiquity. Behind these rows are landscaped grounds—it is here you see those lovely single-brick serpentine walls—and beyond the grounds are additional buildings (Jefferson called them "hotels") that were used as dining rooms and dormitories. They are now known as the East and West Ranges.

Originally Jefferson planned his village as an open-ended square with a green some 800 feet wide, but problems inherent to the site made this impossible to achieve, so instead there is the 200-foot Lawn you see today. In addition, the south end, sadly enough, has been closed off by another Stanford White building, which effectively destroys the view to the mountains and changes the entire character of the original concept.

You can spend a long time there, wandering about, without growing bored. Rather, you will find yourself constantly surprised and refreshed by the whole. For instance, your perspective will be completely changed if you walk along the edge of the Lawn and the buildings. The Lawn itself is terraced, and therefore each section offers a different perspective, too. The gardens, stunningly restored over many years by the Garden Club of Virginia, are worth a trip in themselves, and the undulating brick walls give the whole scene a pleasant feeling of flow and change. The gardens were under the overall supervision of Alden Hopkins, landscape architect for Colonial Williamsburg, for Kenmore (see page 43) and the extraordinary gardens of Gunston Hall (see page 37). It is a unique experience, for no other university in the world is set up in this way. Strange, isn't it, that our most brilliant and beautiful college complex has had little or no influence on what has followed.

Walking tours of the areas Jefferson designed start at the

Rotunda during the school year (except at holidays and during exam periods), Monday–Friday at 10, 11, 2, 3 and 4; May–August, 10 and 2. Admission: Free. Phone: 804-924-1019. The Rotunda is open daily, 9:00–4:45.

Ash Lawn   From 1799 to 1826 this was the home of James Monroe, fifth President of the United States and close friend of Thomas Jefferson. In part, Monroe moved to this spot, then called Highlands and only two and a half miles from Monticello, to be closer to his friend. There even is some speculation that Jefferson helped plan the house, and it also is claimed that he chose the site.

About 1840, part of the house was destroyed—archaeological research suggests that a fire was the cause—and the main part of the house that you now see, including the entrance, was built in the 1870's. Only the wing behind this structure dates from Monroe's time.

Even so, this is a delightful spot. First of all, its setting—a 550-acre estate from which you can see the dome of Monticello —is gently appealing; and it is pleasant to wander about, look- ing at the gardens and the boxwood and generally enjoying the air of rural peace. There are sheep grazing on the lawn, for this is still a working plantation, and the fact that the curator lives in the Victorian section of the house makes it even more home- like.

I quite enjoy visiting here, and one of my fondest memories of Ash Lawn is seeing peacocks spread their tails in courtship. I happened to be there early one soft morning, and consequently was the only visitor. The peacocks, and there are about two dozen of them, were making a fearful racket because it was mating season, and I watched, fascinated, as their tails would rise and spread, the mystical-looking "eyes" on the infinitely long feathers glowing in the clear morning sunlight.

As to the house, its interest lies in the furnishings and Monroe memorabilia more than the architecture, which is that of a typical farmhouse of the early 1800's rather than a distin- guished plantation house; Monroe himself called it his "cabin- castle." But the very simplicity gives it a touching appeal, and some of Monroe's contributions are worth seeing. For instance, in the sitting room—the first room that you enter—there is a handsome bust of Napoleon by Antonio Canova, the great Ital-

The front section of Ash Lawn, built in the 1870's. At the rear is the portion that formed the home of James Monroe. A delightful spot with peacocks and gardens and boxwood and, overall, rural tranquility.

ian sculptor, and some excellent French Empire chairs. But my favorite room, because it is so comfortably intimate, is the Monroes' bedroom, with a magnificent bed (note the feather-and-palm carving on the posts), a Sheraton secretary that belonged to James Madison, and an Eli Terry pillar and scroll mantelpiece clock. Not a bit Presidential; in fact, very republican in feeling, this room, and all the nicer for it.

The remaining rooms have been done with informed imagination, the most unusual being the children's room, with a regal crown canopy bed and a doll's tea table set for a party, the invited "guests" seated around it. Take note, too, of the fine Louis XVI desk in the study, which is almost the twin of the Monroe Doctrine desk in Fredericksburg (see page 47) and the portraits of Hortense de Beauharnais, daughter of the Empress Josephine and Queen of Holland, her brother Eugene and Mme. Campan, headmistress of the school Hortense and Elisa Monroe jointly attended. Large and rather grand for this simple house, they were a gift of Hortense and hang in the dining room, where their presence makes a touching reminder of a long-vanished friendship.

I would suggest that you see Ash Lawn after Monticello. It provides a nice intermediate level between the Olympian heights of Mr. Jefferson's creation and today's world.

Ash Lawn is open daily, March–October, 9–6; November–February, 10–5. Closed: Thanksgiving, December 25, January 1.

Admission: $4; senior citizens, $3.50; children 6–11, $1. Phone: 804-293-9539.

Historic Michie Tavern   Patrick Henry's father, Major John Henry, sold the land this tavern originally occupied to a Scotsman named John Michie. Hardly a major event in the nation's history, but I pass it on to you nonetheless. The tavern opened in 1765 and would remain in the Michie family for more than 150 years.

In the 1920's, it was bought by a Mrs. Martin Henderson to house her collection of antiques. At the time, Monticello had recently opened to the public; realizing the potential value of placing the tavern near Mr. Jefferson's home, Mrs. Henderson had the tavern dismantled, moved and reconstructed on its present site. Then the Depression struck, and she was forced to sell both the tavern and antiques. It would change hands again; finally, in 1968, it was sold to a group of local businessmen who remain the owners.

Today it is a major tourist attraction—how wise Mrs. Henderson was!—that is too commercial for my taste but is, I must admit, cleverly done. The tavern is still the primary attraction, but now there are other restored buildings, a kitchen, smokehouse, gristmill and springhouse—and the owners are creating an eighteenth-century craft village to be staffed by the handicapped, each of whom will be adept in one of the crafts displayed. There also is an "Ordinary," a restored slave house next to the tavern that serves surprisingly good food considering the volume required (fried chicken, corn bread, stewed tomatoes and so forth) at an agreeably modest price. Next to the gristmill is a general store offering Virginia crafts, some antiques and general tourist fare; and, on the second floor of the mill itself, the Virginia Wine Museum that traces the state's wine industry from 1607 to the present.

Still, the tavern remains the primary draw, and the tours of it are packed. Again an agreeable surprise; it's well done and makes an interesting tour.

Historic Michie Tavern is open daily, 9–5. Closed: December 25, January 1. Admission to the Tavern: $3; senior citizens and college students, $2.50; children 6–12, $1. The Ordinary buffet is served daily between 11:30 and 3:00. Phone: 804-977-1234.

Castle Hill (1764/1824)   This unusual house was built in two parts. The first, a wooden Georgian structure, was built by Dr. Thomas Walker, an executor of Jefferson's father's estate and young Tom's guardian. Today Dr. Walker is best remembered as an explorer and land speculator. This building went up in 1764. The second, a red-brick shuttered Federal house with a portico, was built in 1824 by Walker's granddaughter Judith and her husband, William Cabell Rives. Apparently not everyone approved, for as Judith wrote, "It was thought something of a presumption for two such young people to enter plans for remodeling a place which my father and grandfather had thought a suitable residence for them, but we braved all criticism—turned the garden into a lawn, cut down the steeple-shaped poplars already showing signs of decay, added a hall here, wings there, porticoes everywhere; in short," she blithely adds, "[we] made ourselves generally comfortable without reference to the uplifted hands and eyes that sometimes predicted ruin to the venerable place." Later still, in 1840, the two side wings were added. This time not a murmur was heard.

Judith's granddaughter Amélie Rives inherited the estate and also wrote what were considered rather racy (and successful) novels as well as poetry and several plays that wound up on Broadway. Her second husband, to whom she was introduced by Oscar Wilde, was Prince Pierre Troubetzkoy, a Russian who gained some distinction as a portrait painter.

Unfortunately, the family is more interesting than the interior. Although the two sections of the house are connected by a wide hallway that doubled as a ballroom, there was no attempt to integrate them. The result is, at first, rather disconcerting, but the separation into two distinct styles has a kind of perverse charm. The furnishings are moderately interesting, and some of Prince Troubetzkoy's paintings still hang here. Of the two sections, I prefer the earlier; it has some rather nice carved work.

The grounds and gardens are of greater distinction. The upper terrace—there are three—of the formal garden was designed by Alden Hopkins in 1947 and is still very lovely, while the front lawn, modeled by Judith in 1832 after a French estate, contains box hedges that reach almost thirty feet, making them among the tallest of their kind in the world. They also are very old, dating back to the original house. And everywhere you look there are splendid trees—horse chestnut, magnolia, cedar, ash, tulip—that give a very special feel to this place of ancient dignity.

Before you leave, you may wish to see the family cemetery near the parking lot where Judith, Amélie and her prince are buried.

Castle Hill is thirteen miles northeast of Charlottesville and is set in a countryside filled with impressive estates and farms. It is pretty enough to suggest that you take some extra time to explore your surroundings here by getting off on some of the side roads, particularly along Route 250. From Charlottesville, take 250 E to Shadwell. Then bear left on 22 E and continue to Cismont where you will pick up 231. The entrance to Castle Hill is two miles north and on the left. Open: March–November, 10–5. Admission: $3; children 6–12, $1. Phone: 804-293-7297.

A DRIVE

Charlottesville is placed in some of the most ravishing countryside in Virginia. An Eden, Mr. Jefferson called it, and I, for one, am not about to dispute his pronouncement.

Consequently, there are some glorious drives from Charlottesville. The most famous, of course, are the Skyline Drive (see page 84) and the Blue Ridge Parkway (see page 91), but I also particularly enjoy the one described below which, I think, incorporates the best of the best. I would suggest you take a picnic lunch and make a day of it.

Leave Charlottesville going south on 20 to Scottsville, a route that will take you past Monticello and through lush Virginia countryside. Scottsville is a pleasing little town on the James, and here you will go west on 6 to 29, which you will take south, again, until it rejoins 6. Follow 6 to 151, and then take 151 south to 56, which you will then take north to the Blue Ridge Parkway.

The first part of this route, on 6 and 151, will take you through a landscape designed to prove Mr. Jefferson's claim; it will give you glimpses of at least a dozen homes in all their historic splendor and generally make you feel you have entered a time warp and landed back in the nineteenth century. Then, when you begin your ascent to the Blue Ridge Parkway, you go deeper and deeper into country, leaving the civilizing influence of farms well behind. A little more than halfway along this route, you will come to the site of Crabtree Falls, almost 1,500 feet high and supposedly the highest waterfall east of the Mississippi. Stop here—there's a convenient parking area—and follow the Forest Service Trail to the falls, where you can either stop and enjoy the sight or continue up the trail alongside the falls. This is a special, even moving place. The water seems to spring from the earth itself, and you are surrounded by deeply peaceful evergreen trees which, I've always felt, bring a depth to forest silence that is almost cushioning; a pillow for the senses. The water, falling from ledge to ledge, forms constantly changing patterns, and its sound is gentle and refreshing; not here will you know the mighty roar of Niagara. Look up and you will catch little glimpses of the falls through the greenery, a preview of coming attractions should you decide to follow the trail. It is a scene that will awake the latent romantic in the most confirmed cynic. Not extravagant in their beauty, these falls, but deeply, almost atavistically, appealing.

From here the climb to the Parkway becomes more and more like a trail, particularly after you pass the Montebello Fish Hatchery; finally, almost regretfully, you emerge onto the splendor of the Blue Ridge Parkway, which you will take north to the Charlottesville exit, the very beginning of the Parkway. If you really wish to get a panoramic view of the entire area, by the way, hike up to Humpback Rocks, just over six miles from the beginning of the Parkway. Watch the road markers so you'll know when you're approaching the spot. There's a small visitor center here and a hiking trail of less than a mile to the rocks, where the view for once validates the word "breathtaking."

LYNCHBURG

At a bend in the James River, set high above it on seven hills, is Lynchburg, a thriving city of more than 65,000 people that once was a center for tobacco—it is claimed that John Lynch, founder of the city in 1786, built the country's first tobacco warehouse here—but now is a regional industrial center.

In feeling it's a somewhat curious town. Somehow, to me at least, it seems more Northern than Southern. I can't put my finger on the reason. . . . Perhaps it's because so many Northerners have moved here that you can feel their aura. Physically it's pleasant, even appealing. The town suffered little during the Civil War, even though it was the largest Southern armorer after Richmond, and it has some nice examples of domestic architecture from the Federal period onward as well as one splendid urban creation from this century.

Still, the real point of Lynchburg is to use it as a base from which to visit what lies nearby, in particular Appomattox Court House National Historical Park and Poplar Forest, Thomas Jefferson's final masterpiece of domestic architecture. Red Hill, where Patrick Henry spent his last years, is also within driving distance.

WHAT TO SEE AND DO

The most interesting single building in the city is **Point of Honor** (c. 1815), an unusual and striking Federal house set above the James on Daniel's Hill. (Its location is exposed enough that you can see it from many points in the old downtown area.)

The house, originally the center of operations for an almost 1,000-acre plantation, was built by Dr. George Cabell, Sr., a locally eminent physician. Patrick Henry was both his patient and friend, and Cabell married Henry's cousin Sarah Winston. What particularly distinguishes this red-brick house on the outside is the sophisticated front façade with its octagonal bays. Inside is some distinctive carved woodwork, but the house is still being furnished and there is relatively little there at the moment. The rooms, though, are elegantly proportioned and worth seeing for themselves. The name of the house, by the way, came about because it was the site of a duel.

Before you leave you might be interested in exploring Cabell Street, on which Point of Honor resides, and noting some of the other houses. In particular I like the Dabney-Scott-Adams House (1853) at 405. Large—there are twenty rooms—this late stuccoid example of Greek Revival is now owned by the Lynchburg Historical Foundation. I also like the two Victorian houses at 509 and 201. But then, there are several excellent examples of the Victorian here.

Point of Honor, at 112 Cabell Street, is open Tuesday–Saturday, 1–4. Closed: January and February. Admission: $1; students, 50¢. Phone: 804-847-1459.

The other most interesting area of the city is Courthouse Hill, which has the single most original feature in Lynchburg, **Monument Terrace** (1924). Briefly, this ensemble consists of a 139-step staircase with a World War I memorial statue of a soldier at the foot. At the top is the First Unitarian Church, designed at the same time, with a Civil War memorial. The whole makes an extremely successful and dynamic use of a difficult urban space. It has, in purely American terms, some of the feeling of the Spanish Steps in Rome.

At the top of Courthouse Hill is, logically enough, the **Old Court House** (1855), a Greek Revival building loosely based on the Parthenon. Inside are exhibits designed to show Lynchburg's history, which they do rather successfully. (Open: Tuesday–Saturday, 1–4. Closed: January and February. Admission: $1; students, 50¢. Phone: 804-847-1459.) Also of interest is the Old City Hall as well as some of the houses.

In addition, you may wish to see the **Anne Spencer House** (1313 Pierce Street. Phone: 804-845-1313 for an appointment). Spencer (1882–1975) was a rather well-known black poet, and her writing cottage, EdanKraal, is behind the house. The grounds also contain a nice garden. Other sights: The restored **Quaker Meeting House** (5810 Fort Avenue. Open: Daily, 8–4. Admission: Free. Phone: 804-239-2548), the **Miller-Claytor House,** the most interesting fact about which is that Thomas Jefferson once amazed its residents by nonchalantly taking a bite of a tomato, a fruit then considered poisonous. (The house is in Riverside Park.) Riverside Park also has the packet boat *Marshall,* which carried Stonewall Jackson's body from here to a point near Lexington. (Open: Daily, 7–11. Admission: Free.) Finally, Randolph-Macon Woman's College is here and has on its campus the **Maier Museum of Art** (phone: 804-846-7392 for times), which contains ninety American paintings on permanent display and includes such well-known names as Mary Cassatt, Winslow Homer, Edward Hicks, Grandma Moses and Georgia O'Keeffe.

Monument Terrace, dignified and imposing, is one of the primary attractions of Lynchburg. It is so well conceived and executed as to be worth a little extra effort to see.

Point of Honor, with its matched polygonal bays and refined detailing, is a great example of Federal architecture.

NEARBY

Appomattox Court House National Historic Park

General:
   In accordance with the substance of my letter of the 8th
inst., I propose to receive the surrender of the Army of Northern Virginia on the following terms, to wit: Rolls of all the
officers and men to be made in duplicate, one copy to be given
to an officer to be designated by me, the other to be retained
by such officer or officers as you may designate. The officers
to give their individual paroles not to take up arms against
the Government of the United States until properly ex-
changed, and each company or regimental commander to
sign a like parole for the men of their commands. The arms,
artillery and public property to be parked, and stacked, and
turned over to the officers appointed by me to receive them.
This will not embrace the side–arms of the officers, nor their
private horses or baggage. This done, each officer and man
will be allowed to return to his home, not to be disturbed by
the United States authorities so long as they observe their
paroles, and the laws in force where they may reside.

                                    Very respectfully,
                                    U. S. Grant,
                                    Lieutenant-General
                                    [April 9, 1865]

General:
   I received your letter of this date containing the terms of
surrender of the Army of Northern Virginia as prepared by
you. As they are substantially the same as those expressed in
your letter of the 8th inst., they are accepted. I will proceed
to designate the proper officers to carry the stipulations into
effect.

                                    R. E. Lee, General
                                    [April 9, 1865]

Lee's return to his troops after the surrender was recalled by
General James Longstreet: "From force of habit a burst of salu-
tations greeted him, but it quieted as suddenly as it arose. The
road was packed by standing troops as he approached, the men
with hats off, heads and hearts bowed down. As he passed they
raised their heads and looked down upon him with swimming

eyes. Those who could find voice said good-bye, those who could not speak and were near, passed their hands gently over the sides of Traveller."

The formal surrender ceremonies would take place on April 12, four years to the day after the firing on Fort Sumter, and this bloody, rending war, this foretaste of the horrors of the World Wars of this century, this epically tragic and fratricidal struggle whose effects would last for one-hundred years was, for all intents and purposes, at an end.

After the war the tiny village of Appomattox Court House— it probably never had more than 100 or so people—moved on in its own quiet way. Then, in 1892, the courthouse burned and the county seat was moved to the town of Appomattox, three miles distant. In 1893 the McLean house, scene of the surrender, was dismantled by one M. E. Dunlap of Niagara Falls, New York, of all places, who had a scheme that involved moving the house to Washington. His plan failed.

From that time until 1935, when President Franklin D. Roosevelt signed a bill enabling the National Park Service to purchase land and rebuild the village, Appomattox lay a-mouldering. And a good thing, too, for it meant that little had changed in the intervening years. Today the village looks almost exactly as it did when Grant and Lee met to discuss the terms of surrender.

It is difficult to describe how moving it is to visit here. Certainly I wasn't expecting this kind of experience when I arrived

At the left is the McLean house, where, in the parlor, Lee surrendered to Grant, ending, for all intents and purposes, the horror of the Civil War.

on a brilliant day in late October when there were very few other visitors. I had no preconceived ideas of what I would see, but the utter peacefulness, simplicity and great dignity of this brilliant re-creation had an overwhelming effect. This, indeed, is a national shrine, one that every American should visit, for its very simplicity and rural isolation somehow symbolically and perfectly suit it to be the backdrop for the death of the Confederacy and the rebirth of the again united states. The village has been removed from the exigencies of time.

When you visit the village, go first to the **Courthouse.** On the first floor you can get answers to any questions you might have and generally orient yourself to the site. Then be sure to go upstairs to see the two fifteen-minute slide shows; like everything else here, they are superbly done. The first is a chronological account, from April 2–12, of the events leading to the surrender ceremony. The second is based on first-person accounts of the surrender ceremonies and is deeply moving. Then you are on your own to visit what you wish.

Of greatest interest, naturally, is the **McLean House,** the most imposing home in the village and thus the place chosen for Lee and Grant to use. It was oddly appropriate that this family should witness the end of the war, because they had been involved in its first battle at Bull Run/Manassas (see page 67). Wilmer McLean's farm had been on the fields of Manassas, and after the second battle he decided he would move his family to a more secure location. Unfortunately he came here, to this attractive brick two-story house with its inviting porch across the front. Poor man. After Grant and Lee left his comfortable parlor, the Union officers walked away with the furniture.

The remaining buildings, the jail, tavern, store, law office and so on, complete this period re-creation and will be of more or less interest to you depending on your personal tastes. You can also walk or drive northeast from the parking lot to Lee's headquarters (about a twenty-minute walk) and west to the cemetery, with eighteen Confederate soldiers and one unknown Union man, at the edge of the village, and then go on to the North Carolina Monument and Grant's headquarters, a total distance of about a mile. All of this is interesting individually, but it is the whole that is important—this is our history. There is a little bit of the meaning of Appomattox in the makeup of each of us.

Appomattox Court House National Historical Park is on Route 24, which is about twenty miles east of Lynchburg via Route 460. The park is open every day of the year. The buildings are open daily, 9–5. Closed: January 1, Martin Luther King's Birthday, Washington's Birthday, Veteran's Day, Thanksgiving and December 25. Admission: $1 per car; people under 16 or over 62, free. Phone: 804-352-8782.

Poplar Forest Jefferson's buildings at the University of Virginia may be this country's greatest architectural achievement (see page 132), and Monticello may be the most interesting house ever built in this country (see page 127), but this sylvan sanctuary that Jefferson built for himself at a short distance from Lynchburg in Bedford County is a masterpiece and his most perfect creation in domestic architecture.

The land on which the house stands was part of a plantation that came to Jefferson through his wife's family, and his holdings here constituted almost half his estate. During his second presidency he decided, in 1806, just as Monticello was finally nearing completion, to build a new house, which would become Poplar Forest. By 1808 the walls were up. In 1809 Jefferson was able to stay there, but the house would remain unfinished for many years; as at Monticello, Jefferson hated to complete his project.

The house steadily grew in importance for him, particularly after he retired from the presidency. "When finished," he wrote in 1812, "it will be the best dwelling house in the state, except that of Monticello; perhaps preferable to that, as more proportioned to the faculties of a private citizen." For a long period he would make three visits each year to his new house, a distance of ninety or so miles from Monticello as measured by the odometer attached to his carriage wheel. Among other reasons, he loved it for the tranquility it offered, an element completely lacking at Monticello, where guests were never-ending and even strangers would make their way into the house. One story has it that people would approach him on the lawn and then, at a distance of a dozen yards or so, would stare at him as if he were on exhibit. No wonder he liked to get away.

When his grandson Francis Eppes married in 1822, Jefferson presented him with the house and 1,000 acres of land. Several years later Eppes sold the estate to a man named William Cobbs who, in turn, left it to his daughter, Emily Hutter. Poplar Forest remained in the family until 1946. It had two more owners before a nonprofit organization bought it in 1983 and is now working to restore it.

The house is an octagon, believed to be the first in this country. It is one story high on the entrance side, two on the garden side, because it is set on a rise. Both front and back have handsome porticoes, as at Monticello, but the back one here is raised above the garden. There is a square room at the center of the house. This is the dining room, and in its ceiling is a skylight. To either side of this room are two octagonal rooms believed to have had alcove beds set in the middle, dividing the dressing and sitting areas.

Of the alcove beds that Jefferson so admired, the wife of the noted architect Dr. William Thornton (see page 33) remarked of those at Monticello, "When we went to bed we had to mount a little ladder of a staircase . . . into rooms with the beds fixed up in recesses in the walls . . . Every thing has a whimsical and droll appearance." Two other octagonal rooms complete the floor.

As always when Jefferson was the architect, this is an ingenious house. It is also small, airy, wonderfully intimate and very beautiful in a simple way that only a master could contrive. In design it is perfection. When it is fully restored, along with the grounds, one of this country's great houses will stand revealed.

In the meantime, there are no regular visiting hours. To set up an appointment to see the house, you can phone 804-845-5128 or 804-525-1806 or write: The Jefferson Poplar Forest Fund, P.O. Box 1299, 720 Commerce Street, Lynchburg, Va. 24505.

Red Hill Shrine "One of the garden spots of the world," Patrick Henry called this plantation of more than 2,900 acres. Well, every home-owner is entitled to a little hyperbole, and this is indeed an agreeable spot, if not quite the Eden that Henry claimed. But I can understand why he said it, for it was here that —at the age of fifty-seven, old before his time, and tired—Henry retired from the political field and obviously reveled in the peace and tranquility that this countryside radiates even today.

At this time Patrick Henry was far from poor; he was, in fact, one of the wealthiest landowners in Virginia, but nonetheless this is a very simple plantation. You first enter the Patrick Henry Museum where you can see some personal memorabilia as well as a short orientation film on Henry, his life and times. Then you are free to choose a guided or self-guided walking tour of the reconstructed buildings. First look for the huge Osage Orange Tree, the pride and joy of the grounds, for it is the largest in the world: It has a span of 90 feet, is 54 feet high, and could be as old as 400 years.

Now on to the house, which has been rebuilt (the original burned in 1919) to appear exactly as it was when Henry lived there. As I mentioned, it's small. Downstairs there are three main rooms, upstairs only two. A very good thing that his seventeen children never arrived here at one time. All that Henry did to this simple structure built in the 1770's was add the bedroom wing to hear, he said, the patter of raindrops on the shingles as he fell asleep.

The rooms are simply furnished, and some of the pieces—a walnut washstand in the bedroom, a walnut writing desk in the parlor where Henry died in 1799, and others—belonged to him. It's a curious little house—cottage, really—and appropriate for Henry; after all, it would be startling to find that one of our most radical Founding Fathers had lived in a grand, colonnaded mansion à la Mount Vernon.

Two other sites to visit on the grounds: the law office-library

Patrick Henry's last home, Red Hill Shrine, where he liked to hear the patter of raindrops on the shingles as he fell asleep.

and the cemetery. The law office, a one-room building, seems far too small to have contained such an explosive intelligence, and the cemetery, lovingly cared for, is touching in its simplicity. On Henry's gravestone: "His fame his best epitaph."

Red Hill Shrine is about 35 miles southeast of Lynchburg just outside the town of Brookneal. Take 501-S to Brookneal, then get on 600-E to Red Hill. Open: Daily, April–October, 9–5; November–March, 9–4. Closed: December 25. Admission: $2; children 6–13, 80¢. Phone: 804-376-2044.

RICHMOND

"Richmond," Winston Churchill intoned to the Virginia Assembly in 1946, "the historic capital of world-famous Virginia." It's almost a letdown to add that it also is a city with the warmth of a small town, the historic appeal of a capital city not only of a state but also of a nation, and the advantages, cultural and intellectual, of a major urban center.

The city lies at the falls line, the head of Tidewater and that spot on the James beyond which river traffic is no longer possible. For seven miles here the turbulent river flows around great boulders and small islands, its whitecapped course swift and angry. And then, abruptly, just below Richmond, it becomes a wide tidal estuary, placid and peaceful as it flows by the great James River Tidewater plantations and on out to the Chesapeake.

The city was founded in 1737 by William Byrd II, builder of Westover (see page 208), who named it Richmond after the city on the Thames. It became the capital of the state primarily through the efforts of Thomas Jefferson: "I had proposed its removal so early as October '76," he wrote, "but it did not prevail until the [legislative] session of May '79." In 1861 it became the capital of a nation, the Confederate States of America. Today it is a modern Southern city—brand-new buildings attracting the eye, with more on the drawing boards, a center of banking and finance, manufacturing and printing and publishing—that, fortunately, has retained a great deal of its more than two-century-old charm.

You could stay four or five days without exhausting all the

tourist possibilities—particularly if you make it your headquarters for exploring the James River plantations (see page 204), a course I would strongly suggest for your consideration.

Before you explore the riches of Richmond in detail, enjoy what is described below, for it will give you a basic sense of the city and, when you are through, make you feel at home here.

> There is at Nismes, in the south of France, a building called the Maison quarée, erected in the time of the Caesars, and which is allowed, without contradiction to be the most perfect and precious remain of antiquity in existence. . . . I determined, therefore, to adopt this model, and to have all its proportions justly observed. As it was impossible for an foreign artist to know, what number and sizes of apartments would suit the different corps of our government, nor how they should be connected with one another, I undertook to form that arrangement, and this being done, I committed them to an architect (Monsieur Clerissault) . . . who had particularly studied and measured the Maison quarée of Nismes, and had published a book containing most excellent plans, descriptions, and observations on it.
>
> —Thomas Jefferson, Paris (1786)

And so was born the plan for the **Virginia State Capitol,** a Roman temple placed on Shockoe Hill in the (almost) wilder-

Mr. Jefferson's Capitol, modeled after the Maison Carrée at Nîmes, is still among the most beautiful in the country.

ness of 1788 and where the oldest continuous legislative body in the Western Hemisphere still meets. The style of the building would spawn, over the years, hundreds of imitations—on and off hills—all over America, in everything from schools to state capitols to courthouses. This, the first pure Roman temple form built since antiquity, is one of the most influential buildings in our history. Yet, despite its myriad imitators, it is still one of our most beautiful public buildings, its purity and nobility intact and timeless.

The original building, as designed by Jefferson and Clerisseau, can be seen in a plaster model that Jefferson had built in France and that is now on exhibit in the entrance hall of the Capitol. As built, there were differences, primarily in that the steps were eliminated, pilasters were added to the sides, and a window was placed in the pediment. The two flanking buildings were added between 1904 and 1906, where the House of Delegates (east wing) and Senate now sit, as were the steps, while the pediment windows were removed. Today the central building, from the front, is more like Jefferson's original intention then at any time in its history.

Inside, the most interesting architectural feature is the rotunda, with its curious interior dome, the first in the country, that can't be seen from the exterior because it sits twenty feet below the A-line roof. It is here, too, dead center on the checkerboard black-and-white stone floor, that one of Jean Antoine Houdon's masterpieces, the life-size statue of Washington, crowns the interior.

Houdon was among the greatest sculptors of the eighteenth century and without peer in his ability to capture his subjects in portrait busts. Hired by Jefferson in 1785 to make this statue, the sculptor agreed "to leave the statues of kings unfinished, & to go to America to take the true figure by actual inspiration & measurement." In October 1785 he and three assistants were at Mount Vernon. Back in Paris by January 1786, he worked on the statue over the next two years, completing it in clay. The transfer into marble took until 1791, and it was only in 1796 that the statue arrived in the Capitol. (Originally, Washington was to have appeared dressed in a toga. Fortunately he gently but firmly suggested to Houdon that there be "some little deviation in favor of the modern costume," and he appears wearing a simplified version of the Revolutionary uniform.)

As we see it today, Washington exudes that particular dignity and presence yet without hauteur that was so unique to him; "That is the man himself," Lafayette exclaimed when he saw it. Washington's left arm rests on thirteen Roman fasces (rods), symbolic of the thirteen colonies, and his sword hangs here as well. In his right hand he carries a cane. The plowshare of the farmer-statesman is behind him. Indeed, he is represented as the modern Cincinnatus, the citizen-soldier of Rome who, after being granted dictatorial powers, defeated Rome's enemies and returned to his farm.

The head has an extraordinary vitality that gives it a lifelike presence and psychological truth that raises it to the qualification of masterpiece. It *is* Washington, just as Lafayette observed, and then added, "I can almost realize he is going to move."

Around him, in seven niches in the Rotunda walls, are busts of the other Virginia-born presidents: Jefferson, Madison, Monroe, Harrison, Tyler, Taylor and Wilson. The bust of Lafayette, also by Houdon, was commissioned by the Virginia General Assembly in 1784.

The remaining public rooms consist of the Old Senate and House of Delegates chambers. The latter is now a museum and has statuary of great Virginians scattered about, including a bronze, full-length statue of Robert E. Lee placed on the exact spot where he accepted command of Virginia's Confederate forces.

The Capitol is open: April–November, daily, 9–5; December–March, Monday–Saturday, 9–5; Sunday, 1–5. Closed: Thanksgiving, December 25, January 1. Admission: Free.

Capitol Square The grounds are delightful, informal and romantic and very inviting. The first plan, instituted in 1816, disappeared in the 1850's, the only surviving element being the impressive cast iron fence (1818) that surrounds the square. (Cast iron in Richmond is seen in such profusion—and quality —that it is said to be second only to New Orleans. From 1818 almost to the end of the century, when it fell out of favor, local foundries produced enough cast iron to give the city a special quality that lasts to this day.)

The present plan was created by John Notman, a distinguished Philadelphia architect, and although much changed in the intervening years, the basic idea of meandering paths and informal plantings, so inviting to the visitor, still prevails. For many years it was the meeting place for Richmond's infants and their nurses, as Ellen Glasgow so vividly remembered in her autobiography, *The Woman Within*, and I always associate it with that kind of innocent gentleness and pleasure.

If you go west of the Capitol, down Shockoe hill, you will come upon the Old Bell Tower (1824), whose bell served as the fire alarm and to warn of civil disturbances; during the Civil War it signaled Union attacks. Its fish weathervane is a good example of folk art and a wonderfully jaunty touch.

Near the Bell Tower is a statue of Edgar Allan Poe, and statues of other sons of Virginia dot the grounds as well, but the most famous piece of statuary is the large and grandiose Washington Monument created in 1869. Designed by Thomas Crawford—his most famous sculpture is the almost nineteen-foot classical goddess with the feathered headdress on the dome of the Capitol in Washington—it was completed after his death in 1857 by Randolph Rogers, sculptor of the bronze Columbus doors that are also part of the Washington Capitol. I find it rather messy—an equestrian statue of Washington rather wanly pointing off in the distance tops the group. Below, seven Virginians circle the base, and below them seven allegorical figures illustrate their contributions; Jefferson with "Independence," John Marshall with "Justice," and so forth. The whole symbolizes Virginia's role in the Revolution. Two final facts about it: There's a tomb at the base that was to receive the body of Washington, and Jefferson Davis was inaugurated here as president of the Confederacy.

As you walk behind the Capitol, you will see, to the east of it, the Executive Mansion, which was designed by Alexander Parris, a Boston architect who was also the architect for the famous Quincy market. It has been the official residence of Virginia's governors since 1813. The simple neoclassical interior—the east wing is a sensitively accomplished twentieth-century addition —gives no hint of the fine interior with its ornamental plaster ceilings and elegantly carved woodwork. It is open to the public during Historic Garden Week; at other times by appointment only. Phone: 804-786-4537.

Old City Hall (1886–1894) Just behind the extremely dignified

Capitol, at 1001 East Broad Street, is this, the Mae West of Victorian buildings in Richmond. Exuberant, audacious, robust, in fact bursting out all over with turrets and clock tower, pinnacles and finials, dormers and every other architectural detail you can think of; a decorative madness held in check— barely—by an overriding intelligence that, at last, gives it coherent form. It is a fantastical piece of Victoriana.

The architect, Elijah Myers, designed many courthouses and state capitols, including those of Michigan, Texas and Colorado. A good architect, but he became almost as well known for his cost overruns. Here, as seemingly everywhere, he went way over budget, from an estimated $300,000 to $1.3 million; of one courthouse in Illinois it is said that it took more than fifty years to pay off his error in financial judgment.

But how could you not forgive him, especially after you see the interior, a four-story stairhall and court, painted and gilded and staircased and arcaded and skylighted and columned and every centimeter decorated. Fortunately, it has been beautifully restored and now serves as an office building.

New City Hall (1971) Lumpishly placed at 900 East Broad Street, this is just about as boring as a building can be, but it does have an observation deck that offers a twenty-mile, 360° view that makes it an excellent way to see Richmond and its setting in its entirety. Open: Monday–Friday, 9–5. Admission: Free.

Shockoe Slip Historic District, Franklin Street, the Fan District and Monument Avenue

These four areas sum up Richmond in all its periods as well as any in the city. Each is worth exploring for its own inherent worth. Here is a short description of each that will give you an idea of what to expect.

Shockoe Slip Historic District This is the restored area that runs from East Main Street toward the James. Shockoe Slip itself is really a charming, small open space with—at its center —a granite fountain that was used to water horses. It is dedicated to a Confederate officer, "in memory of one who loved animals." This is the center of a restored district that has come bouncing back to life after a long period in the doldrums. Visually, it's immediately appealing—particularly in the cast iron building fronts on East Main and the restored nineteenth-century commercial buildings on Cary Street—and it has become a center of day- and nighttime activity for the city with its likable and widely assorted shops and restaurants.

Franklin Street Running a distance of two miles east to west, this street retains most of its historic character. Some highlights: at 707 is the Lee House (1844), the wartime residence of the general and his family. It is now home to a good restaurant (see page 184). The Bolling Haxall House, at 211 East Franklin (1858), is a splendid Italianate mansion, while Linden Row, 100–104 (1847–1853), is the best grouping of pre–Civil War buildings in the city. And the massive Jefferson Hotel, at the 100 block of West Franklin, is a great building with one of the finest interiors of any hotel in the South. (See page 181.)

The Fan District extends west from Monroe Park, with Franklin Street and Monument Avenue forming its northern edge, Main Street its southern. Mostly comprised of late-nineteenth-century houses of relatively modest origins, it is today undergoing extensive restoration, with little restaurants and shops here and there to meet the needs of the new residents. The totality makes a pleasant and harmonious cityscape that is becoming a rarity.

Monument Avenue The grandest of Richmond's streets, this boulevard, with its impressive monumental statues of Lee, J.E.B. Stuart, Stonewall Jackson, Jefferson Davis and Matthew Fontaine Maury, inventor of the electric torpedo and "Pathfinder of the Seas," is 140 feet broad with Linden trees marching along its sides, a parklike strip running through its center to divide the traffic flow, and large and imposing houses of the late nineteenth and early twentieth century lining it as far as the eye can see. Some are the work of architect William Lawrence Bottomley, one of the great designers of Georgian Revival houses.

Richmond National Battlefield Park As the capital of the Confederacy, Richmond suffered terribly during the war, the final tragedy coming like a thief in the night of April 2, 1865, as government officials set fires to warehouses and supplies before fleeing the city. Wrote one witness of the "terrible splendor," "Three high arched bridges were in flames; beneath them the water sparkled and dashed and rushed on by the burning city. Every now and then, as a magazine exploded, a column of white smoke rose up as high as the eye could reach, instantaneously followed by a deafening sound. The earth seemed to rock and tremble as with the shock of an earthquake . . ." It was, wrote another witness, "as though hell itself had broken loose."

Seven Federal drives were made on the city during the course of the war before the final evacuation. This park commemorates the two that came closest to success, McClellan's Peninsular Campaign (1862) and Grant's 1864 attack.

Go to the Chimborazo Visitor Center at 3215 East Broad Street, where exhibits and an audiovisual presentation will give you the history of the 1861–1865 defense of Richmond. This center is on the site of the razed Chimborazo Hospital, then one of the largest military hospitals in the world. One of the matrons, Phoebe Yates Pember, later wrote of her experiences here from 1862 to the end of the war. She matter-of-factly tells of such events as the drunken surgeon who set the wrong leg of a wounded soldier and thereby caused his death, of the difficulty of being a woman in what had been a man's profession, of the rats that defied all attempts to entrap them, and of the seemingly insuperable daily troubles and worries of this immense operation. But her real theme is her admiration for the common soldier, of whom she wrote, "No words can do justice to the uncomplaining nature of the Southern soldier. Whether it arose from resignation or merely passive submission, yet when shown in the aggregate in a hospital, it was sublime."

Today a park has replaced the hospital where 76,000 patients were treated. Through the presentation here you will see Richmond as the embattled and gallant capital of the Confederacy, the obsession of the North and pride of the South.

The Chimborazo Visitor Center is open daily, 9–5. Closed December 25, January 1. Admission: Free. Phone: 804-226-1981.

Hollywood Cemetery Cemeteries often say something about the cities they are in: Père Lachaise in Paris, for instance, is sometimes interesting, sometimes moving, sometimes beautiful, sometimes grotesque, but always theatrical. In this country, Green-Wood Cemetery, in Brooklyn, New York, one of our more famous resting places, allows the good rich bourgeois of that city to go to his final destination in a beautiful, dignified and discreet natural setting. And, of course, there's always Forest Lawn in Los Angeles, about which no more need be said. This cemetery has its own character, drama tempered by aristocratic restraint in a parklike setting.

Set on a hill, offering lordly views over the James, Hollywood was designed by John Notman, the same man who worked on Capitol Square; both were influenced by the work of Andrew Jackson Downing, the first great American landscape architect. The grounds are stunning, the views still striking. Two American presidents are buried here, Monroe and Tyler, and Monroe's monument of cast iron is so extraordinary as to be unique. Jefferson Davis is buried here as well, as are J.E.B. Stuart and 18,000 Confederate dead, their final resting place marked by a pyramid of granite blocks, a highly effective, simple monument. Other prominent Virginians are also here, and it is interesting to wander through this nineteenth-century place with its strong aura of a Richmond past that still lingers —though fainter and fainter—in the bustling city of today.

Hollywood Cemetery is located at 412 South Cherry Street at Albemarle Street. Open: April–September, Monday–Saturday, 7:30–6:00; October–March, 7:30–5:00; Sunday, 8 to 5. Phone: 804-648-8501.

Major Museums

Virginia Museum of Fine Arts When it opened in 1936, this was the country's first state-supported museum of art. At that time it was a small and limited museum of regional interest only. Today it has grown into a museum of national importance, in large part because of two major gifts from Mr. and Mrs. Paul Mellon and Sydney and Frances Lewis, founders of Best Products. These two collections fill the newest addition to the museum, the West Wing, which in itself doubles the former exhibition space of the old buildings.

The newest jewel in Richmond's crown, the West Wing of the Virginia Museum, which houses two superb collections of art.

The West Wing was designed by the New York architectural firm of Hardy Holzman Pfeiffer Associates and is architecturally the most interesting part of the museum complex. The exterior is splendid, with Indiana limestone finished in four different ways not only giving the wing a pleasing textured quality but also relating it to the older structure it connects with. It is a monumental building but not a cold one. The interior, with one exception, is wonderfully conceived and executed. For instance, strategically placed windows allow natural light to flood in and connect the museum to the ongoing outside world in a natural and relaxed way. From wherever you stand in the galleries, there are tantalizing peeks into other areas, creating a most appealing natural flow. The galleries are superbly designed for their collection: The Mellon works, being small in scale, are displayed in ten intimate galleries that are carpeted and whose walls are covered with fabric; the grander, more contemporary collection of Mr. and Mrs. Lewis is displayed in eight galleries with neutral walls and bare floors, the largest of which is equal to two gallery levels in height and whose spatial appearance can be changed by movable partitions.

The central hall has walls and floors of a particularly warm rose-pink Italian marble from Verona that is, at the same time, both welcoming and formal. What don't work are the four central columns, which are intended to simultaneously divide and unify the space, but which are, instead, insubstantial-looking and overly obtrusive.

The Mellon gift consists of seventy works, mostly French, from the Impressionist period on into the twentieth century, a group of nineteenth-century American paintings, eighteenth- and nineteenth-century British sporting art, a collection of drawings, prints and sculptures concerned primarily with sporting art, and a small room filled with jeweled objects by Jean Schlumberger loaned from Mrs. Mellon's collection. All in all, there are more than fifteen hundred works of art from Mr. and Mrs. Mellon's collection.

The Lewis collection comprises more than twelve hundred post–World War II paintings and sculptures, primarily American, and includes every famous American name of the period. Because of the size of the collection, only a hundred or so of these works can be displayed at any given time. The Lewises also have given six hundred pieces of Art Nouveau and Art Deco furniture and decorative arts created between 1885 and 1935, as well as exceptional objects created by Louis Tiffany and ranging from lamps to windows to a peacock-blue glass punchbowl in a gilded silver mount that is as beautiful as anything the Tiffany studio ever created.

Some impressions (no pun intended): The Mellon British Sporting Art Collection is, not surprisingly, dominated by fox-hunting pictures. But my especial favorite, a masterpiece by any standard, has nothing to do with foxes and horses. It is a small George Stubbs picture of a black-and-white spaniel painted in 1773. Nose to the ground, alert eyes looking to the viewer, this is the quintessential portrait of a dog. . . . Great names abound in the French paintings section, but don't miss the brilliantly witty and charming painting by Kees van Dongen of a Parisian lady and her dog, an enormous black hat obscuring the lady's face, painted in 1910. . . . A group in the Schlumberger collection of six blackamoors, done in 1960 in enamel, black lacquer, rubies, turquoise, sapphires, emeralds and gold, are the equal of Fabergé or any other great master of the gold and bejeweled miniature.

I don't know what I actually expected from the Lewis collection, but whatever it was, it wasn't the surprise of wit, warmth, taste and a very definite intellectual viewpoint that I received. The pictures are of a quality and breadth rarely encountered.

And then there are the Art Nouveau and Art Deco pieces, brilliantly installed and displayed, that include an awesome Sun Bed (1930) by the great French cabinetmaker Emile-Jacques Ruhlmann as well as some flawless jewelry pieces by René Lalique, like a diadem (1900) of leaves of horn, diamonds, gold and tortiseshell. There is stained glass and furniture designed by Frank Lloyd Wright, a carpet by Marie Laurencin, a sideboard by Emile Gallé, a bedroom suite by Marcel Coard designed for Jean Cocteau in 1929.

Obviously, the two collections couldn't be more different, and yet they work together. The reason is that objects of great quality such as these that are displayed with great sensitivity and understanding can only enhance one another.

In the rest of the museum's collection, now in galleries restored and revamped to try and match the grandeur of their new sibling, are some special finds. The Fabergé collection, for one, has over three hundred pieces of imperial jewelry, including five presentation Easter Eggs, and is one of the finest and largest in the world. Another area of some strength is the arts of India, Nepal and Tibet. The European collection, exclusive of the Mellon gift, has one superb painting, a Goya portrait of the French general Nicholas Guye (c. 1810) and several other distinguished pictures, particularly a Salomon van Ruysdael landscape and another, by Jan Brueghel the Elder, that is beautifully executed. Unfortunately, the collection of American paintings from the eighteenth, nineteenth and early twentieth centuries is weak. I hope the museum will now turn its attention to expanding and stengthening this modest gathering.

The Virginia Museum is at Grove Avenue and the Boulevard. Open Tuesday–Saturday, 11–5; Sunday, 1–5. Closed: January 1, July 4, Thanksgiving, December 25. Admission, $2 suggested; senior citizens and children under 16, free. Phone: 804-257-0844. There also is a cafeteria (open: Tuesday–Saturday, 11:30–2:30; Sunday, 1–4) and an interesting gift shop (open Tuesday–Saturday, 10:30–4:30; Sunday, 2:00–4:30).

Valentine Museum   I love museums that specialize in local and regional history because they are invaluable to understanding the particular nature of the place you're in. This one is not to be missed; its offerings make it one of the best of its kind in the country.

The museum is actually a complex of four nineteenth-century residences of which one, the Wickham-Valentine House (1812) ranks among the most interesting houses in Virginia of the period. There is also a formal tiered garden, beautifully restored to the period of the house, and the sculpture studio of Edward V. Valentine, whose masterpiece is the Lee memorial in Lexington (see page 101).

The museum has a permanent exhibit dedicated to the life and history of Richmond, called "Richmond Revisited," and there are changing exhibits based on their extensive collection of textiles, costumes and decorative arts. A stroll through this section makes an enjoyable way to learn about Richmond and even pleasure your senses, but what elevates the visit to an experience is the tour of the interior of the beautifully restored and maintained Wickham-Valentine house, whose architect was Alexander Parris (see page 155).

The 1812 elements of the interior—the cantilevered palette-shaped stairway, curved walls and exquisite detailing—make it one of the finest interiors of its period I have seen.

The Valentine Museum is located at 1015 East Clay Street; the rear portico of a Greek Revival house is the unusual entrance. Open: Monday–Saturday, 10–5; Sunday, 1–5. Tours are on the hour. Closed: Major holidays. Admission: $2.50; children 7–12, $1.50. Phone: 804-649-0711.

Museum of the Confederacy and the White House of the Confederacy Another superb and unique museum with a distinguished, and in this case, famous house.

It is the house that you first notice from the street. This was a building designed by Robert Mills, architect of the Washington Monument in the nation's capital, and it went up in 1818. In the late 1850's it was considerably altered; a third floor was added, a cupola went up on the roof, and Victorian features were introduced into the interior. In June 1861, the City of Richmond bought the house and its furnishings with the intention of presenting them to President Jefferson Davis. He felt that the gift was inappropriate, and ultimately the Confederate government rented the building from the city and used it as the official residence of Mr. Davis.

During Reconstruction, the house was headquarters for Union representatives, and later the city operated it as a school.

In 1890, threats to tear it down mobilized a group of Richmond women—inevitably it was the women who saved our country's heritage—and they turned it into a museum that would collect, preserve, exhibit and interpret everything they could get their hands on during the Civil War period.

In 1976 a new museum building opened, across an attractive courtyard from the White House, to house the collection, now the largest assemblage of Confederate material in existence. It is a unique source of reference not only on the Confederacy but also on how people lived at that time. It seems, quite literally, that at least one of everything created during that period has found its way here. It is a fascinating and priceless trove. Here you will find Jefferson Davis's papers and Robert E. Lee's sword that he wore at Appomattox, a jacket worn by a Louisiana private wounded at Shiloh and furniture from Richmond houses, all sorts of fabric and clothing from the period as well as broadsides, posters, newspapers, photographs and paintings. They even have Mr. Davis's very handsome needlepoint slippers, with crossed Confederate flags.

The White House itself is now being restored. The basement level, where you enter, has exhibits concerning the Davis family and the general history of the building. The first and second floors will be restored as exactly as possible to the way they were during the Davis presidency and will be open to the public.

The Museum, at 1201 East Clay Street, is open: Monday–Saturday, 10–5; Sunday, 1–5. Closed: Major holidays. Admission: $2.50; senior citizens, $2; children 7–12, $1. Phone: 804-649-1861.

The Virginia Historical Society   Organized in 1831 to collect and preserve research materials relating to the history of Virginia and to make these materials available to scholars and researchers, the Society is located in the Battle Abbey, a building near the Virginia Museum.

The floor on which you enter is divided into three parts. The room to the left of the entrance, the Mural Gallery, contains a series of four enormous murals by the French artist Charles Hoffbauer depicting the four seasons of the Confederacy. They were painted between 1913 and 1920. Also on display are portions of a collection of Confederate weapons and military gear.

Beyond the entrance hall is the Library, an almost unbelievably rich depository of material on Virginia, with more than three million catalogued items in the manuscripts division alone, including correspondence of such men as William Byrd II, Robert "King" Carter, George Washington, Thomas Jefferson, James Madison, Robert E. Lee and Stonewall Jackson.

The North Gallery, to the right, is devoted to changing exhibits such as "Virginians in Portraiture," in which seventy portraits drawn from their collection of over six hundred were on display and which also included many of our best-known artists: Charles Willson Peale, Gilbert Stuart, George Catlin and Thomas Sully, among others.

The Society also owns **Virginia House,** a Tudor mansion next to Agecroft Hall (see page 167) that is a reconstructed Warwick, England, house shipped to this country in 1925.

The Virginia Historical Society in the Battle Abbey is at 428 North Boulevard. Open: Monday–Saturday, 9:00–4:45. Closed: Major holidays. Admission: Free to both the exhibit galleries and the library. Phone: 804-358-4901.

Virginia House, 4301 Sulgrave Road, is in the Windsor Farms district of Richmond. Open: By appointment only, Monday–Saturday, 10–4, Sunday, 1–4. Closed: January and major holidays. Admission: $1.50; children 7–12, 50¢. Phone: 804-353-4251. You must give at least two days' advance notice before visiting here.

Science Museum of Virginia (1919)   A wonderful example of how to reuse a grand old building, for the museum is located in the former Broad Street Railroad Station, an imposing Roman-inspired monumental building designed by John Russell Pope, who also was the architect for the Jefferson Memorial and the National Gallery in Washington.

This is a hands-on museum with several unusual exhibits including "Crystal World," the most extensive exhibit of its kind in the country, which explores the crystals that make up solid matter and displays gem specimens; "The Computer Works" and "Growing Up with Computers"; and a fascinating one called "Illusions, Magic and Science."

Universe, which claims to be the world's most advanced planetarium and space theater, is also here and offers large format Omnimax films and planetarium programs with great special effects. Both present kids with a field day of pleasures.

The Science Museum, 2500 West Broad Street, is open: Daily, 11:30–8:00. Universe: Three to five film showings daily and two planetarium programs daily. Closed: Thanksgiving, December 24 and December 25. Admission: For a combined Museum/ Universe ticket, $4; senior citizens and children under 18, $3.50. Phone: 804-257-0000 (Museum), 804-257-8277 (Universe).

Richmond Children's Museum   This is an arts and humanities museum for children from two to twelve, and offers both hands-on and participatory exhibits. Well done. Open: Tuesday–Friday, 10:00–4:30; Saturday and Sunday, 1–5. Closed: Easter, Thanksgiving and December 25. Admission: $1.50; children 3–12, $1; under 3, free.

House Museums

Both the Valentine Museum and the Virginia Historical Society have houses that are on exhibit (see above), but Richmond also offers several houses that are, in themselves, museums.

Wilton   This magnificent Georgian house, probably completed in 1753, and the only completely paneled house in Virginia, was built by William Randoph III, a member of one of the most famous families in the colony. This is not its original setting; it was moved here by its current owners, the Colonial Dames of America, when it was threatened by surrounding commercial development. Its setting, overlooking the James and surrounded by complementary plantings and lovely flower beds, is perfection. Its exterior, brick with a severely symmetrical, elegantly proportioned façade and four tall chimneys, is textbook Georgian. Its interior is breathtaking, not only for its magnificent paneling but also for the museum-quality splendor of its furnishings. The restorers have been fortunate, for there is an early inventory of the house that helped them in selecting representative furnishings; and some personal pieces (the secretary in the library, the desk in an upstairs bedroom) as well as family portraits are back. The remaining furniture and accessories, though, are gifts, and the Colonial Dames and others who have given to the house have given of their best. Rarely will you see such a consistently great collection, and if you have any interest in eighteenth-century furnishings, this is a house that must be seen.

Wilton, on Wilton Road in Windsor Farms, is open Tuesday–Saturday, 10:00–4:30; Sunday, September–June, 2:30–4:30; Monday, by appointment only. Closed: Major holidays, Sundays in July, second Thursdays October–May and the month of August. Admission: $2; children, 75¢. During Historic Garden week the fee increases to $2.50.

Agecroft Hall This is not another plantation house on the James. Not at all. It's a half-timbered English Tudor manor house built about 1480 near Manchester. In the 1920's it fell on hard times—it was surrounded by industry and factories—and was about to be razed. America to the rescue, in the person of Mr. T. C. Williams, Jr., of Richmond, who dismantled the house, shipped it here in 1926, and thereafter made it his home. Good for him; it is a house worth preserving.

The house and grounds are beautifully maintained—Mr. Williams obviously left a generous endowment—and, because of the quality of both, you really should visit here. The house is an excellent example of domestic Tudor architecture and is filled with top-quality period furnishings, pictures and accessories. The leaded crown-glass window in the Great Hall, twenty-five feet long and ten feet high, is spectacular in itself, while the staircase, interestingly enough, comes from Warwick Priory, source of a very good part of neighboring Virginia House (see page 165).

Agecroft Hall, c. 1480, was moved lock, stock and barrel from England to Richmond in 1926. Its Great Hall is, in itself, worth a visit.

The gardens are very special and are divided into four distinct period units: the Sunken Garden, Knot Garden, Herb Garden and Formal Garden.

Agecroft Hall is at 4305 Sulgrave Road in Windsor Farms. Open: Tuesday–Friday, 10–4; Saturday and Sunday, 2–5. Closed: Major holidays. Admission: $2; senior citizens, $1.50; students, $1. Phone: 804-353-4241.

John Marshall House   A modest but appealing Federal house that was completed in 1791 for John Marshall (1755–1835), Chief Justice of the United States Supreme Court from 1801 to his death. This is the only surviving eighteenth-century brick house in Richmond; today it stands in lonely, even slightly forlorn isolation in the center of the downtown area. The interior contains many of the original furnishings and family possessions and has some good paneling. The house is located at 818 East Marshall Street. Open: Tuesday–Saturday, 11–4. Closed: Major holidays. Admission: $2. Phone: 804-648-7998.

Edgar Allan Poe Museum   This museum is contained in five buildings and includes the Old Stone House, the oldest dwelling in Richmond. No one is sure when it actually was built, but it certainly was before the Revolution and may have been as early as 1736. Poe himself never lived in any of these buildings, which contain mementoes of his life, including a sad little collection of his possessions found at his death (his trunk, a walking stick and a pair of boot hooks, and his wife's mirror and trinket box). There also is the rather bizarre Raven Room, filled with illustrations of his most famous poem done by a man named James Carling in the 1880's. After this it's an even greater delight to go into the entrancing walled garden, a refreshing surprise and delightful oasis in the middle of Richmond.

The Edgar Allan Poe Museum, 1914–16 East Main Street, is open: Tuesday–Saturday, 10–4; Sunday and Monday 1:30–4:00. Closed: December 25. Admission: $2, students $1. Phone: 804-648-5523.

Maymont Park and the Dooley Mansion   This 100-acre park and its accompanying Victorian mansion was once the private estate of Major James Dooley and his wife, Sallie May. Dooley, son of an Irish immigrant family, was born in Richmond in 1841 and died in this house in 1922. His wife died in 1925, and the estate passed to the city of Richmond.

The park is lovely, and the Japanese and Italian gardens in particular are enticing and well maintained. I especially like the Japanese garden that is in an area once part of the old James River and Kanawha Canal System. (This was a canal originally envisioned by George Washington and meant to eventually stretch to the Rocky Mountains, following the Ohio, Mississippi and Kansas Rivers. In fact, it never got out of the state and was done in by the railroad.) The version you see today is a modern redesign of the garden the Dooleys installed and is as tranquil a spot as any I know in Richmond. Also on the grounds near the house is a Nature Center, a collection of horse-drawn carriages, a children's farm and the Virginia Wildlife Exhibit.

The house, completed in 1892, is a late-Victorian curiosity, unusual in that it still contains all its original furniture and accessories. I don't like it. I find it . . . "laide," as the French so expressively put it. It is filled with all those things I associate with bad Victorian—copies of eighteenth-century French furniture, acres of shiny wood, mediocre stained glass, bad statuary and pictures, ceilings painted in sugary imitation of the already confectionary French rococo. Mrs. Dooley, like Mad Prince Ludwig of Bavaria, had a passion for swans, and her bedroom, decorated with furnishings from their summer home (called— you guessed it—"Swannanoa"), has a swan bed, swan rocker, and so forth. Here too is the most bizarre Tiffany piece, a silver and narwhal tusk dressing table and chair. (In the Middle Ages, you might like to know, narwhal tusks often passed for unicorn horns.) Visiting here is, indeed, an experience.

The house is open Tuesday–Sunday, 12:00–4:30. Closed major holidays. Admission: Free. Phone: 804-358-7166.

The gardens, children's farm, carriage collection and park are open daily, April–October, 10–7; November–March, 10–5. Admission: Free. Phone: 804-358-7166. The entrance to Maymont is at Hampton Street and Pennsylvania Avenue.

Maggie Walker House   Maggie Walker (1867–1934) was a very interesting woman. The daughter of former slaves of Elizabeth Van Lew, a famous spy for the Union in the Civil War, she would eventually become the first woman bank president in America. Her National Historic Landmark home, at 110½ East

Leigh Street in the Jackson Ward section of Richmond, the oldest black neighborhood in the country, has been preserved with all of her furniture as well as many of her personal possessions. The house is open: Thursday–Sunday, 9–5. Admission: Free. Phone: 804-226-1981.

Tuckahoe The approach to this house, about seven miles west of Richmond, is over a mile-long lane bordered by cedars; it is redolent of romantic nostalgia. At the end is Tuckahoe, a large, rather plain early Georgian H-shaped house—the shape is unusual—of clapboard and Flemish bond brick. Tuckahoe was built by a Randolph—among Randolph descendants can be numbered Thomas Jefferson, John Marshall and Robert E. Lee —in two sections (c. 1712 and c. 1730). Today this house is more than worth a visit for the startlingly lovely paneling of the interior, in particular that of the north stair hall, with its exceptional carving incorporating acanthus leaves, scrolls, flowers— even a wicker basket of them—and, on the staircase itself, the delicately turned, spiraling balusters.

The plantation has another unique feature: It is the most complete plantation layout left in this country and has its original outbuildings still standing on its plantation street: the kitchen, stable, smokehouse and so forth. To the west of the house is a schoolhouse (whether original or reproduction is not known) where young Thomas Jefferson studied. He lived here from 1745–1752 while his father looked after the estate and the children of the house, whose own father had died. It is possible that the arrangement of Tuckahoe's plantation street inspired Jefferson's own Mulberry Row at Monticello.

The house is privately owned; and as the owners live in it, a sense of family and life pervades both house and grounds. This, for me at least, always gives a house added interest. The garden is informal and pleasant; the grounds may need work here and there, but it's all on a human scale, one we can empathize with and feel at home in.

Tuckahoe Plantation, on River Road, is open by appointment only. Admission: $5. Phone: 804-784-5736.

Churches

Richmond has several important churches, some for their history, some for their architecture, some for both. Here are the most important.

St. John's Episcopal Church (1741) This and the Old Stone House (see page 168) are the only two pre-Revolutionary Richmond buildings still at the same site. But what has guaranteed a spot in history for St. John's is that here Patrick Henry, during the Virginia Convention of 1775, ended his famous speech with, "Is life so dear, or peace so sweet as to be purchased at the price of chains and slavery? Forbid it, Almighty God. I know not what course others may take, but as for me, give me liberty or give me death!"

The church has been considerably altered since Henry's time and its primary interest is its historical role. In the churchyard is buried Edgar Allan Poe's mother, Elizabeth, and George Wythe, a signer of the Declaration of Independence and the first law professor in this country. His house in Williamsburg can still be visited. He was poisoned by a nephew who was overeager for his inheritance.

Take some time to wander through the Church Hill area. It has more than seventy antebellum houses and is undergoing extensive restoration. Be sure to see both the **WRVA Radio Station** at 22nd and Grace Streets, a small, stunning building designed by Philip Johnson in 1968 and the mews off 24th Street that was restored by the Garden Club of Virginia in 1965.

St. John's Church is at 25th and Broad Streets. Open: Monday–Saturday, 10–4; Sunday, 1–4. Closed: Thanksgiving, December 25. Admission: $1; students, 50¢, children, 35¢. Phone: 804-648-5015 or 649-7938.

St. Paul's Episcopal Church (1845) On Sunday morning, April 2, 1865, President Jefferson Davis was in his pew, No. 63, for the eleven o'clock service. The minister, a much-beloved German immigrant named Charles Minnigerode, had to raise his voice to be heard over the not-so-distant gunfire. Suddenly a courier came down the aisle and handed Davis a message from General Lee advising him to flee Richmond. It was the death knell for Richmond and the Confederacy. Davis rose and left the church. That night a train took him and his cabinet to the south. Union forces, exactly one week from this day, would be firing 200 guns just across the street in Capitol Square to celebrate Appomattox.

This expressive and graceful Greek Revival church was designed by Philadelphia architect Thomas S. Stewart, the architect, too, for the excellent Egyptian Building, also in 1845. The seventy-foot tower originally was topped by a spire that rose a further 225 feet, but that was removed in 1906 and replaced by the present octagonal dome. (All the Richmond church spires were removed at that time because the authorities were afraid, after one particularly severe hurricane, that they could topple to the streets in another such serious storm.) The iron fence is superb and was designed by the architect, as was the more expressive fence of the Egyptian Building. One of the reasons the façade is so appealing, of course, is the portico with its slender columns and beautiful Corinthian capitals of prefabricated cast iron.

The interior has been changed from the time that Jefferson Davis and Robert E. Lee—he sat in pew No. 111—worshiped here. The stained-glass windows, some by Tiffany (as is the mosaic reredos of the Last Supper), were not there, for instance, and the chancel has also been remodeled. (You may wish to note, too, that the 1889 pulpit was put there "in recognition of nearly 33 years of pastorate of the Rev. Charles Minnigerode.") But the major—and most spectacular—element of the interior is the plaster ceiling. At the center is the Hebrew symbol for Yahweh (God), which is enclosed by the symbol for the Trinity and a radiating star. Around all this is a complex and admirably executed design of classical leaves. The result is the most splendid church interior in Richmond.

At 800 East Grace Street is **St. Peter's Church** (1835), the oldest Catholic church in Richmond. The interior is dignified and unpretentious, quite in contrast with its neighbor.

St. Paul's is across from Capitol Square at 815 East Grace Street. Open: Monday–Saturday, 10–4; Sunday, worship beginning at 8. Closed major holidays. Admission: Free. Phone: 804-643-3589.

Monumental Episcopal Church (1814) On the night of December 26, 1811, many of Richmond's most important citizens were at a play being performed in the theater then on this site. Suddenly, with a terrifying whoosh, the scenery went up in flames and, within minutes, the building was engulfed. Seventy-two people died in this tragedy, one of the worst theater fires in our history. Wrote one witness fortunate enough to escape: "I myself saw a crowd standing at one of the windows when they were well surrounded by the flames, their clothes took fire and they perished in the general conflagration." Monumental Church was built as a memorial to those who perished in this fire.

Robert Mills (see page 163) was the architect for this building, his best work in Richmond and, many feel, among the best building of his career. On the outside, I find the building odd: It is a brick and stucco octagon surrounded by a dome, while the plain porch is square, with columns fluted just below the Doric capitol and, again, at the base. The two structures do not blend into each other, nor does the porch seem a natural extension of the octagon, but this was intentional for the "monument" is the portico.

The inside, though, is a very different story, and in its unaffected, masculine feeling, it is one of the finest interiors in Richmond. Look at the two cantilevered stair halls, for example. Mills was something of a genius at staircase design—the Treasury Building and the National Portrait Gallery, both in Washington, contain other examples of his brilliance in this area—and these can be matched with his best in the genre. The room itself is filled with light, from both the cupola and the triple windows that pierce the octagonal drum. The horseshoe-shaped balcony gives a visual sweep to the room that is stopped dramatically at the apse, where the pulpit is flanked by dark green marbleized columns. It's very exciting, walking in here, particularly after examining the almost stolid exterior.

The building, at 1226 East Broad Street, is now owned by the Historic Richmond Virginia Foundation, who are restoring it. It no longer serves as an Episcopal church. Open: by appointment. Admission: Free. Phone: 804-786-9734.

Behind Monumental Church is Richmond's most curious landmark and one of my personal favorites, the **Egyptian**

Building (1845) at 1223 East Marshall Street. Designed by Thomas S. Stewart, it was the first building of the Medical College of Virginia and is still in use today. Bernard Baruch's father was a student here, and the son, in the 1930's, provided funds for major interior renovation. In any case, it is one of the finest examples of Egyptian Revival architecture in the country. The best touch: the iron fenceposts are in the form of mummies. The façade is superior, the lotus-topped columns as good as any in the genre, while its inclined walls, massive concave cornice and Egyptian decorative touches make the building completely successful. Both the grounds and the distinctive lobby are open to the public.

One other building in the immediate area deserves some attention, the original **First Baptist Church** (1841) at 302 North 11th Street, which was designed by Thomas U. Walter, architect of the United States Capitol dome. An austere, inward-looking building, its proportions and great dignity caused it to have a profound effect on Richmond church architecture. It too is now owned by the Medical College of Virginia.

OTHER THINGS TO SEE AND DO

Sixth Street Marketplace Yet another in the long line of James W. Rouse creations. Among other credits of his Enterprise Development Co.: Boston's Faneuil Hall Markets, Baltimore's Harborfront and New York City's South Street Seaport. This is less elaborate than its brethren, a $25 million, three-block area with shops, restaurants, kiosks, galleries and landscaped plazas. Its most distinctive feature is a Victorian-inspired, glass-enclosed, elevated pedestrian bridge that spans Broad Street between the Marriott Hotel and the city's major department stores. The bridge also has a symbolic meaning, as it is the physical manifestation of the bridging of racial differences between black and white sections of the city. The Marketplace, like all Rouse developments, is cleverly put together and has become a major factor in the revival of downtown Richmond.

Nearby is the **Virginia Center for the Performing Arts** (1927), 600 East Grace Street, a former Loew's theater that now houses, after a $6 million restoration, the Richmond Symphony and the Richmond Ballet. I mention it because it is a marvelous example of movie architecture at its most grandiose. The Spanish exterior is so exaggerated and transformed that it becomes an extravaganza exactly suited to the entertainment it once housed. Inside, the auditorium is a fantasyland, with statues in niches, pavilions, lights everywhere, and not an inch undecorated. And, it's great fun and wonderfully evocative of its era.

Main Street Station (1901) Another example of creative reuse for a grand old building, this time a French Renaissance railroad station that saw its last train depart in 1975. Behind it is a 400-foot-long metal shed that is a marvel of engineering. Now all is transformed into a discount shopping outlet and theme mall. And the restoration has had a snowball effect; just look at the 17th Street Farmer's Market, which not so long ago appeared to be on its last legs. This section of East Main Street, which the station really dominates, is in the Shockoe Bottom area. Smell the tobacco still here? This was—and is—Richmond's tobacco road, and with the renewal efforts, it will soon be on the way to a new life.

Richmond offers some first-rate examples of contemporary corporate architecture. I am thinking in particular of the **Philip Morris Factory,** 3601–4201 Commerce Road, designed by Skidmore, Owings & Merrill, and, especially, the **Best Products headquarters,** which was designed by Hardy Holzman Pfeiffer Associates and contains especially fine examples of contemporary art based on the collecting efforts of Sydney and Frances Lewis (see page 159).

Both buildings can be visited. Philip Morris offers free tours, Monday–Friday, 9–4, except the weeks of July 4 and December 25. It is also closed on company-recognized holidays. Phone: 804-274-3342. The Best Products Building is open weekdays, 9–5. For an appointment, phone: 804-261–2000.

PETERSBURG

When we got home, we laid the foundation of two large cities: one at Shacco's, to be called Richmond, and the other at the point of Appomattox River, to be named Petersburg.

These Major Mayo offered to lay out in lots without fee or reward. The truth of it is, these two places, being the uppermost landings of the James and Appomattox Rivers, are naturally intended for marts where the traffic of the outer inhabitants must center. Thus we did not build castles only, but also cities in the air.

—William Byrd II (1733)

I see no prospect of doing more than holding our position here [Petersburg] till night. I am not certain that I can do that. If I can I shall withdraw north of the Appomattox, and, if possible, it will be better to withdraw the whole line tonight from the James River.

—General Robert E. Lee to John C. Breckinridge, Confederate Secretary of War, April 2, 1865

From the time it was first settled in 1645 to the Civil War, Petersburg was a prosperous town and then city that, in the early nineteenth century, even had pretensions to rivaling its neighbor Richmond, only 23 miles to the north. During the Civil War, Petersburg, by now a major rail center, became crucial to the welfare of the capital as the entrepôt for its supplies. When Grant began his siege on June 15, 1864, then, it became only a matter of time before the city would fall; and if Petersburg went, Richmond would immediately follow. The outlines of the end of the war were forming.

But still it went on, for another ten months, as Grant relentlessly closed his circle around the beleaguered city: "When our armies were in front of Petersburg I suffered so much in body and mind on account of the good townspeople," Lee would later write. When it ended, Petersburg's economy was in a shambles. The city would recover, but never again would it be that shining aspirant for the city in the air of Byrd's dreams.

Petersburg National Battlefield

The primary reason most people visit Petersburg, of course, is to see where the South made its last stand. They will not be disappointed here, for as with all national park facilities in the state, the presentation of this 2½-square-mile park is first-rate.

The Visitor Center has maps and information as well as an excellent exhibit concerning the siege. (Open: Daily, June–Labor Day, 8–7; rest of year, 8–5. Closed: December 25, January 1. Admission: Free. Phone: 804-732-3531.) Then you are ready to drive through the park, stopping at points of interest and listening to the thorough and well-presented "living history" programs. The park is so quietly lovely it's almost troubling, especially in the spring, when flowering dogwood and the fresh green of the trees make it hard to believe so much tragedy took place here.

The most famous site is The Crater, where the best-known and most horrifying battle of the siege took place. It started with Lieutenant Colonel Henry Pleasants of the 48th Pennsylvania Volunteers, many of whose members had been coal miners, who had an idea. The idea was to tunnel 400 feet from the Union lines under the Confederate position known as Elliott's Salient, blow it up, and then follow through with an attack that would sweep them into Petersburg.

Work began on June 25 and was completed on July 23. The explosion was set for July 30. At 4:45 that morning, the 8,000-pound charge was detonated, one of the largest explosions ever known on this continent. "And as the mass of earth went into the air," wrote one witness, "carrying with it men, guns, and carriages and limbs, and spread out like an immense cloud as it reached its altitude, so close were the Union lines that the mass appeared as if it would descend immediately upon the troops waiting to make the charge." From that moment on, thanks to incredible mishandling on the Union side, potential victory turned into hideous mayhem in this newly created crater 170 feet long, 60 to 80 feet wide and 30 feet deep.

"It was a sickening sight," another officer remembered. "Men were dead and dying all around us; blood was streaming down the sides of the crater to the bottom, where it gathered in pools for a time before being absorbed by the hard red clay." At one point 15,000 men were in the crater. It became a slaughter pen. That day the Union suffered more than 3,700 casualties, the Confederates about 1,500. Now it's only a grassy depression, still in the sunlight. Only the reconstituted entrance of the Union tunnel casts the slightest shadow of remembrance over this pretty rural scene.

A Walking Tour of the City
and Old Blandford Church

Petersburg is small enough—slightly more than 41,000 people—that you can easily walk through it, seeing the major buildings of interest, in a few hours. As you enter the town you will see signs directing you to the Information Center/Farmers Bank, conveniently located at 19 Bollingbrook Street in Old Towne. (If they insist on adding an *e* to *Town*, why not one to *Old*? Better yet, why not drop the whole damn thing?) Park your car here. The Information Center (c. 1817) is open Monday–Saturday, 9–5; Sunday, 12:30–5:00. Closed: Thanksgiving, December 24 and 25, January 1. Phone: 804-733-2400. They publish a perfectly adequate "Places of Interest" map that will help guide you on your tour.

When you leave, go to the **Siege Museum,** 15 West Bank Street, a good-looking Greek Revival building devoted to exploring the siege period from the point of view of the citizens of Petersburg. Even now, many long years later, it is deeply moving to read the personal accounts of what they suffered and how they struggled to keep their lives as normal as possible. There is also a short film here, "The Echoes Still Remain," narrated by Joseph Cotton, a native son, which further details the effects of the war on the civilians. It's a museum with a different angle on the war.

The Siege Museum is open Memorial Day–Labor Day, Monday–Saturday, 9–5; rest of year, Monday–Saturday, 9–5; Sunday, 12:30–5:00. Closed: Thanksgiving, December 24 and 25, January 1. The film is shown every hour on the hour. Admission: $1; children, 50¢. Phone: 804-733-2400.

Trapezium House (1817)   The next stop on your grand tour of Petersburg. This eccentric house has no right angles and no parallel lines because the owner-builder believed that ghosts and evil spirits inhabited right angles. It has now been restored to its period.

The Trapezium is open Memorial Day–Labor Day, Monday–Saturday, 9–5; Sunday, 12:30–5:00. Admission: 50¢; children 6–12, 35¢. Phone: 804-733-2400.

From here you can go to **Centre Hill Mansion,** the grandest house in Petersburg. On the way, you can't miss the courthouse, built in the 1830's, which has an octagonal steeple topped with a statue of the goddess of Justice. It may seem a bit clumsy, but it certainly makes an effective landmark and creates the most interesting exterior in the city.

Centre Hill Mansion, on Centre Hill Court, was originally built in 1823, extensively remodeled in the 1840's and then again in 1901. It now has been restored and furnished with Victorian antiques. I find the house more engaging outside than inside.

You should also stroll down Old Street, which has several antique shops and some interesting vernacular architecture.

Old Blandford Church (1735) With the Siege Museum, this is the most interesting sight in Petersburg. At one time this Episcopal church was abandoned when the congregation moved to a later, larger building. Then, in 1901, the Ladies Memorial Association of Petersburg took the building over from the city and developed it as a memorial chapel and Confederate shrine to honor the 30,000 men buried in the surrounding cemetery.

You first enter a neighboring building, the Blandford Church Interpretation Center, which offers you a multimedia program to give you a background on the memorial. Then you go to the church, which is distinguished by fifteen Tiffany windows, almost all given by the Confederate states as a memorial to their war dead. One was given by Mr. Tiffany himself. Of all the Confederate memorials, this, certainly, is one of the most beautiful, dignified and moving.

Old Blandford Church, 321 South Crater Road, is open Monday–Saturday, 9–5; Sunday, 12:30–5:00. Closed: Thanksgiving, December 24 and 25, January 1. Admission: $1; children, 50¢. Phone: 804-733-2400.

WHERE TO STAY AND EAT
Area Code: 804

WHERE TO STAY

Charlottesville

Boars Head Inn, Box 5185, Charlottesville 22905. Phone: 296-2181. Rates: For a single, from about $73; for a double, from about $83. European plan. Credit cards accepted. Reserve in advance, particularly when the university is in session.

The Boar's Head has a golf course, jogging trail, tennis courts, swimming and even hot-air ballooning over the Virginia countryside. It is a strange mixture of the personal and the attractive and the anonymity of a motel. Let me explain. The exteriors of the complex of buildings that make up the inn, colonial in style, are well designed and welcoming. The most important of these is an old gristmill moved here when the inn was built and now housing the Old Mill Restaurant downstairs, guest rooms upstairs. It's a fine-looking room with its 43-foot beams and pleasant decoration. The lobby is pretty, too, with oak paneling and antique furniture, and most of the public rooms are on this level. But at some point it begins to feel contrived; there isn't that sense of invitation to relax and enjoy these rooms that is essential to success. As for the guest rooms, there are 175 of them, and I would suggest that you ask for one of the older rooms—some even have wood-burning fireplaces. The newer rooms are comfortable enough but smack too much of motel production.

Guesthouses Bed & Breakfast, Inc., P.O. Box 5737, Charlottesville 22905. Phone: 979-7264 or 979-8327, Monday–Friday, 12–5. Rates: From about $44 for a double. Includes breakfast. No credit cards.

This is one of the best-run Bed & Breakfast organizations in the East. You make your choice from one of three categories: Budget, Moderate or Deluxe, and you can also choose a town or country location. Complete privacy is available, but if you would like to see something of your host or hostess, that also can be arranged. I would suggest that you call them first before deciding where to stay; no matter what your need, chances are they can meet them.

Prospect Hill, Route 613, Trevilians 23070. Phone: 703-967-0844. Rates: From about $90 for a double. Includes breakfast in bed. Credit cards accepted. (See page 183.)

A comfortable-looking yellow frame manor house (1732) with later wings (c. 1840). It is a very likable spot, with pleasant gardens and trees and lawns, and inviting and comfortable rooms. Guests can also stay in the renovated slave quarters and carriage house. Even though it is about fourteen miles from

Charlottesville, if you want some peace and quite in a civilized setting, this is definitely the place for you. I, for one, love it here.

Wintergreen, Wintergreen 22958. Phone: 325-2200. Rates: From about $108 for a double. Higher rates during the ski season. Credit cards accepted. Reserve well in advance in the skiing season and holiday weekends.

The magnificent setting is similar to Big Meadows (see page 87) and Skyland (see page 87), but there's much more comfort here. Set on 10,800 acres, this resort offers everything you could wish for. There's a great deal for children to do, so this is a good family resort, and the staff is both pleasant and efficient. In short, it is a first-rate mountain resort.

Lynchburg

There are no pretty inns or little bed and breakfast "finds" here, so I therefore would recommend either the **Hilton Lynchburg** (2900 Candler's Mountain Road, Lynchburg 24502. Phone: 237-6333. Rates: For a single, from about $43; for a double from about $63. Credit cards accepted) or the **Sheraton Inn** (Odd Fellows Road, Lynchburg 24501. Phone: 847-9041. Rates: For a single, from about $42; for a double, from about $48. Credit cards accepted).

Richmond

Commonwealth Park, P.O. Box 455, Richmond 23205. Phone: 343-7300. Rates: For a single, from about $95; for a double, from about $115. Credit cards accepted.

Beautifully situated on Capitol Square, this is Richmond's most sumptuous hotel. All accommodations have a spacious living room and bedroom as well as a luxurious bath, and all are tastefully appointed. The hotel is relatively small, and the general feeling is that of a European hotel. Highly recommended.

Jefferson-Sheraton Hotel, Franklin and Adams Streets, Richmond 23205. Phone: 788-8000. Rates: From about $90 for a double. Credit cards accepted.

The grand old lady of Richmond has had a multi-million-dollar face lift, and the public rooms now are among the most beautiful in the South. The bedrooms are on the small side but are nicely furnished. Contrary to legend, the grand staircase did not figure in the last scene of *Gone With the Wind.*

Bensonhouse of Richmond (A Bed & Breakfast organization), P.O. Box. 15131, Richmond 23227. Phone: 648-7560. Rates: From about $40 for a double. Includes breakfast. No credit cards.

Another highly professional service that caters to your needs and places you where you will be happiest and most comfortable. Be as specific as you like; chances are they have it. As is true of the organizations in Charlottesville and Alexandria, I invariably find the hosts and hostesses to be considerate, pleasant people whom I've enjoyed meeting.

The Carrington Row Inn, 2309 East Broad Street, Richmond 23223, phone, 343-7005, and the **Catlin Abbott House,** 2304 East Broad Street, Richmond 23223, phone, 780-3746, are both in the Church Hill District. Both are restored Federal houses that operate as bed and breakfasts and both are owned by the same family. The rooms are both attractive and comfortable. Rates: From about $45 for a single, $55 for a double. Breakfast included. Credit cards accepted.

WHERE TO EAT

Charlottesville

C&O, 515 East Water Street. Phone: 971-7044. Credit cards accepted.

This is one of my two or three favorite restaurants in Virginia. Don't be shocked at its location, a dingy hole in the wall, for once up the narrow stairs you're in a small, smart-looking dining room, all white, while the waiters wear contrasting black aprons. The emphasis is on superb food and service, and generally both are achieved. The menu changes with what's on the market, and the waiters take great care in explaining each selection. A good wine list completes your dining needs. No matter where else you choose to eat in Charlottesville, one night at least must be spent here. I have only one complaint—the chairs are uncomfortable. Expensive. Downstairs is a comfortable, much more casual bar with tables where you can have a pub lunch or dinner. It is moderately priced and good and is open from 11:30–2:00 A.M. Monday–Saturday; from 5–1 A.M. on Sunday. The upstairs dining room serves at two sittings, 6:30 and 9:00, Monday–Saturday. Reservations required. The restaurant is closed two weeks in January and again in August.

Prospect Hill, Route 613, Trevilians. Phone: 703-967-0844. Credit cards accepted. (See page 180.)

If you arrive here a half-hour before dinner, you will be served a glass of wine which you can enjoy outdoors in good weather or in the parlor—a pleasant prelude to the dinner, which is the same for everyone. This is what I would call comfortable dining, with fresh food served in good-sized portions and thoughtfully prepared to bring out the best of its qualities. Very nice. Moderately expensive. Dinner is served Wednesday and Thursday at 7:30, Friday and Saturday at 8:00. Reservations required.

The Galerie, Route 250-W. Phone: 804-823-5883. Credit cards accepted.

A country restaurant offering good food and efficient service in pretty surroundings, this is a gratifying dining experience. Slightly off the beaten trail, it is a short drive from Charlottesville. Moderately expensive. The restaurant is open Wednesday–Sunday from 6:00–9:30. It closes for three weeks each winter. Reservations suggested.

Le Snail, 320 West Main Street. Phone 295-4456. Credit cards accepted.

Owned and operated by a Viennese chef who serves standard continental food in a setting with acres of velveteen. Old-fashioned, comfortable, not very exciting. Moderately expensive. The restaurant is open for dinner from 6–10. Closed on Sunday, major holidays and for three weeks in January and again in August. Reservations suggested.

The Old Mill Room at the Boar's Head, Route 250-W. Three miles from Charlottesville. Phone: 296-2181. Credit cards accepted. (See page 179.)

The food here is not very interesting. It's not bad, just dull. Stick with plain old meat-and-potato entries, they're the best. One bright spot: The wine list has some fine Virginia entries you should definitely try. Expensive. Lunch is served 12–2, Sunday brunch 10:30–3:00. Dinner is 6–9. Reservations required for dinner.

As is true in all college towns, near the campus you will find several restaurants serving good and filling food at modest prices. I can recommend three here: **Graffiti's** at 16 Elliewood for soups and sandwiches, **Martha's Café** at 11 Elliewood for the best vegetable salad in town and good desserts, and the **Virginian,** 1521 West Main Street, for all of the above but the salad.

Lynchburg

Crown Sterling 6124 Fort Avenue. Phone: 239-7744. Credit cards accepted.

This restaurant serves beef and trout only. The beef is beautifully flavored and cooked exactly to your wishes. If you desire a larger size than their standard on the menu, they will bring the meat to your table for you to indicate exactly how thick you wish it to be. The restaurant is comfortable, with straightforward service. It's quite good. Moderate. Dinner is served Monday–Friday, 6–10; Saturday, 5:30–10:00. Reservations necessary.

Richmond

Traveller's, 707 East Franklin Street. Phone 644-3976. Credit cards accepted.

You enter the basement of Robert E. Lee's house, now a pleasant and convivial bar, and go through to the restaurant, which is located where Lee's horse Traveller was stabled. It is surprisingly big and comfortably decorated, with paneling and paper, hunting prints and a Victorian brass chandelier. There's a small menu—steaks, beef, crab, scallops, shrimp, the service is friendly and the food is good. Expensive. Lunch: 11:30–2:30; dinner: 6–10. Closed on Sunday, reservations suggested.

The Butlery, Ltd., 6221 River Road. Phone: 282-9711. Credit cards accepted.

Off the beaten path and cozily informal, you enter through a store that sells first wine, and then food beyond. The food is French, light and fresh and well prepared, and the prices are moderately expensive. An inviting restaurant. Lunch and dinner are served, Monday–Saturday. Lunch: 11:00–3:30; Sunday brunch, 10–3. Dinner: 5:30–9:00. Reservations suggested.

The Aviary, 901 East Cary Street. Phone: 225-8219. Credit cards accepted.

Owned by the same man who operates The Butlery, Ltd., this is a more splendid setting in one of Richmond's newest buildings. The food, though, has not changed in terms of quality and innovative approach. Very good. Moderately expensive. Lunch: Monday–Friday, 11–3. Dinner: Monday–Saturday, 5:30–9:45. Reservations suggested.

La Maisonette, 3343 West Cary Street. Phone: 355-7264. Credit cards accepted.

This small, cheerful restaurant has a menu offering carefully prepared food with a nouvelle orientation. Go here for an intimate dinner. Also in their favor is the well-chosen wine list. Moderately expensive. Dinner: Tuesday–Saturday, 6–10. Reservations suggested.

La Petite France, 2912 Maywill Street. Phone: 353-8729. Credit cards accepted.

Every town seems to have a fancy French restaurant. This is Richmond's. The food and service are good, but it strikes me as one of those "special occasion" places that people go to without really knowing why. I think the kitchen could stand a little spicing up—pun intended. Expensive. Lunch and dinner are served. Lunch: Tuesday–Friday, 11:30–2:00. Dinner: Tuesday–Friday, 5:30–10:00; Saturday, 5:30–11:00. Reservations suggested.

The Tobacco Company Restaurant, 1201 East Cary Street. Phone: 782-9555. Credit cards accepted.

This is what its name says, an old tobacco warehouse, and there are dining rooms on several floors. It's likable, but it's also crowded and noisy and doesn't offer interesting food. Right in the heart of the Shockoe Slip Historic District, which is a great location, but it also guarantees the aforementioned crowds. A major tourist attraction. The restaurant is open for lunch, Monday–Friday, 11:30–2:30; Sunday, 10:30–2:00; dinner, Monday–Friday, 5:30–10:30; Saturday, 5–12; Sunday, 5:30–10:00. The bar is open until 2:00 except on Sunday when it closes at 1:30. Reservations necessary.

Nearby

Fox Head Inn, Route 621, Manakin-Sabot. Phone: 784-5126. No credit cards.

A down-home Southern inn in the country in what was once a farmhouse (1880). Make the extra effort to go there—it's about a half-hour from Richmond—and have some good food in one of their four distinctively decorated dining rooms. Owned and operated by a family, food and atmosphere both have that "welcome to our house" appeal you can't find in more commercial establishments. Moderately expensive. Dinner: Monday–Friday, 6:30–8:00; Saturday, 6:15–8:30. Reservations required.

Half-Way House, 10301 Jefferson Davis Highway. Phone: 275-1760. Credit cards accepted.

This old inn has been here since 1760 and is halfway between Richmond and Petersburg. The dining room, in the basement, is hospitably warm, and the food is reasonably good. If you have visited Petersburg and need a restaurant on the way back to Richmond, this makes a good solution. Moderate. Dinner: Sunday–Thursday, 5:30–10:00; Friday and Saturday, 5:30–11:00; Sunday Family Dinner, 11–3. Reservations suggested.

Petersburg

I can offer no recommendations in Petersburg. See Richmond.

TIDEWATER

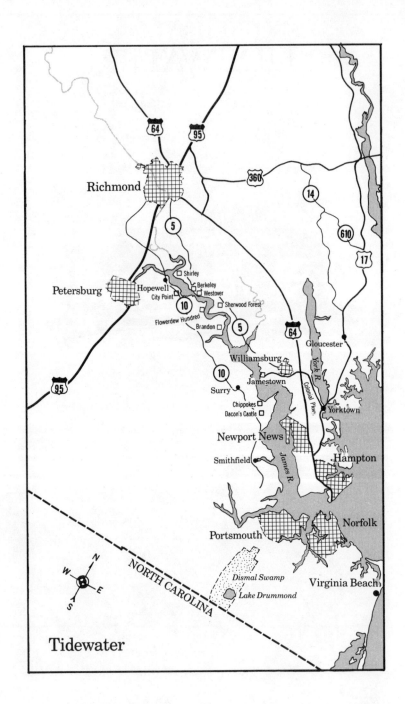

Tidewater

T HIS is where it all began, in 1607, when Jamestown was first settled. This, too, is the heart of Virginia; it was from here that settlers fanned out to the rest of the state. Williamsburg is here and the splendid James River plantations. Dismal Swamp, that eerily beautiful, primeval setting, anchors the area to the south and is almost cheek by jowl with Virginia Beach, very definitely a late twentieth-century beach resort. The U.S. Navy has its biggest base in the world here, but it can also encompass one of the most charming and rural of all Virginia towns, Smithfield, which is very comfortably ensconced on the south side of the James River. Obviously, then, it is an area of contrasts, vastly rewarding no matter where your interests lie.

WILLIAMSBURG

When I first went to Colonial Williamsburg I was about ten or eleven, and I didn't return until I was an adult. For some reason or reasons, I had developed, in the meantime, the attitude that it was boring, commercial and crammed with tourists, even though I had enjoyed it as a kid. So I went back with some reluctance. I shouldn't have worried. I loved it. Every minute of it. And I can't conceive of where my prejudices had come from, for the whole thing is brilliantly conceived and presented. Sure, there are lots of tourists, but there's so much to see and do that there's plenty of room for everyone. Go—it's truly extraordinary—and plan to stay at least three days to enjoy it all at leisure.

To get tickets and generally orient yourself to what you can expect in the Historic Area, you must first go to the **Visitor Center** (8:30–8:00), enormous and groaning with information. Here you can see the orientation film, "Williamsburg—the Story of a Patriot" (8:45–5:20, ticket required), which is also shown at many of the hotels in the area. If you've been to Tuckahoe, by the way (see page 170), you'll recognize the house in the opening sequences of the movie. You also should watch for Westover (see page 208). Here, too, you can get your admission tickets and make lodging and dining reservations, but don't wait this long for lodgings (see page 237). There is also bus service to the Historic Area from here (8:45–5:20), should you wish to leave your car.

Several kinds of tour tickets are available, but I would suggest the Patriot's Pass, which is valid for one year and gives you unlimited admission to all of the daily exhibits and everything you will want to see; it also includes a one-hour introductory tour of the Historic Area. I would buy the *Official Guide to Colonial Williamsburg,* an invaluable paperback that will give you complete information on every building, open to the public or not, in the historic district.

If there's one thing that Williamsburg offers, it's information; for me to add to it by covering the same ground would be ridiculous. At the same time, attention is drawn to certain aspects of the restoration that people specifically come for: architecture, gardens and greens, furniture and furnishings and crafts. I would add two more to the list, museums and Carter's Grove, that, I think, should be treated separately. By telling you some of my observations in these areas, I can give you a sense for and flavor of the delights in store for you that is not to be found in the more official and impersonal literature.

Architecture In this category I would include the brilliant overall plan of the town, the most sophisticated in colonial America. The basic schema is of an off-center, upside-down T like this: ⊥. The bottom is Duke of Gloucester Street, known as Dog Street by the natives, which is just under a mile long and a generous 99 feet wide. At the east end of the street is the Capitol; at the west the Wren building at William and Mary College. The leg is the Palace Green, an imposing 210 by 825 feet, with the Palace at its northern end. What a perfect sense of civilized order at the three focal points—government, crown and college. Within this broad, eminently satisfying plan, houses were to be placed on half-acre fenced plots, and subsidiary streets form a grid to the plan.

The effect is of an entire space filled with movement and of areas to explore. Trees and fences and gardens and greens and houses and public buildings all work together to create constantly changing views and perspectives, while gates invite you to move behind the street front. The plan emphasizes depth and gives a delightfully rural aspect to its overall makeup.

Nor does the street seem like an outdoor museum, amber-preserved for the contemporary world, for the Colonial Williamsburg Foundation strives valiantly to make it as much as possible like a living eighteenth-century village, and they do, indeed, create the aura of hustle and bustle vital to the success of the illusion: shops display period wares and are staffed by costumed attendants . . . down the street comes a drum and fife corps tootling and banging away . . . a cannon is fired near the Magazine . . . carriages and carts pass back and forth . . . costumed "villagers," looking perfectly natural, hurry on their ways to and from jobs and duties . . . costumed workmen, on a ladder and roof, perform maintenance chores in the manner of the eighteenth century. . . . It works because it's serious and is, indeed, real; the people are performing actual functions, not just playacting.

The result is that you've barely entered Duke of Gloucester Street before you're swept up and away, back to the eighteenth century, in an open-air setting as enchanting and dynamic as any in this country. No wonder children always like it so much; it's real and inviting enough (what's behind that gate? that door?) to bring "pretend" to reality.

As you familiarize yourself to the landmark buildings and the general aspects of Duke of Gloucester Street, your eye will begin to take in more detail. First, perhaps, will be the fences, picket and Chinese Chippendale, wattled and split rail, a great abundance of form and materials, that outline the plots and define the boundaries. There's something very cheerful about them; they don't seem meant to keep you out but rather to frame the settings and their buildings.

And then there are the houses, mostly wood with shutters, but some of brick, that are a source of endless delight because they are so diversified. I'm particularly aware of roofs here—gambrels and gables, hipped and shed and pyramidal—they, and more types, make a "roofscape" of infinite variety to explore. The chimneys too are fascinating, their designs ranging from the simplest to the very distinctive outline of the Public

Records Office chimney caps to the handsome massiveness of
the exterior chimneys at the Powell-Walker House or the
Bracken House.

Next you begin to explore behind the houses and walk on the
subsidiary streets, and then you see a whole new aspect of the
town, with the wonderful outbuildings—smokehouses, kitch-
ens, dairies, privies—and here again the design becomes a delight; the bell-roofed office of the Tayloe House being the most
captivating.

The interiors of the buildings are perfection, the care and
research that has gone into each is awesome. And again, certain
impressions remain—watching the flickering light cast by the
sconced candles at evensong in Bruton Parish Church as it
illuminates the high, white box pews, or first entering the Hall
of the House of Burgesses in the Capitol and thinking how small
it is to have contained such seminal events, or examining the
library of the Peyton Randolph House, so comfortable and
warm in feel and filled with such splendid furnishings, or spying
the beautiful staircase at the Brush-Everard House or drawing
in your breath at the first sight of the smashing display of
swords, pistols and muskets filling the entrance hall of the Governor's Palace . . . it is caviar for the senses.

Gardens and Greens The gardens of Williamsburg, more
than a hundred of them, are an endless delight. After all, you
can quickly enough absorb the general forms of the interiors
and then study them in detail, as you please, but the gardens
and greens are constantly changing. Indeed, this aspect of Williamsburg was the most surprising to me both in its beauty and
in its extent; of the 175 acres that make up Colonial Williamsburg, ninety of them are devoted to gardens and greens.

On my first visit I sensed this magic when I left the Brush-
Everard House and decided to enjoy its pretty garden for a
moment or so. I soon discovered a gate at the back, opened it,
and immediately found myself in an allée of boxwood, the loveliest imaginable. It's a secret place, scented and silent, away from
the activity of the town, and it is absolute perfection, one of
those surprises that Williamsburg proffers to the interested
explorer. I love, too, the little gardens, each a world of its own,
beside the houses, with their signs inviting you to enter and
enjoy their charms. Strangely enough, not many people do, at

I love the backyards of Williamsburg and their wonderful feeling of an almost rural domesticity. I can spend hours wandering in them and enjoying their endless diversity.

least not the times I've been there. I wonder why—not enough time? too little interest? a sense of intruding? Whatever the reasons, the result is that the gardens afford a sense of repose and quietude that is blissfully welcome. Perhaps that's the answer: no one wants to disturb those who are enjoying the tranquility and beauty; after all, there are plenty enough to go around for everyone.

Loveliest of all, as you might expect, are the gardens of the Governor's Palace. And here is my second-favorite place in Williamsburg; on the Chinese footbridge overlooking the canal. These and the other Williamsburg gardens make this one of the great garden settings not only of this country but of the world.

Furniture and Furnishings No matter what you've been told of the quality of the interiors, don't believe it. It's better. The sum total of the collection in the public buildings and in the DeWitt Wallace Decorative Arts Gallery makes this one of the great museums of the world for its period. Equally important, the presentation has been done with exquisite taste and sensibility. I suppose we've all heard the complaints that it's too perfect and therefore unrealistic, but it just doesn't hold water when you see everything *in situ.* Weeks could be spent here getting to know the collection in depth, but for those of us with only a short period of time or lack of interest, even, it is still an unforgettable experience being exposed to so much from the past in so many settings. There is nothing to match it.

Crafts One of the most unusual aspects of Colonial Williamsburg is its twenty or so craft shops, where over one hundred people using period tools create wigs and bookbindings, printed materials, silver and brass objects of supple beauty, baskets and all those necessary eighteenth-century forged items from hinges to nails to andirons, saddles and harnesses, casks, boots, guns, even musical instruments. All are for sale in the shops, and you can watch many of the men and women at their work. Children, of course, are fascinated by this, but then I found it hard to tear myself away from several demonstrations, too.

Museums These three I group together: the **DeWitt Wallace Decorative Arts Gallery,** the **Abby Aldrich Rockefeller Folk Art Center** and **Bassett Hall.**

The most important of the three in terms of size and scope is the DeWitt Wallace Decorative Arts Gallery, which displays about eight thousand objects from the Colonial Williamsburg Collection of seventeenth, eighteenth and early nineteenth century English and American antiques in ten galleries.

Kevin Roche John Dinkeloo & Associates was the firm assigned to the task of planning this building, with Mr. Roche the principal designer. The problem was to make sure that the building in no way intruded into the historic atmosphere, and this was ingeniously solved by placing the gallery behind a brick wall 12 feet high, 46 feet long and 90 feet wide behind the public hospital, where it looks like a part of the hospital complex. From the exterior, then, the brick façade totally conceals its purpose.

Inside, the gallery is divided into a Lower Level and a Main Level, the whole totaling 61,788 square feet. The gallery spaces occupy about 26,000 square feet. As for the collection, it is superb. The Masterworks Gallery, for example, a dramatic, even glamorous space with a skylit atrium, is reserved for the finest pieces in the collection. Here are found such period masterpieces as Thomas Tompion's great tall case clock (c. 1699), made for King William III and one of the most beautiful clocks ever created; the Charles Willson Peale full-length portrait of George Washington after his triumph at Princeton, done on bed ticking; splendid examples of silver by the great Paul de Lamerie; an extraordinary and unique Masonic chair carved with symbolic tools of the order and crafted in Williamsburg—all told, as many as 150 masterpieces can be found here.

But the Decorative Arts Gallery is more than just the Masterworks Gallery. It was designed with three specific criteria in mind: (1) to create an area for the visitor with only a casual interest; (2) to include galleries for those with more specialized knowledge and greater interest in the periods covered, from both a cultural and historical standpoint; (3) to allow space for the individual or scholar with a profound interest in a single or group of objects to study. That the gallery achieves these three objectives makes it a brilliant success.

Abby Aldrich Rockefeller Folk Art Center If nothing else, folk art is a friendly art, and after you have seen this collection you will leave with a warm glow of happiness that will last for the rest of the day—for here, in this small, pleasant building, is one of the great collections in the country. More than two thousand works of American folk art—including wood and metal sculpture, quilts, paintings, toys, fraktur, household items and calligraphic drawings—make up this collection, and not a few are masterpieces in the genre.

Visiting this museum is always a pleasure. The comfortable-looking building is found in a parklike setting, and the ensemble looks like nothing so much as a comfortable Georgian country house and garden. Inside is this same lack of pretension, giving the collection a chance to speak in its own gentle terms and not compete with its surroundings. Some of the things here are familiar enough through reproductions to almost be old friends, but there are also some splendid surprises, and I defy anyone, whether or not they've seen pictures of it, not to be thrilled by the Carolina Room, taken in its entirety from a home in North Carolina and painted with a vivacity and delight that does your heart good. This museum is one of the great joys of Colonial Williamsburg.

Bassett Hall For many years this was the Williamsburg home of Mr. and Mrs. John D. Rockefeller, Jr. It now has been

given to Colonial Williamsburg and is open to the public. Again
you will find some exciting folk-art paintings as well as Turkish
rugs, Chinese porcelains and other handsome furnishings from
the Rockefellers' private collections. When the tour of the house
is over—and, frankly, I found it a bit too long—wander out to
the Teahouse, where some terrific weathervanes can be seen,
and then take some time to walk in the grounds, first exploring
the fourteen acres of gardens and then wandering through the
woodlands behind the house. It's a very satisfying and peaceful
experience to walk through these woods, particularly on a soft,
sunlit day when you want to enjoy the outdoors and escape the
crowds on Duke of Gloucester Street. It's hard to believe that
such tranquility is so close to the center of activity. Another
Williamsburg surprise to savor.

Carter's Grove (1750–55)   Six miles from Williamsburg, overlooking the James from its eighty-foot bluff, lies the great mansion of Carter's Grove, which many consider to be America's
most beautiful house. I can't go that far, but I certainly would
rank it among the greatest houses in our country.

As it is today, it reflects changes made by its last owners, Mr.
and Mrs. Archibald McCrea, who, among other things, raised
the roof of the main house to provide a full third floor, added
dormers and changed the roofline and built half-story brick
hyphens between the two outbuildings whose general aspects
were also modified. These and other changes, performed in the
1930's, were done completely in the spirit of the original, and the
result is very pleasing.

For me, though, the great and overwhelming glory of Carter's
Grove is, was and always will be the entrance passage and
staircase. Who can ever forget the soaring elliptical arch that
sweeps across almost the entire length of the room? Or the
buttery richness of the pine paneling and walnut stairs? Or the
exquisite carving of the Ionic pilasters and stair balusters?
There is a sense of proportion and a mastery of execution that
takes your breath away. (But not everyone felt it: in 1881, to
celebrate the centennial of the Battle of Yorktown, the then
owner painted the paneling red, white and blue!)

The house is now owned by the Colonial Williamsburg Foundation, which decided to leave it as it was when Mrs. McCrea
died in 1960, so you do not see an architectural and furnishings

Carter's Grove, which has been called the most beautiful house in the country, can be approached by a special and enchanting drive from Williamsburg.

restoration, but rather a lived-in house. I think it was a good decision in this particular instance, and a thoughtful memorial to the McCreas' preservation efforts.

While here, you may also wish to take some time to go down to the river and explore the site of Martin's Hundred, a site established in 1618 only to be totally destroyed in an Indian uprising of 1622 when so many Virginia colonists were massacred. It lay hidden until 1970, but now tours of the excavated site are given daily from March–October.

To reach Carter's Grove, be sure to take the country road that begins on South England Street between the Williamsburg Lodge and the Abby Aldrich Rockefeller Folk Art Center. It traverses woods, swamps and open fields, all very much as they might have been two hundred years ago, and it is an especially nice way to get to the house while enjoying delightful and varied scenery.

NEARBY

Jamestown, Yorktown and Williamsburg are all connected by the Colonial Parkway, a particularly scenic drive that makes traveling between the three historic sites almost as enjoyable as being in them.

A small, surprisingly elegant little garden tucked away off Main Street.

JAMESTOWN

There are two parts to the Jamestown complex. The first and most important is the site of the original settlement, now called Colonial National Historical Park and operated by the National Park Service and the Association for the Preservation of Virginia Antiquities. The second, just before you reach the Jamestown site, is Jamestown Festival Park, a re-creation of seventeenth-century Jamestown.

Both commemorate the event that happened on May 14, 1607, when, from three frail vessels that had left England the previous December with 144 men, some of whom had since died, landing was made to establish the first permanent English settlement in the Americas. Here, too, in 1619, the first blacks arrived in British North America on a Dutch ship out of the West Indies. And, in the same year, ironically enough, the meeting of the first representative legislative assembly in the New World took place in the Jamestown church.

From 1607 until 1699, when the government moved to Williamsburg, this was the capital of their colony. When the capital was moved, though, the settlement never recovered and the buildings disappeared. Today all that is left of the original settlement is part of the brick tower (c. 1647) of the church.

You begin your visit by seeing a fifteen-minute orientation film. (Open: Phone 804-229-1733 for hours. Admission: $3 per car.) There is also a small museum with artifacts recovered from digs undertaken in the 1950's.

The site is now landscaped, with a splendid view across the James River. You can see the church tower and Memorial Church (1907) behind it, a stately Tercentenary Monument (1907), from whose terrace you can survey the settlement, and statues of Pocahontas and Captain John Smith. Sites of houses and public buildings are marked, and there are paintings that depict what the buildings might have looked like.

When you are through, you can take a five-mile-long loop drive through the nearby woods and marshes that is not only beautiful but also offers paintings and historical material to help you interpret what you are seeing and to further understand the settlement.

Festival Park is adjacent to Jamestown. It was built in 1957 by the state to commemorate the 350th anniversary of the Jamestown settlement. I have a somewhat ambivalent feeling about it. The most effective part is the re-creation of the settlement, including the three original ships tied to the wharf. (They

The church tower is the only seventeenth-century structure still standing. Behind it is a memorial church built in 1907.

were named *Godspeed, Susan Constant* and *Discovery.*) The reconstructed town is inside a palisaded fort and contains seventeen wattle and daub buildings. It has been done with historical accuracy, and the result is moving in its very primitiveness; it is hard not to feel great admiration for the men who struggled here in those first grueling years filled with hunger, disease and travail.

Other areas of the park include an Information Center, Old and New World Pavilions with interesting graphic and multidimensional displays, a re-creation of a Tidewater Virginia Indian Village, a fort and a craft exhibit area.

My problem with Festival Park is that it leans a little too much toward the commercial, but I must admit that overall it is professionally done, and it is certainly a place that children go for.

Jamestown Festival Park is open daily, 9–5, closes later from June 15–August 15. Closed: December 25, January 1. Admission: $5; children 6–12, $2.50. A combination ticket to include the Yorktown Victory Center (see below) is $7.50; children 6–12, $3.75. Phone: 804-229-1607.

YORKTOWN

I have a real fondness for Yorktown. First of all, it's charming; second, there aren't so many tourists here as in other areas; but mostly it's simply that I feel comfortable and happy strolling its lovely Main Street and side streets and following the battlefield tour. An afternoon here can be gratifying indeed.

Go directly to Main Street, park and begin your stroll. Far and away the most interesting house is the early eighteenth-century Georgian **Nelson House** (Open: Daily, mid-June–Labor Day; Easter–Memorial Day, weekends only. Admission: Free). The exterior has a pleasing richness of detail—the elegant outline of the chimney caps; the prominent, strongly stated quoins and keystones; the simple but beautifully proportioned entrance; the contrast in brick colors. The interior, restored in 1976, has several paneled rooms, of which the dining room is particularly impressive. You may be interested in knowing that the grandson of the builder, Thomas Nelson, Jr.,

Yorktown is a delightful spot, particularly Main Street. This great Georgian house, home to Thomas Nelson, Jr., signer of the Declaration of Independence, has a fine interior and welcoming garden.

was a signer of the Declaration of Independence. While you're there, be sure to take a few minutes to explore the well-maintained garden, which also offers excellent views of the house.

Behind the house, on Nelson Street, are two other houses you should stroll by, the Edmund Smith House and the Ballard House. And then just enjoy Main Street and its other buildings, being sure not to miss the **Monument to Alliance and Victory** (1881), the 95-foot elaborately decorated column at the eastern end designed by Richard Morris Hunt, and **Grace Episcopal Church** and **Swan Tavern** at the western end. Swan Tavern, at 104 Main Street, is a reconstruction of a colonial tavern (1722). The current tenant is **Swan Tavern Antiques,** a superb shop, among the best in Virginia, that offers a large and beautiful selection of eighteenth-century American and English furniture and accessories. Don't miss it. (Open: Monday–Saturday, 10–5. Phone: 804-898-3033.)

After this relaxing interlude, go to the **Yorktown Battlefield Visitor Center** at the east end of town. There's an interesting exhibit on the Revolution and a good film. (Open: Phone 804-898-3400 for hours. Admission: Free.) Then you are ready to take the self-guided battlefield tour, which I thoroughly enjoyed and that is so well presented that those final days of the Revolution come through to your mind's eye with

Grace Church was damaged both during the siege of Yorktown in 1781 and in the Civil War; during the latter, more battles were fought in Virginia than in any other state.

etched clarity. Be sure to take the longer of the two tours—the difference isn't that much—and, as an extra bonus, you will go through some lovely countryside.

As far as I'm concerned, this completes the most interesting part of Yorktown, but there is one more thing to visit, the **Yorktown Victory Center.** Particularly if you are traveling with children, you may wish to stop here. (Open: Daily, 9–5, closes later from June 15–August 15. Closed: December 25, January 1. Admission: $4.50; children 6–12, $2.25. A combination ticket to include Jamestown Festival Park (see above) is $7.50; children 6–12, $3.75. Phone: 804-887-1776.)

The center is devoted to multimedia exhibits that cover the course of the Revolution from the Boston Tea Party through the surrender at Yorktown. There is also a half-hour film, "The Road to Yorktown," on the battle itself. After that you can visit an outdoor encampment where costumed men and women strut their eighteenth-century stuff—demonstrations of cooking, crafts, musketry and so on.

Legend has it that this cave was the last headquarters of General Cornwallis in the Revolution.

GLOUCESTER

Rosewell (begun c. 1725) Fabulous Rosewell, probably the largest and finest of all the houses built in the colonies before the Revolution. Today it is a sad but fascinating ruin, the remains left by a fire that gutted the house in 1916. Still, if you are interested in architecture, and particularly in colonial architecture, this is a house worth visiting, and the drive from Yorktown takes less than an hour.

The original thirty-room house overlooking the York River stood three stories above a high basement 60 by 60 feet. It was built of brick laid in the Flemish bond pattern. The roof had two cupolas and four T-shaped chimneys with exceedingly well-modeled Portland stone caps. Portland stone imported from England also served as keystones for the windows. The façades on each side were five bays long, and the windows on the first floor were of great height. The main house was flanked by two dependencies, each 24 by 60 feet, which were intended to be connected to the curved passageways. These were never built. It is generally agreed that the craftsmanship in both brick and woodwork was the finest in the country, and evidence of that quality can still be seen in the ruins.

The interior, on the main floor, consisted of an off-center hall and three main rooms, the latter elaborately paneled with walnut and mahogany, the former exhibiting a staircase that was without peer in North America.

There was also a garden—there are plans afoot to eventually restore it—and it is probable that Thomas Jefferson, who often visited here, copied its design. Among his papers is the plan of a garden 240 feet wide and 450 feet long, extending from the façade of a house that is most likely Rosewell.

A visit here requires interest and imagination, but for those who have both, it is a compelling glimpse into our past.

Rosewell is difficult to find, but in any case, a visit needs to be arranged in advance. Phone 804-693-4042 for information and directions.

Ware Church (1693–1715) This simple rectangular structure is small yet refined in its execution. It is about two miles east of Gloucester on Virginia Route 14, and as long as you are here it is handsome enough to deserve a short visit.

ALONG THE JAMES RIVER BETWEEN RICHMOND AND WILLIAMSBURG

As Egyptian civilization was nourished along the banks of the Nile, so did seventeenth- and eighteenth-century colonial Virginia Society develop along the James. And still today great monuments are left of that long lost, legendary civilization; the distance involved, about fifty miles, seems very short to contain such a historical cornucopia.

The Great Plantations on the North Bank

All those that follow are off Route 5, one of our country's most historic roads. If you exclude Carter's Grove as I have—it seems so much a part of Williamsburg (see page 196)—you can see the remainder relatively comfortably in one day. I have listed these in geographical order from Richmond to Williamsburg, unlike my usual listing by preference. In order of preference they

would be: Shirley, Westover, Berkeley and Sherwood Forest. If
your time is limited, then, see Shirley and Westover above all
else.

Shirley Plantation (c. 1740) There is a view of Shirley, both
from the river and land side, that sums up its special feeling
very quickly—it is the sight of the huge carved pineapple, symbol of hospitality, that dominates the top of the roof and sits
between the two massive chimneys. Shirley is a welcoming
house and, for all its grandeur, very definitely a family's home;
in this instance, the same family, the Hill-Carters—R. E. Lee's
mother was Anne Hill Carter of this family, and it's one of the
proudest names in Virginia—have lived here for nine generations and have owned the plantation since 1660. (The name
probably derived from Sir Thomas Sherley, father-in-law of
Lord Delaware and one of the first owners of this property.)

Shirley is unique. Not only has it remained in the same family from the time it was built (c. 1723), but it is still a working
plantation; the fields come up almost to the dependencies; this
is how a plantation must have looked in the eighteenth century.
Shirley is also uniquely beautiful; with one of the three or four
loveliest interiors, and an exterior with features you will not see
anywhere else in the state.

First look at the plantation as a whole, a primary composition
of five buildings which has no peer in the state. Two L-shaped
buildings flank the north entrance. Next are the kitchen and
the overseer's house, two-story brick with steep gabled roofs and
enough architectural refinement to make them worthy of note
by themselves. At the head of it all, at the south end, stands the
mansion, large, almost square, two and a half stories with a
mansard roof unique for its time and place and pierced by over-
sized dormers. Front and back also have porticoes added in 1831
that are elegantly carved and well suited to the building. (The
present owner, Mr. Hill Carter, feels the roof may show Hugue-
not influence; there was a settlement nearby at the time the
house was built.)

The splendidly furnished interior is also different from most
plantation houses in that there is no central hall. Instead,
there is a hall "room," and here is found Shirley's most famous feature, the magnificent carved walnut staircase that
has no visible means of support. (But it does have invisible

Shirley is a very special heirloom in American history: The same family has lived here for nine generations and includes in its ranks Robert E. Lee's mother, while the interior is one of the most captivating in Virginia.

ones, iron bars that have been driven into the twenty-two-and-a-half-inch-thick walls of the house.) This first floor has three other rooms—a parlor, a dining room, and a bedroom—that are open to the public. These too are unique, for they hold family possessions accumulated over three centuries, a richly varied collection of silver, china, furniture and portraits of museum quality; the wonderful portrait of Washington, now in the DeWitt Wallace Decorative Arts Gallery in Williamsburg, came from here (see page 194). It gives the house a sense of continuity and tradition that can be matched by very few other houses in this country.

Before you leave, explore the river views, the best of any from these plantations, and also the glorious trees, some as gnarled and craggy as age itself. You can also see the plantation kitchen and others of the outbuildings—including the delightful round, fat pigeon-house, just before the forecourt entrance.

Shirley is open: Daily, 9–5. Closed: December 25. Phone: 804-795-2385 for admission fees.

Berkeley (1726)   Historically, Berkeley is the most interesting of these plantations. It stands on land that was part of a grant awarded by James I in 1619 to the Berkeley Company and was first known as Berkeley Hundred and Plantation. On December

14, 1619, Captain John Woodlie, leader of the small colony, wrote: "Wee ordaine that the day of our ships arrival at the place assigned for plantacon in the land of Virginia shall be yearly and perpetually keept holy as a day of thanksgiving to Almighty god."

Therein lies Virginia's claim to the first Thanksgiving.

Berkeley was built by Benjamin Harrison IV, father of Benjamin Harrison V, a signer of the Declaration of Independence, and was the birthplace of William Henry Harrison. The latter, of "Tippecanoe and Tyler Too" fame, rather ignored his antecedents by running as a log-cabin-born frontiersman.

Later, during the Civil War, the estate grounds became a Federal encampment for the Army of the Potomac of 140,000 men—President Lincoln twice visited the troops here—and it was here that General Daniel Butterfield, in the summer of 1862, wrote that most haunting of all melodies, "Taps."

After the Civil War the house fell upon sad days, eventually being used as an animal barn. But in 1907 a Scottish immigrant, who had been a drummer boy during the war, bought the estate. His name was John Jamieson, and his son and daughter-in-law, Malcolm and Grace, live there today, operating the plantation and continuing the restoration of the house and gardens that they began many years ago.

It is the grounds here that I particularly like. The plantings

The grounds and gardens of Berkeley are of a tender, old-fashioned beauty that makes them particularly appealing.

are some of the best along the James and include five beautifully landscaped terraces leading down to the river as well as
distinguished boxwood gardens. It is extremely agreeable to
wander among them, enjoying perspectives and coming upon a
surprise or two: the reproduction of the ship that brought the
original settlers, for instance.

Berkeley has other faint overtones of the theatrical: in the
cellar you can see a slide show that describes the history of the
place, and paintings on the surrounding walls give you an idea
about how life was on the plantation. The house itself, while
well-proportioned, is rather severe in its straightforward approach to the Georgian. As for the interior, it is comfortable
with hand-carved Adam woodwork; a pleasant dwelling. The
original paneling has unfortunately disappeared, but the Ja-
miesons have worked hard to bring the house back to its one-
time splendor. Come, then, for the gardens; stay to see the
house.

Berkeley is open: Daily, 8–5. Closed: December 25. Admission:
$6; children 6–12, $3. Phone: 804-795-2453. Berkeley also offers
a reasonably priced and good lunch (see page 242), making this
the perfect spot to have a quick bite with an accompanying
Virginia wine. And don't forgo the rum cake.

Westover (c. 1730)   When you leave Berkeley, you will see a
sign for Westover, probably the most famous Georgian house in
America. Follow it, for if Shirley has the most beautiful and
accomplished interior of the river plantations, Westover has the
greatest Georgian exterior—including that of Carter's Grove—
in all of Virginia, perhaps in the country.

It was built by William Byrd II (1674–1744), planter, speculator, public official, one of our first important writers and *grand
seigneur* of one of Virginia's noblest families. The estate's spectacular setting by the James, among boxwood and lawn and
ancient tulip poplars, is appropriate to the splendor of the
house. Byrd loved this spot and, as well as his great house, he
created here the famous library of four thousand volumes, the
largest and finest in the colonies that, years later, Thomas Jefferson would so avidly peruse. Wrote Byrd to a friend: "A Library, a Garden, a Grave and a purling stream are the innocent
scenes that divert our leisure."

His pleasures may have been innocent (notwithstanding his

secret diary), his house is not. This is a superlative and sophisticated dwelling. (Only the main building and west wing are original, the hyphens and east wing were added about 1900. These have not been connected to the main building with the same sensitivity and care as was used at Carter's Grove.)

The exterior of the main building, seven bays wide, is topped by a high-pitched hipped roof pierced by dormers. On the river (south) side, you immediately notice the doorway, the most famous and most copied in this country, carved in Portland stone and imported from England. (The pediment is a scroll or swan's neck type, the curve ending in rosettes. At the center is a pineapple. The flute pilasters flanking the door have finely carved and proportioned Corinthian capitals.) The north side also has a highly sophisticated doorway, although not quite so showy. The doors are the exuberant exclamation points in an exceptionally elegant but restrained façade. The brick of the walls is in the Flemish bond pattern, a lovely rich red-orange that can't be captured by photographs. The wedge-shaped bricks over the window are of a slightly different shade and give a feel of suppleness to the wall surface. Most subtle of all is the wall treatment: The segmented windows are repeated on the second floor, but as they rise, the individual pane size decreases ever so slightly. This kind of sensitivity and refinement makes the house a joy to the eye, a building to look at with ever-deepening pleasure.

The interior of the house is open to the public only during some days of Garden Week each spring, and if you can go at that

Westover, perhaps the most famous of all the plantation houses along the James. This is the greatest Georgian exterior in the state.

time, do, for the entrance hallway with its elaborate plaster ceiling and sweeping staircase, and the stunning mantelpieces —particularly the marble one in the drawing room—will be highly rewarding of your efforts.

The gardens at Westover and the grounds are always open to the public. The flowers here are what could be called intimate shades, nothing flashy or pressing, but as quietly rewarding in the aggregate as any garden you can think of. Crape myrtle and roses, violets, peonies . . . old-fashioned flowers that still create magic in the heart. Many years ago a visitor wrote that Byrd spared no expense "in new Gates, gravel walks, hedges and cedars finely twined and a little green-house with two or three orange trees with fruit on them; in short, he hath the finest seat in Virginia." Today, still, it is a very fine seat. Be sure to examine those finely wrought iron gates, mentioned by that gentleman so long ago, also made in England in the eighteenth-century, that are on the north side of the house. Each is surmounted by a spread eagle. Finally, before you leave, examine the epitaph on Byrd's grave, which he wrote: It makes the proud claim that he was "the constant enemy of all exorbitant power and hearty friend to the liberties of his country."

The grounds of Westover are open daily, 9–6. Admission: $2; children under 16, 50¢.

A little east of the mansion on Route 5 is **Westover Church** (c. 1730). If you have a moment, stop in to see this fine restored

Westover Church, the very quintessence of a serene country church.

eighteenth-century Virginia church. And note, too, its beautiful boxwood.

Sherwood Forest (c. 1730) This is the only frame house among the James River plantations open to the public and, at three hundred feet in length, it is the longest frame house in the country. Of more interest is the fact that John Tyler, tenth president of the United States, bought it in 1842 as his retirement home. It remains in the Tyler family today.

Tyler named it Sherwood Forest because he had been outlawed from the Whig Party, and it was here that he brought his second wife, Julia Gardiner of New York, one of the richest women in the country and a member of one of America's proudest and most ancient families. She added to the house and, more important, had the famous landscape artist Andrew Jackson Downing redesign the grounds. Her aristocratic pretensions also continued unchecked. For instance, she had a bright blue rowboat named the *Pocahontas* to ferry her across the James to see friends and neighbors. She was attended by four black oarsmen in livery that she describes as "bright blue and white checked calico shirts, white linen pants, black patent leather belts, straw hats painted blue, with 'Pocahontas' upon them in white, and in one corner of the shirt collar is worked with braid a bow and an arrow (to signify from the Forest) and in the other the President's and my initials combined." Farewell to the dear old Republic and the days when Abigail Adams strung up her wash in the White House. Still, Julia had gumption and is appealing even now; though ruined by the Civil War, she never gave up. There's a touching story that at the end of the war she saw two down-at-the-heels Confederate soldiers coming up the drive and offered them all that she had, bread and water and a place to sleep. "Mother," said one, "don't you know us?" She hadn't seen them since they left four years previously.

The grounds are still of interest and display more than eighty varieties of trees, including a large gingko behind the house that was presented to Tyler by Admiral Perry. There also is a rare seventeenth-century tobacco barn; walking here is enjoyable. The interior of the house is comfortable, and furnished with eighteenth- and nineteenth-century heirlooms, but it is the ballroom that I find most appealing, perhaps because of its airy simplicity.

The grounds of Sherwood Forest are open daily, 9–5. Closed: December 25. Admission: $2; children under 12, 50¢. The house is open by appointment only and a minimum of four people is required to see it. Admission: $6.75. Phone: 804-829-5377.

Southside from Hopewell to Smithfield

It's hard to believe that two banks of a river could be as different as are these. Southside is certainly not as well known as its northern neighbor, but it has more than its share of glamour and history; and in the village of Smithfield, it has one of the most delightful villages in Virginia—and one of its best-kept secrets. In fact, if you intend to explore Southside, make your quarters Smithfield. But in any case, take some time to enjoy it here. All the places discussed are either on or just off Route 10.

Hopewell and City Point

Hopewell, with a little more than 23,000 people, could be either a smallish city or a large-ish town depending on your mood; I lean toward a large-ish town. On the outskirts are chemical and other plants, reminders of what makes the area tick. More interesting is the history, for Hopewell also includes City Point, at the junction of the James and Appomattox rivers, Grant's headquarters during the Petersburg siege (see page 176), and, for a time, one of the world's busiest ports and the largest Civil War supply depot.

City Point Unit of the Petersburg National Battlefield
Grant arrived here on June 15, 1864. From then until March 29, 1865, when he decided to move closer to the front for the final campaign of the war, City Point was the nerve center of the Union's efforts in Virginia. From here 100,000 soldiers were supplied, and thousands of civilians were brought in to build the necessary railroad lines, wharves storehouses, barracks . . . a grand total of 280 structures. There was even a prison capable of holding four hundred men. All in all, an extraordinary effort for its time.

Lincoln visited here twice, arriving the second time on March

24, 1865, and staying for almost two weeks before making his famous trip to see fallen Richmond. It was here, aboard the president's steamer *River Queen,* that Lincoln began to formulate his generous terms for the approaching peace.

Of primary interest today is the simple cabin of timbers and mortar that served as Grant's headquarters and is on the lawn of Appomattox Manor, which, with its surrounding acres, was the heart of the Union operation. The house and land belonged to the Eppes family, who received it in 1635 and lived there for the next 340 years. After the Civil War, Dr. Richard Eppes, then head of the family, had to borrow money to pay the U.S. Government $641.50 to purchase the buildings and wharves on his own property. That's always struck me as mean-spirited.

City Point Unit is administered by the National Park Service. As always within this service, the staff is ready, eager and very able to answer any questions you may have about the period. Open: Daily, 8:30–4:30. Closed: December 25, January 1. Admission: Free. Phone: 804-458-9504.

Weston Manor (c. 1735) This Georgian frame house on the banks of the Appomattox also belonged to the Eppes family. Both the house and its situation qualify it for consideration of a visit. During the Civil War, by the way, the house served as headquarters for General Philip Sheridan, and you can still see the names of Union soldiers scratched into a windowpane.

The house is open by special appointment. Phone: 804-458-4829. Admission: $2.

Five miles east of Hopewell and worth a stop is **Merchants Hope Church** (1657), which claims to be the "oldest Protestant church still standing in America and used as a House of Worship." It's very similar on the outside to Westover Church (see page 210), a quietly dignified brick structure, but the brickwork, in the Flemish bond pattern, is of a rare beauty. The flagstones in the aisle were brought over from England as ballast.

The key for the church is at the neighboring superintendent's house. Admission: Donation. Phone: 804-458-8657.

Flowerdew Hundred For the general public—us—this is the most interesting archaeological investigation currently under way in Virginia, because of the great variety of the sites discovered. Evidence, for instance, has been discovered of Indian occu-

pation here as far back as 9000 B.C. In 1618 the first English
settlement was established here, and there are plans to rebuild
it based on archaeological evidence found at the site. (A stone
foundation, 41 feet by 24 feet, is only one instance of this dig.)
The first windmill in America was built here, and although no
one knows what it looks like exactly, a replica of an eighteenth-
century windmill has been built.

This is, then, an outdoor living history museum. It is well
done and seems to have managed a successful mix of the scholarly with the more commercial: There is a museum shop and
bookstore. You can watch archaeologists at work, and some of
the thousands of artifacts discovered are on display and presented in a thoughtful, interesting way. You can buy cornmeal
ground at the mill and watch a thirty-minute film on the windmill. The Charter of the Flowerdew Hundred Foundation states
that its purpose is "to preserve and study the cultural history
of the plantation and its region and especially to interpret the
past to the general public." They are succeeding admirably.

The plantation is open April–November, Tuesday–Sunday,
10–5. Admission: $2.50; children 6–12, $1.50. Phone: 804-541-8897.

Brandon Plantation (c. 1765) I almost hate to spread the
news after enjoying it pretty much to myself so many times, but
this is one of the most handsome estates on the James and also
has the most beautiful gardens open to the public along the
river. It shouldn't be missed.

The history of the estate goes back to 1616, when John Martin
received the patent to the Brandon property. But he probably
had been farming the property already because he brought
farm produce, including tobacco, to England in the same year.
That makes Brandon the oldest continuous agricultural enterprise in the country.

From 1630 to 1720, the estate was owned by a group of families
that originally included Richard Quincy, whose son had married Shakespeare's daughter Judith. In 1720 it passed to the
Harrison family, who built the house you see today and who
remained until 1926. The new owners, the Daniel family, have
been there since. One anecdote about a Harrison that should be
passed on: A widowed Mrs. Harrison, known as "old Miss," was
once asked to entertain President James K. Polk. She called her
cook in to discuss the meal, but the man seemed to take it all

too much in his stride. "You must remember that this is the President of the United States," she finally remonstrated. "And you, Madame, must remember how blest we are in your cook," he replied.

The 210-foot-long house, red brick with white trim, is made up of five parts constructed at different times; parts of the two dependencies at each end may go back to the late 1600's. The three-part central building (c. 1765) has been attributed to Thomas Jefferson, but almost the exact plan can be found in Robert Morris's "Select Architecture" of 1757. Jefferson owned this book and may, therefore, have suggested this particular plan. The two-story dependencies and central house are connected by low hyphens. This is one of the finest and purest examples of the Palladian style in Virginia. Unlike the straightforward Georgian, this also is a very supple and elegant house, sophisticated and almost feminine in its complexity.

The interiors have been much altered: The center hall's triple arch and staircase, admittedly handsome, were added in the early nineteenth century, and much of the paneling was damaged in the Civil War, to cite two examples. Nonetheless, there is much to admire, the Chinese trellis stair in the central hall of the west wing in particular.

And now for the gardens, with their enormous, centuries-old tulip poplars and dwarf boxwood and hardwoods, their row of pecan trees and mulberry and crape myrtle, their wisteria and old-fashioned shrubs and 300-foot-wide close-cropped and emerald-green lawn. Flowers are everywhere, and very beautiful they are; but it is the trees and the shrubs that make this garden uniquely memorable. At the end of it all is the James, wide and old, the perfect coda to this almost mystically splendid chambered space.

Unfortunately, the house is only open to the public during Garden Week, although groups and tours can go through at other times by appointment. Phone: 804-866-8486 or 866-8416. The grounds are open daily, 9:00–5:30. Closed: December 25. Admission: $2.50; children 6–12, free.

Not far from here, on Route 610, is **Martin's Brandon Church** (1856), a nice example of ecclesiastical architecture of its time that looks as if it belongs in a long, gossipy nineteenth-century novel.

Soon after you enter Surry County, you will see, on your

right, the ruins of **Lower Southwark Parish Church** (c. 1754), which was gutted by fire in 1868, and its accompanying cemetery. I have a great weakness for ruins—it's the Sir Walter Scott Romantic within me—and these are special. The old brick walls have been stabilized so that you can walk in and about the shell; the interior is full of secondary undergrowth but has a path. The sense of the place is more European than American. A five-minute stop here, including a short visit to the little cemetery, evokes an aura of nostalgia, a remembrance of some secret place we all harbor deep in our souls.

You next come to **Smith's Fort Plantation,** whose history goes back to the arrival of the English. Captain John Smith, in 1609, built a fort here to defend Jamestown. Later, in 1614, the great and mighty Indian chief Powhatan gave the land to John Rolfe when he married Pocahontas, Powhatan's "dear and darling daughter," as John Smith wrote, "who exceeded all; not only in her feature and countenance and proportion, but in her wit and spirit." No wonder that John Rolfe, the first successful developer of a mild strain of tobacco that the English loved— "the bewitching weed," they called it—wanted to marry her "to whom my heart and my best thoughts are and have a long time

The ruins of Lower Southwark Parish Church. "There's a fascination frantic / In a ruin that's romantic; / Do you think you are sufficiently decayed?" Sir William S. Gilbert, The Mikado.

been entangled and inthralled in so intricate a labyrinth, that I was even awearied to unwind myself there-out," as he wrote to the Governor in his petition to marry the beguiling creature.

Their son, Thomas, inherited the land, and he sold it to a Thomas Warren, who in 1652 built a house here. The building that stands today, though, goes back only to the first half of the eighteenth century, and is a small but high-style Georgian dwelling. It's worth a visit, for it has, for the time, a sophisticated interior (note the paneling in the dining room) and is interestingly furnished (William and Mary, Jacobean and even Elizabethan pieces). There also is a well-executed English garden, a rare example of its type.

Smith's Fort Plantation is open April–September, Tuesday–Saturday, 10–5; Sunday, 1–5. Admission: $2; students, $1.50. Phone: 804-294-3872.

Chippokes Plantation State Park   This is a 1,683-acre park (hiking, bicycling, fishing, picnicking, swimming) and working farm (corn, peanuts, wheat, sheep, soybeans, honeybees and more), which also includes plantation dwellings. I had never been terribly interested in seeing it, but when at last I did go, I thoroughly enjoyed it; it is both scenic and absorbing.

The entrance is through a wide and splendid stand of loblolly pines, tall and straight, with that seemingly three-dimensional, exquisite soft green shade that only pine trees possess. Be sure to stop at the visitor's center, which has first-rate displays on agriculture and this plantation. (It was here that I learned that the word *barbecue* may come from an Indian word, *barbacoa*, which they used to describe a meat-smoking technique.) When you leave, go behind and to the right of the center, passing into the woods with holly trees flashing their dull-brilliant green, and almost immediately you will hear the waves of the James breaking against the sandy shore below.

Now continue the driving tour around the plantation, stopping where you please. There are some good-looking buildings, including the River House, with its four wonderfully silhouetted chimneys, and the Mansion (1854). In addition, the gardens at the Mansion are gratifying and have seats placed just where they should be for viewing the plantings. Inside, though, I found the building to be uninteresting in its furnishings; you can easily skip that part of the tour. How dreary, then, after all that beauty and gentle civilization to come across this sign "You are within 10 miles of the Surry Nuclear Power Station. In the event of a serious accident . . ." At that point I stopped reading.

Chippokes Plantation State Park is open daily. The Visitor's Center is open daily, April–October. Admission: Free. Phone: 804-294-3625.

Bacon's Castle (1655) This building lays claim to being the "oldest documented brick house in English North America," and that alone would make it of great interest. But there is more, for some of its architectural features are outstanding and define it as a Jacobean manor house—the sole survivor in this country, according to the National Trust. (The period is named after James I of England.) Not only that—its English-style Renaissance garden, dating from 1680, is the oldest documented formal garden in America. And then it has a glamorous history as well.

The house was actually built by Arthur Allen. Its name came later, from Nathaniel Bacon and his 1676 rebellion called, aptly enough, Bacon's Rebellion. At that time, Sir William Berkeley was governor of the colony, and a more autocratic, unpopular man would have been hard to find. For fourteen years he had refused to allow elections to the House of Burgesses. To make matters even worse, he was refusing to provide the settlers with adequate protection against the Indians, who were growing increasingly threatening. One group of settlers from Charles City County, home county of Shirley, Berkeley, Westover and Sherwood Forest, asked the governor to allow them to go after the Indians. He refused. A mistake, for the settlers now looked for someone who would lead them out of their troubles, and they quickly found Nathaniel Bacon, Jr., a twenty-eight-year-old English immigrant who was related to the great Sir Francis Bacon as well as Governor Berkeley himself through Lady Berkeley. He was not your ordinary down-and-out rebel; he even had a place on the governor's council, a signal honor for such a young man.

Bacon—whose favorite oath was said to be "God damn my blood!"—accepted the proffered leadership and immediately went out into the field against the Indians. Affairs went from bad to worse, and soon the governor captured Bacon, but pardoned him and his followers on Bacon's word that he had re-

Bacon's Castle, the sole surviving Jacobean manor house in this country, and its garden, the oldest documented formal garden in America.

pented. The truce didn't last long, and soon Bacon was out in the field again, this time in full rebellion against Berkeley's government; he even burned the capital of Jamestown. Suddenly he was brought down by dysentery. In a few weeks he was dead. The revolt quickly petered out and Berkeley took his revenge by executing 23 men. "That old fool has hanged more men in that naked country than I did for the murder of my father," said King Charles II when he heard of it. Charles, one of the most appealing of England's monarchs, had pardoned all but Bacon before he heard of Bacon's death and Berkeley's executions. How wise of him; here was an early indication that the colonists' rights could be tampered with only at great risk.

About a month before Bacon died, and after burning Jamestown, Bacon retreated to Gloucester and directed one of his lieutenants, William Rookings of Surry County, to fortify a stronghold in his home county. He chose the Allen house, and rebel forces would remain there almost to the end of the rebellion, when loyal forces captured the castle. From that time on, it has been known as Bacon's Castle.

The house looks exactly the part of a headquarters for a rebellious underdog fighting for the weak. In fact, it would fit beautifully into a Romantic or even Gothic novel. Although much has changed over the last three hundred years, it is still rather glamorous. The best feature is the elaborate Flemish gable at the end of the house with that wonderful grouping of three chimneys, so strong as a unit that it overwhelms the building. The architect obviously knew what English houses with this kind of grouping looked like but didn't quite know how to integrate it into the body of the house. It is very similar to a folk artist's effort in painting—strong, exuberant, even daring, but lacking educated know-how. I love it.

Inside, you first see a video program giving the history of the house. Then you are taken through the building—which is, incidentally, quite small—to see the rooms, which have been restored to different periods. This is an excellent solution, for the house has so changed over its lifetime, and this approach recognizes that fact. It is very well accomplished, I might add, and extremely absorbing. Off to the right of the house, by the way, look for a tree with the most magnificent roots—what seems like dozens of them—looking like some primordial living, twisting mass.

The garden, rediscovered in 1985, is said to be not only the earliest but also the largest (360 feet long and 195 feet wide), best preserved, and most sophisticated, for its time, in North America. It comprises six rectangular planting beds with outlying brick garden pavilions and a twelve-foot-wide central broad walk of sand. Bordering the sides of the garden are six-foot-wide planking beds. When it is fully restored, it will be unique in this country and should be one of our great gardens.

Bacon's Castle is open mid-April–October, Tuesday, Friday and Sunday, 12–4; Saturday, 10–4. The remainder of the year is by appointment. Admission: $4; students, $1. Phone: 804-357-5976 or 866-8483.

Smithfield

What a wonderful little town. I like it so much that I would rank it as one of the five most delightful towns in Virginia. This is the home of the world-famous Smithfield ham, and there is more interesting architecture than is found in many cities three times the size, a picturesque little harbor, friendly people . . . they even have the oldest church in the country, St. Luke's. I would spend the night here, at least, and make this my headquarters to more closely explore Southside.

Here are some highlights of Smithfield, beginning with the
Courthouse. This, with similar ones in Hanover, King William
and Charles City, is, as far as I know, a unique and very handsome design. It's of brick, with a simple five-arched arcade
across the façade forming a loggia-style porch. Two chimneys
are at either end, and the roof is hipped. Inside, the main court-
room has a rounded end that gives the room a grace that the
other courthouses don't have. It is believed that this was copied
from the old Capitol in Williamsburg, and when that building
was being reconstructed, the Foundation sent men to study this
room and its circular roof. The building has been beautifully
restored and today houses the Isle of Wight/Smithfield Chamber of Commerce and Smithfield Visitor's Center (Open: Monday—Thursday, 10–3). It has a presence and a dignity, this
building, that makes it stand out as one of the best buildings in
the town.

Smithfield has more than fifty buildings of historic note, and
the result is a "townscape" of great appeal. Some of these buildings would be outstanding anywhere. For instance, one of the
finest late Victorian houses in Virginia is here, at 304 South
Church Street. It was built in 1901 by P. D. Gwaltney, Jr., whose
family packages the hams that have made Smithfield famous,
and it has everything—towers and tiles and porches and pillars
and bays and recesses and balusters and pilasters and stained
glass and . . . and . . . and somehow it all coheres. The house is
beautifully maintained, fortunately, but according to "Smithfield: A Pictorial History," by Segar Cofer Dashiell, a fascinating book on the town and its buildings, the interior has been
completely changed. What a pity! Dashiell tells us that originally the house had "cabinet mantles inlaid in mother-of-pearl,
parquet floors, dark oak paneling, inside shutters, plaster frieze,
and walls decorated with cherubs, garlands and ribbons, hand
painted on silk by an artisan from Baltimore." And here is my
favorite touch: "On the wall of an alcove in the master bedroom,
among cupids and swags, was painted a dove bringing in its
beak a letter addressed to Mrs. P. D. Gwaltney, Jr."

From a much earlier time is the Grove (c. 1790) at 22 Grace
Street, the most handsome house of its period in Smithfield.
(Segar Cofer Dashiell tells us the name came from a nearby oak
forest that was cut down and sold to the Russians in 1854,
during the Crimean War.) I particularly admire the three

Board and batten and gingerbread and cozy little windows nestled under the eaves—just one of the many enticing houses of Smithfield.

porches that grace this brick house, and especially their beautifully formed Doric pillars. Another handsome touch is the large stone lintels over the windows. This is one of those houses that, in its entirety of design, proportion and detail, is deeply satisfying.

These are three extremes of architecture represented in Smithfield, but there's so much in between to enjoy: the Gingerbread Cottage on Grace Street or the Wentworth-Barrett House (c. 1752) at 117 South Church with its handsome steps from either side leading to the front door, or the Andrew Machie House (c. 1796) at 338 South Church, a wonderful frame house with a pretty Chinese Chippendale fence and a glorious backyard. And Hayden Hall (c. 1807) another agreeable building at 222 Grace, was the home of Mr. Walker Warren, last owner of Bacon's Castle (see page 218).

St. Luke's Church is two miles south of Smithfield on Route 10 and is that greatest of all rarities in this country, an original Gothic building. In fact, it is the only one in the country. The brick church was built in 1632, the top section of the tower and the quoins came later, sometime after 1657. It is our oldest surviving church.

You approach the building through the graveyard, and with each step you seem to be entering more deeply into space that is otherworldly, for the church does not look Virginian or American. Instead it looks like one of those timeless medieval English parish churches. And that, in essence, is what it is. Buttresses support the side walls. Round arched windows are divided into lancets by brick tracery. The tower, square and Norman, is pierced by a round arched entrance, thick as the wall and topped by a primitive triangular pediment. It is a sturdy building, one to last the ages.

The interior has been carefully restored. Its most interesting feature is the ceiling of timber trusswork and the three massive tie beams that cross the church and meet the walls where the outside buttresses are located. Behind the altar, windows—both round arched and pointed Gothic—pierce the thick wall, and here is my one—admittedly minor—quibble with the restoration: if such great care was taken to be completely authentic, why not replace the not very interesting nineteenth-century stained glass with the clear glass of the original?

St. Luke's is open Tuesday–Sunday, 9:30–5:00. Closed: January. Admission: Free. Phone: 804-357-3367.

St. Luke's Church is the only true Gothic building in this country. The interior has been carefully restored and has a ceiling of timber truss-work.

NORFOLK

Norfolk—deservedly—used to have a terrible reputation. It was, not to put too fine a point on it, one of the dreariest, tackiest, raunchiest cities on the East Coast, mainly because of the huge nearby naval base. No more. What once could compete with the Whore of Babylon is now a bustling, growing, typical late-twentieth-century coastal city that is pleasant to visit and offers a great deal to see and do. Congratulations to the citizens; their herculean efforts on behalf of their city have more than paid off.

Norfolk was founded in 1682, and as trade with the West Indies and North Carolina expanded, the town grew into a thriving port. By the time of the Revolution, some 6,000 citizens resided here. But when the Revolution began, the last royal governor, Lord Dunmore, in January 1776 ordered his ships to fire on the town. In retaliation, the rebels set their own fires. By the end of the war not one building was left whole and only St. Paul's was rebuilt.

From then until the Civil War, Norfolk went through a series of economic ups and downs, never achieving sustained prosperity. But it came through that war intact physically, and from then on it prospered, shipping cotton and coal, becoming a vital rail center, milling lumber and textiles, and becoming increasingly important as a center for retail business and finance. And always, of course, there was the Navy and shipbuilding.

With one of the finest natural harbors in the world, the Navy was here as early as 1801. It was from here that Commodore Perry sailed to Japan in 1853 and the Great White Fleet sailed around the world in 1893, showing America's new global potential. Here, too, on March 9, 1862, the Confederate *Merrimac* sallied forth, "a submerged house, with the roof only above the water," to engage the Union's *Monitor* and change forever the history of naval warfare. By the time World War I began in 1914, the port and shipyards were vital to our nation's defense. From 1910—when Norfolk had about 67,000 people—to 1920, the population increased to 115,000. Much of this was due to huge Army and Navy installations, and the Navy base became a permanent legacy of that period. It happened again in World War II when, from 1939 to 1943, the population increased from 144,000 to 200,000.

When that war ended, the city took a good hard look at itself and was nut pleased. In 1950 they began a cleanup and rebuilding program that won an All-American city award in 1960 and that still continues. In some ways it may have gone too far in tearing down, but there's no denying that the city has been immeasurably improved overall. As one example, consider the area known as Ghent, originally developed as a suburb beginning in 1890 and completed about 1910. Its underlying appeal, then as now, is in its pleasant period architecture—Queen Anne, Colonial Revival, Shingle Style, and so forth—the streets that conform to the land contours and the water that is central to it all.

Soon it became one of the nicest places to live in Norfolk. But after World War I, it went into a decline and grew shabby. The process was reversed in the 1970's, though, and today Ghent is, once again, a most attractive and livable area. It is typical of what can only be called Norfolk's Renaissance.

And, before I forget, there's also a wonderful antiques shop here, **Family Tree Antiques** at 420 West Bute Street, a pretty street in any case, that has wonderful examples of nineteenth-century English silver in particular. Phone 804-625-6250 for hours. Nearby, in Hampton, is the sister shop of Swan Tavern Antiques (see page 201) at 2538 West Pembroke Avenue. It is, needless to say, a superior shop. Phone 804-244-2613 for an appointment.

One final note—and a wonderful example of Norfolk's sincere commitment to excellence: if the Virginia Opera Association is performing, go. This is one of the most exciting regional groups in the country—they performed the world premiere of Thea Musgrave's *Harriet Tubman,* for instance—and is well worth taking in.

Norfolk is still growing. Today the city has a population of about 267,000. If you also include Virginia Beach and Newport News, the figure rises to more than 1,600,000. Of these, more than 475,000 are connected in some way with the Navy; this is the largest U.S. Naval installation in the world.

WHAT TO SEE AND DO

The Chrysler Museum   One of the two best museums in Virginia—and my personal favorite—primarily thanks to Walter P. Chrysler, Jr., who in 1971 gave a large portion of his collection to the museum. It was subsequently named after him, and he has continued to donate works of art and to support the museum in other ways. It is he who has given this museum its unique quality and individuality. As the museum itself states, "The Chrysler Museum houses an unusually varied and interesting collection of important artworks ranging from Chinese bronzes dated circa 2500 B.C. to paintings and sculpture of the 1980's. Nearly every important culture, civilization and historical period from the past 5,000 years is represented. The collection comprises works by Gauguin, Rubens, Boucher, Cassatt and Picasso. The Chrysler Institute of Glass collection contains approximately 10,000 objects dating from the Roman empire period to the present—including more than 2500 pieces of Sandwich glass and 220 works by Tiffany." To that impressive statement I would add that there are masterpieces here by other world-famous artists as well, and first-rate paintings of lesser-

The Chrysler Museum has an unusually varied collection for a museum of its size and a glass collection that ranks among the finest in the world. I like it very much.

known artists that make this museum a trove of distinguished riches.

The collection of **Italian Art,** which ranges from the fourteenth century well into the eighteenth century, is what I would call superior eclectic; that is, there seems to be no prejudice as to period or style, but rather a broad range, intellectually informed taste with particular strength in the Baroque.

Some asides: the huge (112 inches by 66½ inches) *Virgin and Child with Angels Appearing to Saints Anthony Abbot and Paul the Hermit* (1562) by Veronese, one of the greatest pictures in the collection, was commissioned with two companion pieces for an altar in a monastery church in Mantua. Veronese completed all three in the incredibly short period of three months. . . . *Samson Bringing Honey to his Parents,* c. 1625, was painted by il Guercino. In the upper middle section, flying in formation, as it were, are bees, a graceful allusion to the coat of arms of the Barberini family, which included Pope Urban VIII, who commissioned this picture. Aside from that, note the brilliant psychological presentation of the three heads. . . . *Memorial to James, First Earl Stanhope,* c. 1720, by Pittoni, came about because a bankrupt Irish impresario named Owen McSwiny got Pittoni and other famous painters of the time to collaborate on a series of allegorical tombs of British "worthies" that included Isaac Newton, John Locke and the Duke of Marlborough. . . . And finally, there is the great Bernini masterpiece, the *Bust of the Savior* (c. 1679), the last work by that great artist. He wanted to give it to his patron, Queen Christina of Sweden; but because she felt she had no comparable gift to give him for such a great masterpiece, she refused it. Bernini then willed it to her. It disappeared in the eighteenth century and was only reidentified in this collection in 1972. It is one of the greatest sculptures in an American collection.

The **French Nineteenth Century painting** collection is very strong in that still-neglected area, French salon painting. It has some fascinating pictures: *The Acis et Galatée,* 1833, by Gros—in which the two melodramatic figures huddle in a grotto, terrified at the approach of the Cyclops—looks like nothing so much as a frame from an early film, a nude *Perils of Pauline.* Perhaps because the picture was so heavily criticized, Gros killed himself. . . . The Millet, *Le Sommeil de l'enfant,* c. 1855, is one of the most beautiful maternal studies he ever created and is devoid of the overwrought sentimentality so often associated with the genre. . . . A mystical and serene Gérôme, *L'Excursion de l'Harem,* 1869, had a strong impact on Gérôme's student, Thomas Eakins, whose *John Biglin in a Single Scull* (1870–71) at Yale was strongly influenced by it; the two artists even corresponded about Eakins's picture while he was working on it. . . . But of all these pictures, the most interesting is *Portrait de Léon Maitre,* 1886, by Fantin-Latour, an artist best known for his flower paintings. It is a great portrait, beautifully conceived and painted and strongly influenced by photography, and the arrogant but intelligent intensity of the subject's gaze can be unsettling.

The other paintings by Degas, Cézanne, Matisse, Gaugin, Manet, Renoir and so forth are much more along the lines of what we are accustomed to, but even here it is interesting to note Mr. Chrysler's catholic approach: the contrast, for instance between two stunning masterpieces, Degas' *Danseuse aux Bouquets* (c. 1890–1895) and Gauguin's *La Perte du Pucelage* (1890). The former is illusionistic, a moment caught as the dancer emerges from her stage persona into her real one; the latter is deeply symbolic, thematically eternal, with great washes of flat color. And in contrast to both is Renoir's *Les Filles de Durand-Ruel* (1882), a light-filled picture, the quintessential manifestation of the Impressionist movement, depicting two little bourgeois girls in their snug garden. There are also unexpected works from famous artists: for one, there's Cézanne's early *Le Baigneur au Rocher* (c. 1864–68), whose force and even sensual power, underlined by the energetically applied paint, struggles to free itself from the canvas.

The **American Collection** is very strong and includes a large number of folk art pictures from the Edgar William and Bernice Chrysler Garbisch collection. In fact, after the National Gallery in Washington and the Metropolitan Museum of Art in New York City, the Chrysler Museum was the major recipient of gifts from this collection, and almost every great painter in the genre is represented. But it is the nineteenth-century paintings by our trained artists that steal this show through their superior quality. One of my favorite Benjamin Wests is here, *Mary, Wife of Henry Thompson of Kirby Hall, as Rachel at the Well* (1775), a painting of supreme dignity. Thomas Cole's *The Angel Appearing to the Shepherds* (1833–34), his largest canvas, is also one of his most moving, while *God's Judgment upon Gog* by Asher B. Durand (c. 1851), is a splendid example of the Hudson River School at its most dramatic, with God a tiny, rather lost figure in the brooding, all-important mountain landscape, with its flash of lightning and eerily threatening wheeling birds. Here again is that lovely Chrysler discrimination, in *Still Life, 1856* by George Henry Hall, an exquisitely rendered Ruskinian study in jewel-like tones that eminently qualifies as a minor masterpiece, if only for its painterly qualities.

The later pictures by Cassatt, Hassam, Homer, Sargent and others are excellent, but the collection of pictures by The Eight, Glackens, Davies, Henri, Lawson, Luks and Prendergast, Shinn and Sloan is particularly noteworthy. (The Eight were formed in reaction to the restrictive exhibition policy of the National Academy and exhibited together in 1908 at the Macbeth Galleries in New York City; one of the paintings here, Glacken's *The Shoppers,* was in that show, and Mrs. Shinn is the woman portrayed to the right. Their individual styles varied considerably, but generally speaking they were interested in the realistic portrayal of urban life.)

From that period to today the collection continues, with selections ranging from Walt Kuhn and Thomas Hart Benton to Charles Burchfield and Stuart Davis to Leonard Baskin, Josef Albers and Milton Avery to Louis Nevelson, Roy Lichtenstein, Frank Stella and Red Grooms. It is a great collection.

The museum has other strengths as well, an **oriental art collection** that is particularly strong in Japanese and Chinese art and whose most endearing works are a series of watercolors by a Japanese artist of Commodore Perry's visit to Japan. Two —the portrait of Perry and that of Samuel Wells Williams—are brilliant and hilarious caricatures, really, and what could the Japanese have made of the "Minstrel Show"? The **art deco collection** is also impressive, an enormous grouping that includes several pieces by Emile-Jacques Ruhlmann and others such as Jean Dunand, Louis Sue and André Marc as well as sculpture, glass, pottery and metalwork of superior quality.

Last, but hardly least, is the great **glass collection,** one of the finest and most comprehensive in the world. I happen to be particularly fond of Sandwich glass, made by the Boston and Sandwich Glass Company of Sandwich, Massachusetts, from 1825 to 1888. It is glitteringly represented here, with everything

from lamps and bowls and goblets to whiskey jugs, compotes
and banks. All the well-known patterns are here, and many of
the rarest, too. It is a feast for the mind as well as the eye. As
for the Tiffany glass, there are some extremely rare examples
in this large collection, and particularly beautiful examples of
French Art Nouveau are in the collection, too. The entirety is
good enough to make it of international significance.

The Chrysler Museum is open Tuesday–Saturday, 10–4; Sunday, 1–5. Closed: Mondays and major holidays. Admission: Free.
Phone: 804-423-2052.

Norfolk Botanical Gardens   These gardens, now ranked as
among the finest in the country, were begun as a Works Project
Administration (WPA) project in 1938. They have expanded
continually over the years and now cover 175 acres and can
boast of 100,000 azaleas, 4,000 roses and 3,000 camellias, this last
being one of the finest in the country. Rhododendron, laurel and
dogwood are found here in great profusion too, as well as other
shrubs and trees. There is a Japanese Garden and a Sunken
Garden. There are twelve miles of pathways, and thirty-minute
guided tours by either boat or train. There also are a Statuary
Vista (boring), a Rose Garden, a scented garden for the sight-
impaired, the Colonial Garden and the Flowering Arboretum.

When the azaleas are in bloom, the sight is nothing short of
spectacular, one of the great things in the state, but at any time
of the year this is a very beautiful spot that should be seen.

The Information Center is open Monday–Friday, 8:30–5:00;
Saturday, Sunday and holidays, 10–5. Closed: December 25, January 1. The gardens are open daily, 8:30–sunset. Admission: $1.
Boat and train tours, $1.50, each; combination ticket, $2. Phone:
804-853-6972.

General Douglas MacArthur Memorial   First the building,
then the rest, for the building is one of the landmark buildings
in the city.

The Classic Revival design of a pillared portico and a handsome dome is by William R. Singleton, although Thomas U.
Walter, architect of the U.S. Capitol extension and the cast-iron
dome, made some suggestions that were incorporated in the
building. It was completed in 1850. From 1961 to 1963, the interior was gutted and then rebuilt as a mausoleum for MacArthur

—his mother was a native of Norfolk—and he was buried here in 1964. It now serves as a museum of his life. Six of the eleven display rooms have murals by Alton S. Tobey that depict major events in his life, and in front of the building is a replica of the MacArthur statue by Walker Hancock at West Point.

Three other buildings are also part of the complex: The Theater, where a twenty-two-minute film biography made up of newsreels is continuously shown; a gift shop; and the library and archives, which contain four thousand volumes and over two million items of scrapbooks, motion pictures, correspondence, messages, photographs, newspaper files and reports.

To be quite honest, I didn't burn to see this memorial. MacArthur has never been one of my heroes. I felt I knew enough about him, and I certainly never wanted to hear "Old Soldiers Never Die" again. Still, there's no getting around the fact that he was a fascinating, brilliant and complex man, at the nerve center of every important period in our history, and this museum treats him in a respectful and thorough manner, with well-chosen displays and memorabilia. The result is a historical feast that wound up keeping me fascinated for some time. And yes, I did hear "Old Soldiers Never Die" again.

The MacArthur Memorial is open Monday–Saturday, 10–5; Sunday, 11–5. Closed: Thanksgiving, December 25, January 1. Admission: Free. Phone: 804-441-2965.

Waterside Norfolk has made a valiant effort to restore its waterfront. To that end it has hired the Rouse organization (see page 174) to design a two-story, 130,000-square-foot pavilion with more than a hundred shops and restaurants as the centerpiece of their efforts. It's lively and crowded—all Rouse projects seem to have huge amounts of these qualities—and if you're in the mood, it can be fun. I don't find this one as successful, though, as other Rouse projects; somehow it all seems forced. Busy it certainly is; festive it is not.

Norfolk Naval Station and Norfolk Air Station You can tour this behemoth base and, on Saturday and Sunday, visit certain ships. The Hamptons Roads Naval Museum is here, too. Part of the base occupies the old 1907 Jamestown Exposition Grounds—the Exposition was to honor the three-hundredth anniversary of the founding of Jamestown—and some of the buildings constructed to house state exhibits still stand, all in the Colonial Revival style. They house officers today. There's no question that the nearly one-hour tour is interesting, but like an institutionalized way of living, and particularly on this vast scale, it can leave you feeling slightly depressed and happy to get back to the outside world.

Tour buses leave from the Naval Tours and Information Office, 9809 Hampton Boulevard. Tours operate May 28–Labor Day, daily, 10–2, on the half-hour; April 8–May 27, and day after Labor Day–October 29, 10–2 on the hour. There are also tours from Waterside. Admission: $3; children 6–13, $1.50. Phone: 804-444-4791 or 444-4795.

Adam Thoroughgood House (c. 1630–40)   In itself, this house is not of any particular importance, but historically it is one of the most important houses in Virginia, for it probably is the oldest house in the state—perhaps in the country—and therefore uniquely important in our history.

Adam Thoroughgood came to this country as an indentured servant in 1621. By 1629 he was a member of the House of Burgesses, and when his house was built he was the master of an estate of 5,350 acres, achieved by bringing 150 indentured servants to Virginia. This, then, would have been one of the great houses of its time, yet it is a very simple brick English house, largely medieval in style, with chimneys at each end (note the formidable exterior one at the south end), a sharply gabled roof and windows of diamond-shaped glass panes set in lead. Inside, there are only two rooms on each floor.

The city of Norfolk has restored the house as accurately as possible, and has furnished the rooms with seventeenth-century objects. There also is a seventeenth-century garden with box hedging.

The Thoroughgood House is open April–December, Tuesday–Saturday, 10–5; Sunday, 12–5; January–March, Tuesday–Saturday, 12–5. Closed: Major holidays. Admission: $2; children 6–18, $1. Phone 804-460-0007 for directions, as the house is outside the city limits.

The **Myers House** and **Willoughby-Baylor House** (see below for both) are within walking distance of each other. As you look at them, also take note of the **Freemason Street Baptist Church** (1849), on Freemason at Bank, and the **Old**

Norfolk Academy Building (1840), 420 Bank. The former is a handsome Gothic Revival building; the latter—Greek Revival in style—is pleasingly simple. Both are by the same architect. Thomas U. Walter (see page 230).

Two other buildings within walking distance that are of special interest: the first, **St. Paul's Church** (1739), 201 St. Paul's Boulevard at City Hall Avenue. This is the only pre-Revolutionary structure left in Norfolk. The interior was restored in 1892 and 1911 and the tower was added in 1901. The churchyard has bucolic charm and the interior is pleasant. There's also a small museum. Guided tours are available of the building and the yard, Tuesday–Saturday, 10–4. Admission: Donation. Phone: 804-627-4353.

The other building, and, I think, the best in Norfolk, is the circular hall at the **Scope Convention and Cultural Center** (1971, 1972) at Brambleton and Monticello Avenues. What makes it so breathtaking is the dome, and the engineer for this awesome achievement was none other than Luigi Nervi. From the exterior, the "cap" of the dome is supported by stunning, ribbonlike and seemingly weightless buttresses. The interior of the dome has a span of 336 feet (!) and is composed of 2,500 precast concrete triangles that, combined, give a feeling of dignity, quality and monumentality that is brilliant. This is a great building.

The other building in this complex is **Chrysler Hall,** a 2,500-seat theater and concert hall with another, smaller theater of 350 seats. Not of the quality of the Nervi building, but perfectly acceptible.

Moses Myers House (1791/2, 1796) This is the most impressive period home in Norfolk, and it is made more interesting by the fact that, because the house remained in the Myers family until 1931, many of the original furnishings remain—including Moses Myers' collection of eighteenth-century musical instruments and manuscripts.

Myers was an interesting man. A shipping merchant and the first Jewish citizen of the city when he arrived from New York City in 1787, his Federal house was among the first of brick construction to go up after the Revolution. Later, in 1796, he would add his Adam-inspired dining room of considerable elegance and refinement (in particular, note the cornice and twin sideboards). The famous architect Benjamin Latrobe may have been the designer of it. For the rest of his career, Myers would serve as a diplomat in Denmark and Holland and, in 1828, would become Collector of Customs for the Port of Norfolk, an appointment he would receive from President John Quincy Adams.

Some of the original furnishings are special. Of particular interest, from a curiosity standpoint as well as an artistic one, are the Gilbert Stuart portraits of both Moses and his wife Eliza, painted c. 1803. There also is a Thomas Sully portrait of their son, John, painted in 1808. An interesting house, then, and worth a visit. In fact, if you have time for only one such visit, this should be it.

The Moses Myers House, 325 Freemason Street at Bank, is open April–December, Tuesday–Saturday, 10–5; Sunday, 12–5; January–March, Tuesday–Sunday, 12–5. Closed: Major holidays. Admission: $2, children 6–18, $1. Phone: 804-622-1211.

Willoughby-Baylor House (1794) The house, brick with a later porch (1824), has been furnished with antiques based on an inventory made after the original owner's death in 1800. Small, it is a pleasant and cheerful house to visit and also boasts a large —for a city—garden, a welcome oasis planted with herbs and flowers popular at the time the house was built. The ensemble, then, is unpretentious and relaxing.

The Willoughby-Baylor House, 601 East Freemason Street, has the same hours, fees and phone number as the Moses Myers House.

Hermitage Foundation Museum (1908) This forty-one-room house in the Tudor style is attractive in itself and has one of the loveliest settings you could ask for on twelve landscaped acres by the Lafayette River.

The house was built by William and Florence K. Sloane—he made a fortune in textiles—and displays, in thirteen galleries, oriental bronzes and ceramics, twentieth-century American paintings, oriental rugs, tapestries, works of art from Russia (including some from the last czar's collection), Spain, France, and so on. Go to see the Chinese collection, which includes tomb figures from the T'ang Dynasty, and forget about the paintings, except for one very nice de Chirico, rather out of the way on the second floor.

The Hermitage Foundation Museum, 7637 North Shore Road, is open Tuesday–Saturday, 10–5; Sunday, 1–5. Closed: Thanksgiving, December 25, January 1. Admission: $3; children 6–18, $1. Phone: 804-423-2052.

Lafayette Zoological Park   This claims to be Virginia's largest zoo, but it's quite small. Still, it has charm—who can resist even a small zoo?—and if you're traveling with children, it will be enjoyed by them, as much of the zoo is, naturally, geared to them. As for me, I liked the Virginia Farmyard and the sea lion demonstration.

The zoo is open daily, 10–5; from the second week of April–September 2, Saturday and Sunday 10–6, and on holidays as well. Closed December 25, January 1. Admission, $1, children 2–11, 50¢. Free admission daily between 10 and 11. Phone: 804-441-2706 or 441-5227.

Finally, I would heartily recommend a **harbor cruise.** Several are available, including one that offers a dinner cruise (phone: 804-627-7771), but the one that I like best, because it's the least crowded, least pretentious and has an engaging boat that is a replica of a nineteenth-century Mississippi riverboat, is Harbor Tours' offering on the "Carrie B." (Phone: 804-393-4735). The harbor is fascinating, and it gives you an understanding of Norfolk that you can achieve no other way.

NEARBY

One of the more pleasant things to do here is take the ferry from Waterside to **Portsmouth** and then spend an hour or so walking around the old town enjoying the architecture that goes from the late eighteenth century through the late nineteenth century. The area is well marked with historic Portsmouth plaques, and it claims to have "the largest concentration of antique houses between Alexandria and Charleston."

Newport News has one of my favorite specialized museums in this country, the **Mariners' Museum,** whose collection celebrating maritime history has an international reputation. From the dazzling and awesome one-and-a-half-ton gilded eagle figurehead (1880) shooting into the sky that you see as you enter the museum lobby through the stunning marine paintings and the sixteen tiny vessels that depict the history of sailing ships to the proud, large and brilliantly detailed models of great ships to figureheads and carvings and scrimshaw and posters and ceramics and photos and films and a 67,000-volume library, this museum will catch you up in as romantic a subject as you can think of. Both children and adults are happy here. Outside there's a 550-acre Mariners' Museum Park and Wildlife Sanctuary that includes a fishing lake and where you can picnic. Delightful.

The Mariners' Museum is open Monday–Saturday, 9–5; Sunday, 1–5. Closed: December 25. Admission: $3; children 6–16, $1.50. Phone: 804-595-0368.

Hampton offers Hampton Institute, founded in 1868, and its **Virginia Hall** (1874), designed by Richard Morris Hunt, which was paid for by concerts performed by the Hampton choir. (Phone: 804-727-5254.) It also has Fortress Monroe, the largest stone fort ever built in this country (completed in 1834) and the **Casemate Museum,** whose most famous exhibit is the casemated cell that held Jefferson Davis after the Civil War. (A casemate is a chamber with embrasures for artillery.) Davis was treated with no little cruelty through the orders of Secretary of War Stanton, who falsely accused him of being involved in the Lincoln murder plot. A grim, sad spot.

The Casemate Museum is open daily, 10:30–5:00. Closed: Thanksgiving, December 25 and January 1. Admission: Free. Phone: 804-727-3973.

Probably the most famous of all attractions in the area is **Virginia Beach,** with its twelve-mile strip of lovely beach (good news) that is packed to the gills with people, hotels, fast-food places, bars and restaurants (bad news). In my opinion the developers have run riot here, turning what had the potential of being one of the great glories of the East Coast into a honky-tonk area that has lost any and all claims to being a quality resort.

Great Dismal Swamp National Wildlife Refuge Dismal may be its name, but it certainly doesn't describe the quality or appeal. Twenty-five miles long and twelve miles wide, this is one of the most fascinating natural areas in Virginia. Even George Washington got involved here through his interest in constructing a canal that would run from the Chesapeake Bay to Albemarle Sound in North Carolina. The canal actually was begun in 1793 and was cut through the swamp by 1805.

Life is incredibly rich in this swamp, not only in mammals and birds but also in trees and shrubs, vines, ferns and flowers. At the heart of it all is Lake Drummond, five square miles, whose average depth is only six feet. Its water is unusually pure, and in the nineteenth century it was taken on by ships; it was not only pure, it would last a long period of time. The remains of the great cypress forest that once dominated the swamp are here, at the lakeshore.

There are several walking trails through the swamp, including a particularly interesting boardwalk trail. Black bear and bobcats are still here—only a few miles, really, from Norfolk—as are copperheads, rattlesnakes and cottonmouths. The last are not among my favorite sights. There's nothing else like it in Virginia, and I found it fascinating.

WHERE TO STAY AND EAT
Area Code: 804

WHERE TO STAY

Williamsburg

Williamsburg Inn, Francis Street, Williamsburg 23185. Phone: 229-2141 or, for reservations made from outside the state, 800-447-8679. Rates: From about $100. Credit cards accepted.

Far and away the nicest place to stay in Williamsburg, it also is located in the Historic Area so that everything is within walking distance. The rooms are attractive, the service impeccable. In addition, the inn has rooms in twenty-eight restored houses in the Historic Area, and it would be hard to imagine a more pleasant way to visit Williamsburg. Reserve as far in advance as possible, especially if you want to be there for Christmas.

Tennis, swimming, golf and lawn games are available, and you can also rent bicycles. (For food, see page 239.)

Williamsburg Lodge, South England Street, Williamsburg 23185. Phone: 229-1000 or, for reservations made out of state, 800-582-8976. Rates: From about $75. Credit cards accepted.

If you can't get in the Inn, call here immediately and hope for the best, for this is the second-nicest place to stay. The same sports are available as at the Inn, and this too is in the Historic Area.

If you can't stay at either place, then I would suggest the **Sheraton Patriot Inn** (3032 Richmond Road, Williamsburg 23185. Phone: 565-2600. Rates: From about $70. Credit cards accepted), or the **Fort Magruder Inn and Conference Center** (6945 Pocahontas Trail, Williamsburg 23185. Phone: 220-2250. Rates: For a single, from about $60; for a double, from about $70. Credit cards accepted), which are acceptable. Do not stay at the **Williamsburg Hospitality House**, which, though convenient, is among the worst-run hotels I have ever visited.

Yorktown

Ideally, you would visit Yorktown from Williamsburg, as the distance between the two is minimal. If you wish to stay here, though, there is one adequate motel: the **Duke of York** (100 Water Street, Yorktown 23690. Phone: 898-3232. Rates: April–October, for a single, from about $28; for a double, from about $34. Rates are higher June–September, lower during the rest of the year. Credit cards accepted). It faces the water, and there is a public beach across the road. One real advantage: If you're on a budget, you could stay here and use it as your headquarters for visiting Williamsburg.

The Great Plantations on the North Bank

There is no place I can comfortably recommend in this area. The best thing, then, is to make either Richmond or Williamsburg your headquarters or to stay in Smithfield (see below).

Southside

Smithfield

Isle of Wight Inn, P.O. Box 486, 1607 South Church Street, Smithfield 23430. Phone: 357-3176. Rates: From about $49 for a double. Credit cards accepted.

This is a bed and breakfast, but with a difference; this is not a house but a one-time office building, Colonial in design, that has pretty and very comfortable rooms. It seems much more like an inn to me, but the breakfast is included in the fee. In any case, this is the place to stay for the greatest comfort.

Norfolk

Omni International Hotel on the River, 777 Waterside Drive, Norfolk 23510. Phone: 622-6664 or, for reservations made from outside the state, 800-228-2121. Rates for a single, from about $79; for a double, from about $99. Credit cards accepted.

A satisfying hotel and currently the best Norfolk has to offer. Be sure to ask for a room with a view of the water.

Madison, 345 Granby Mall, Norfolk 23501. Phone 622-6682 or, for reservations made out of state, 800-552-6353; in Virginia, 800-552-0976. Rates: For a single, from about $65; for a double, from about $75. Credit cards accepted.

An old downtown hotel that has been completely done over. It's centrally located and has a relaxed, friendly atmosphere. Worth considering, especially if you want something a little less grand (and expensive) than the Omni.

WHERE TO EAT

Williamsburg

Three Favorites

I group these three restaurants because they are all outstanding but so different that it really is a matter of mood, not quality, that will decide your choice. None should be missed.

The Regency Room, Williamsburg Inn. Phone: 229-2141. Credit cards accepted.

This is the most elegant and formal of the three. It also is the most conservative, not in a derogatory sense but simply that it hasn't changed much in its approach to food over the years. I kind of like that. The food is very good and is conscientiously prepared and served. No surprises, just good, solid dining. Expensive. Lunch: Daily, 12–2. Dinner: Daily, 6:30–9:30. There is dancing on Friday and Saturday. Reservations necessary for dinner.

The Trellis, Duke of Gloucester Street in Merchant's Square. Phone: 229-8610. Credit cards accepted.

I find this restaurant enormously appealing. It's lively, it's pretty, it has an imaginative menu. What more can you ask? Crowded and noisy—but not loud—the service is very good, yet relaxed and informal. The wine cellar is exemplary and the food has a nouvelle bias; I have yet to be disappointed in the menu selections. Most enjoyable dining. Expensive. On the other hand, if you wish only a light supper, you can eat outdoors for a moderate price. Lunch: Daily, 11:30–2:30; from 2:30–4:00, a limited menu is available. On Sunday, brunch is served to 2:30. Dinner: Daily, 6:00–9:30. Closed Thanksgiving, December 25, January 1. Reservations necessary for dinner.

Le Yaca, 1915 Pocahontas Trail. Just off Route 60-E in the Village Shops at Kingsmill, a few miles outside Williamsburg. Phone: 220-3616. Credit cards accepted.

If the Regency Room is formal, and The Trellis is chic and nouvelle, this is down-home French, warm and cozy and of the most satisfying kind. It is family owned and operated, and you feel much more like a valued guest than a mere customer. The food is top-notch, perfectly prepared and with that extra little touch that makes it memorable. Expensive. Lunch: Daily, 11:30–2:00. Dinner: Daily, 6:30–9:30. Closed: Sunday and the last two weeks of February. Reservations suggested for dinner.

Colonial Williamsburg itself owns three restaurants in the Historic Area that are fun to eat at and also offer pretty good food. In the warm months, all have outside dining.

Chowning's Tavern, Duke of Gloucester Street at Queen Street Phone: 229-2141. Credit cards accepted.

Of the three, this is probably the best. They serve a reasonably good Brunswick stew for dinner, as well as the more standard prime ribs and duckling. When I like it best, though, is later in the evening when the tavern is overflowing with people and you can play eighteenth-century games or just relax and be entertained by the strolling musicians and magicians. It's good fun. Moderate. Lunch: Daily, 11:30–3:30. Dinner: Daily, three sittings, 5:00, 6:45, 8:30. Reservations necessary for dinner.

Christiana Campbell's Tavern, Waller Street, which is just behind the Capitol. Phone: 229-2141. Credit cards accepted.

Because this is a little off the beaten track, it seems more private to dine or lunch here, and that gives it a slight edge for

me. I particularly like to have lunch outside and feed crumbs
to the demanding birds. Moderate, but slightly more expensive
than Chowning's. Lunch: Daily, 10:00–2:30. Dinner: Daily,
5:30–9:30. Reservations necessary for dinner.

King's Arms Tavern, Duke of Gloucester Street. Phone: 229-
2141. Credit cards accepted.
My least favorite of the three from the point of view of both
food and ambiance. Moderate. Lunch: Daily, 11:30–2:30. Dinner:
Daily, 5:15–9:30. Reservations necessary for dinner.

Three other restaurants outside the Historic Area deserve a
mention.

Cascades, opposite the Information Center and in the Motor
House Motel. Phone: 229-1000. Credit cards accepted.
The food, particularly the seafood selections, is good and the
price is moderate. Lunch: Monday–Saturday, 12:00–2:30; Sunday
brunch, 8:00–2:30. Dinner: Daily, 5:30–9:00. Reservations suggested for dinner.

Lafayette, 1203 Richmond Road. Phone: 229-3811. Credit cards
accepted.
Not very attractive, but the food is reasonably good; the selections are what is usually referred to as "Continental." Moderately expensive. Dinner: Daily, 4:00–10:30. Closed December 25.
Reservations suggested.

Kingsmill, 100 Golf Club Road. Off Route 60-E, a few miles
outside Williamsburg. Phone: 253-3900. Credit cards accepted.
The setting is pretty in a rather cold way, the food moderately
good, as at Lafayette. Expensive. Lunch: Daily, 11:30–2:00. Dinner: Daily, 6–9. Closed December 25. Reservations suggested for
dinner.

Yorktown

Nick's Seafood Pavilion, Water Street. Phone: 887-5269.
Credit cards accepted.
Lavender walls. Green ceiling. Chandeliers. Venetian lan-
terns. Salmon-colored chairs and booths. Waitresses in Greek
costume. Statuary. Mottoes that include "Never return a kindness—pass it on"; "A good man dies when a boy goes wrong";
"No one hates a job well done." Canaries going crazy. Me going

crazy. But . . . the food is really good and the portions generous. You've never been in a place quite like this, that I can guarantee. Moderate. The restaurant is open: Daily, 11–10.

The Great Plantations on the North Banks

Carriage House, Berkeley Plantation. Phone: 795-2453. No credit cards accepted. (See page 206.) Moderate. Lunch: Daily, 11:00–2:30.

Southside

Hopewell

Wheelhouse Restaurant, 700 Jordan Point Road, Prince George. Phone: 541-2600. Credit cards accepted.

The restaurant offers a striking view of the James, but only so-so food. Still, there's not much else around here, so enjoy the view. Moderate. The restaurant is open Monday–Friday, 11–10; Saturday, 5–10; Sunday, 12–10. Reservations requested for dinner.

Surry

Surrey House, on Route 10 in Surrey House Motel. Phone: 294-3389. Credit cards accepted.

Some people think this offers the best Southern-style food in the area. It sure is good. My test in this area is crabcakes; theirs come pretty high up on the Mulligan Crabcake Scale—a 6.8 out of 10. And the prices are so cheap you'll smile with pleasure— they get a 10. Except for December 24 and 25, the restaurant is open Monday–Saturday, 5:30 A.M.–9:00; Sunday, 6:30–9:00.

Norfolk

The Ship's Cabin, 4110 East Ocean View Avenue. Phone: 480-2526. Credit cards accepted.

Certainly the best seafood restaurant in Norfolk. Not a large menu, but the fish is the freshest you can find, the preparation is generally straightforward and meant to enhance the natural flavor. They also mesquite-grill steaks and chops as well as a seafood grill, there's a pretty view, and the service is excellent. Expensive. Dinner: Sunday–Thursday, 6–10; Friday and Saturday, 6–11. Closed: December 25 and January 1. Reservations necessary.

L'Esplanade, Omni International Hotel, 777 Waterside Drive. Phone: 623-0333. Credit cards accepted.

An elegant, highly decorated room offering fancy food. Too fancy, in fact. The food is quite good and this is indeed one of Norfolk's best restaurants, but they try a little too hard and the strain shows. That's what keeps it from being *the* best. Expensive. Dinner: Monday–Saturday, 6–11; Sunday, 5–10. Reservations recommended.

Le Charlieu, 112 College Place. Phone: 623-7202. Credit cards accepted.

Norfolk's best French restaurant, but that doesn't mean much, unfortunately. The food is boring—not bad, just dull. Someone needs to shake up the chef or get one with some imagination. And a little more attention to the clients wouldn't hurt, either. Expensive. Lunch: Daily, 11:30–2:00. Dinner: Daily, 6:00–9:30. Closed: Thanksgiving, December 25, January 1 and, in summer, Sundays. Reservations suggested for dinner.

THE
EASTERN SHORE

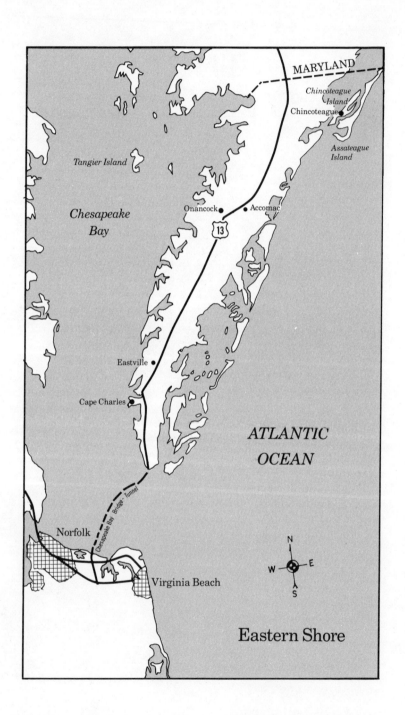

MARYLAND

*Chincoteague
Island*

Chincoteague

*Assateague
Island*

Tangier Island

*Chesapeake
Bay*

Onancock

Accomac

13

Eastville

Cape Charles

*ATLANTIC
OCEAN*

Chesapeake Bay Bridge-Tunnel

Norfolk

N
W   E
S

Virginia Beach

Eastern Shore

THIS seventy-two-mile peninsula that separates the Chesapeake Bay from the Atlantic Ocean stands aloof from the rest of the state, totally unto itself. It's not that it has a selfish or insular attitude—the people are both warm and friendly—it's the way it is. That, of course, is one reason it's so fascinating, and not only is it unique in the state but also unique in the country. Even the architecture is special. The typical Eastern Shore house is usually frame and usually has a central house two rooms deep with what looks like little afterthought houses added on, higgledy-piggledy, so that you have gabled roofs at different heights topping a long, rambling structure; if you see one with four different roof levels, the natives will instantly identify the parts as big house, little house, colonnade, and kitchen. It has great charm, this style, and the houses look snug, yet full of corners and surprises.

I also love the names of the towns, which, when you repeat then to yourself, sound like an American litany: Chincoteague and Assateague, Onancock and Accomac, Wreck Island and Hog Island, Nassawadox, Machipongo, Oyster and Modest Town, Temperanceville and Birdsnest.

Captain John Smith first discovered this peninsula and explored it in 1608. It was he who named Cape Charles, the southernmost point, after his king; one hundred years later, another famous visitor, Blackbeard, would arrive and use the barrier islands along the Atlantic coast as protection against the English fleet.

There are no cities here. The peninsula is very beautiful in an unspoiled—and therefore rare—way, and the fishing is superb, the beaches white and usually pristine. The livin' is easy.

THE CHESAPEAKE BAY

This noble body of water, the nation's largest estuary, has fascinated men since it was first discovered. A few facts: Its main

branch is slightly more than 195 miles long and reaches widths
of up to 35 miles. It drains a basin of 64,000 square miles in three
states, Pennsylvania, Maryland and Virginia, and is fed by
roughly 150 rivers, creeks and streams. It teems with marine
life, providing the largest oyster harvest in the country and
more than half the soft-shell crab catch, for example, and is the
habitat of vast numbers of water fowl and other wildlife, which
makes it of great economic importance, as well as a paradise for
the aquatic sportsman.

About 11,000 watermen, a breed threatened by the increasing
pollution of this incredible natural resource, sail the bay, a few
still using the specially designed boats called skipjacks. Help is
on the way for them; the bay is now the object of one of the most
extensive reclamation projects in our history, which is being
undertaken by Virginia, Maryland and Pennsylvania with the
help of the federal government. The purpose is to "improve and
protect the water quality and living resources of the Chesapeake Bay estuarine system and restore and maintain the bay's
ecological integrity, productivity and beneficial uses and to protect public health." It will cost hundreds of millions of dollars,
but everyone agrees it will be money well spent.

In the meantime, the bay is a source of endless fascination to
the casual visitor. Given half a chance, this bay will mesmerize
you into a state of timeless suspension. Everyone has his favorite part; for me it's the salt marshes. Read my favorite description of them from *The Living Chesapeake* by J. R. Schnebel (The
Johns Hopkins University Press, 1981), in which he describes
them as "among the Bay's most scenic assets, adding a gentleness to the Bay's eastern shore that contrasts sharply with the
rugged bluffs of the western shore and with those of the upper
bay. Haunting, eerie, peaceful, lonely. Constantly changing in
form and mood, in pattern and outline, in flora and fauna, in
sound and smell. The marshes lie along the shoreline like jade
beads on a precious necklace."

The Chesapeake Bay Bridge-Tunnel   The ideal way to approach the Eastern Shore is across this 17.6-mile-long engineering marvel, the world's longest bridge and tunnel complex,
which has made access to the peninsula vastly easier from the
Virginia shore. (The two end points are Virginia Beach and
Cape Charles.) It is nothing less than astounding to be driving

over a seemingly endless expanse of water while watching, a little ahead of you, a large battleship pass before your windshield. The drive includes a stop with a restaurant and fishing pier, and it's worth getting out here, if only to enjoy the exhilarating sight of the surrounding bay. The toll, to attend to more mundane affairs, is $9 per car.

THE PENINSULA

Although the area is relatively small, the diversity within it is remarkable. I shall go from south to north, assuming you will reach the shore via the Chesapeake Bay Bridge-Tunnel.

There is a central road, Route 13, that runs up and down the spine of the peninsula. The more interesting roads, of course, lead off this, and almost anywhere you drive from 13 will be of interest; the best advice I can give you, then, is to explore your surroundings as the mood moves you.

While you drive, keep an eye out for one of the blue crab fisheries and stop in to see how they operate. If you share my taste, you will agree that this particular crabmeat is very special, delicate and sweet. If you are here during the right time of year, soft shells will be in season and you can gorge yourself to your heart's content. One of my most sybaritic memories is of eating soft-shell crab sandwiches, an experience no crab lover should miss in this life. And then there are the Chincoteague oysters . . . Food is not among the lesser reasons to come to the Eastern Shore. Some interesting trivia I picked up about crabs, those succulent delicacies: Male crabs are called *jimmies,* females *sooks,* and you can tell the sex by looking at the underside of the crab; mature females have a U-shaped segment called a telson. To grow, the crabs must shed their shells, and just before they do, the crab is known as a *peeler.* The minute the crab sheds, you have a soft shell, but after a few hours it will begin to harden—unless you remove it from salt water.

The Custis Tombs (1695)   John and Frances Custis, parents of Martha Washington's first husband and ancestors of Robert E. Lee's wife, Mary, lived in Arlington (hence the name of the estate outside Washington) on the Eastern Shore. They became famous for their detestation of each other. One day, while out riding in their carriage, John Custis began driving into the Chesapeake. Frances asked him where he was going. "To hell, madam," he replied. "Drive on," she retorted, "any place is better than Arlington." Hoisted by his own petard, Custis turned back to shore, saying bitterly, "I believe you would as lief meet the devil himself if I should drive to hell." "Sir," she answered coolly, "I know you so well I would not be afraid to go anywhere you would go."

John did have the last word, though—he outlived Frances by seven years. To drive home his triumph for posterity, he had this inscribed on his tomb: "Aged 71 years, and yet lived but seven years, which was the space of time he kept a bachelor's home at Arlington on the Eastern Shore of Virginia."

I should add that John's tomb is very imposing and has been cited by the Virginia Landmarks Registry as "one of the finest examples of English mortuary sculpture in Virginia."

Eyre Hall (c. 1733. Additions: c. 1760, 1790's) One of the loveliest homes and settings on the peninsula. The house, on Cherrystone Creek, is part of a 1,500-acre grant given to the Eyre family in 1662 by Governor William Berkeley (see page 218). The present owner, a direct descendant, is the tenth generation of the family to live here.

The frame house, painted white, is a charmer. Inside, the furniture (Queen Anne, Chippendale, Hepplewhite), family portraits (Sully and West), enchanting entrance hall (with striking French block wallpaper from 1816) and, overall, fine woodwork and furnishings make an exceptionally warm impression. As for the boxwood garden, it is one of the oldest in the country and is enclosed by brick so mellowed by time as to glow. It was brought from England as ship's ballast. Unusual trees and shrubbery—a cucumber tree, parsley-leaved hawthorne—and ancient plantings approached by well-raked shady walks make this an unusually alluring and private place.

The house is only open during Historic Garden Week in April. The grounds, though, are open all year.

Eastville Of primary interest here is an unusual grouping, the old Courthouse (1730), Clerk's Office (1719) and Debtor's Prison (1644). Of particular importance, though, is that the earliest (1632) continuous court records in America are here and can be inspected.

Onancock

I particularly like one spot here, **Hopkins & Brother Store** (c. 1840), a building now owned by the Association for the Preservation of Virginia Antiquities (APVA) and leased to a young couple who operate it as a most amiable store—food "plain and fancy," wine, crafts and gifts—and restaurant. If you're on the peninsula this is a must, for the view out over the water is delightful, the food is very good (see page 254), and it's downright homey to sit here enjoying your surroundings. The store is fun to browse in, too. It's a fine example of creative reuse. You can also visit Tangier Island from here (see page 266). Phone: 804-787-8220.

Onancock's other prime attraction is **Kerr Place** (1799), which also is the Historical Society Museum. A dignified Federal brick building, it probably is the most formal and sophisticated mansion on the Eastern Shore; the architectural detail of the exterior is of superior quality, and the interior rooms have good proportions and tasteful plaster and woodwork. Combined with tall windows and a fine curving staircase, this is a light and airy house that wears its elegance gracefully and naturally. For some reason it reminds me of Jane Austen—perhaps because it displays a clean, lucid intelligence. As for the gardens, they have been restored by the Garden Club of Virginia, so you can be assured of their choice quality.

Kerr Place is open March–December, Tuesday–Saturday, 10–4. Admission: $1; children under 12, 25¢. Phone: 804-787-3394.

Accomac

The greatest pleasure here is to walk about enjoying those wonderful Eastern Shore houses, but you can also take in the **Debtor's Prison** (1782), a small brick two-story building that has a well-executed design of some sophistication; **St. James Episcopal Church** (1838), with an agreeable though unprepossessing Greek Revival façade, but whose interior has interesting work done by Jean G. Potts, a nineteenth-century itinerant painter, that covers walls and ceiling and, at the altar, creates a trompe l'oeil of columns and an archway; and **Makemie Presbyterian Church** (1838) with its monument to Francis Makemie (1908), the founder in America of Presbytery.

Chincoteague and Assateague

Most people think of these two islands when the Eastern Shore is mentioned. Chincoteague is an island resort, Assateague an island wildlife refuge of transcendent beauty that includes the famous wild ponies who inspired Marguerite Henry's children's books, beginning in 1948 with the wild pony Misty. I have read none of them, nor have I seen the movie; but after my first visit here I felt I had more than a passing acquaintance with Misty, particularly after I saw her stuffed and mounted and in a mock stall and looking—oh, why not say it—rather mystified at her bizarre situation. She is in something called the **Chincoteague Miniature Pony Farm** (Open daily, Memorial Day–Labor Day, 10–9; February–May and September–November, 12–5. Admission: $2.50; students, $1.50. Phone: 804-336-5533), from which I fled wild-eyed and which I only mention for those of you with a child who is a Misty fan.

Physically, Chincoteague, as far as I'm concerned, is an overbuilt resort on a narrow island. Assateague, though, converts the dross to gleaming gold. This thirty-seven-mile barrier island has walks, drives and bicycle paths as well as glorious beaches, forests and marshes. Sika deer, introduced many years ago, forage here with the ponies, and the birds are innumerable. Snow geese, Canada geese and whistling swans winter here. Heron sometimes seem as common as robins; falcons and hawks, and the occasional eagle, grace the sky in arcing flight; terns and cormorants and frigates and egrets—all are here in this resplendent natural aviary. It is a bird-watcher's paradise, beachcomber's dream, hiker's delight, fisherman's joy. It is special to everyone who comes here.

As for the ponies, you do see them and they are fun to watch. There are several theories as to how they arrived here, but the most widely accepted one is that, in 1670, during a violent storm, a Spanish ship sailing past the island, and carrying horses cruelly blinded for work in the great gold mines, foundered and sank. Somehow a few horses managed to swim to the island, the ancestors of the animals you see today. Their reduced size—smaller than a horse but larger than a pony—has come about through their island diet of marsh grasses and through inbreeding.

The celebrated event of the year is the annual pony run, the last Thursday in July, for which the ponies are herded together in a holding pen and then driven across the bay to the carnival grounds on Chincoteague, where the foals are auctioned off—"Here's one of the Misty line"—for prices ranging from as low as $150 to $1,500. The unsold ones swim back to Assateague.

It's an interesting event in more ways than one, for the Chincoteaguers consider this a prime time to hold family reunions, and members stream back from all over the country. They're a feisty bunch, these islanders; their members speak four dialects, and don't even think of becoming a Chincoteaguer unless your mother or father was one. Still, they're friendly and funny and warm.

Two other annual events, the Oyster Festival (Columbus Day weekend) and the Seafood Festival (first Wednesday in May) serve food that is mind-boggling in quality and quantity, but you must reserve months ahead. For further information on the Oyster Festival, write Chincoteague Chamber of Commerce, P.O. Box 258, Chincoteague 23336. For the Seafood Festival, write Eastern Shore of Virginia Chamber of Commerce, Inc., P.O. Box 147, Accomac 23301.

I enjoy coming here even if it is overdeveloped and even overblown. I can always escape to Assateague and live the dream of a better place.

WHERE TO STAY AND EAT
Area Code: 804

WHERE TO STAY

Cape Charles

America House, P.O. Box 472, Cape Charles 23310. On Route 13. Phone: 331-1776. Rates: June–August, for a single, from about $45; for a double, from about $52. Lower during rest of year. Credit cards accepted.

A standard motel with one plus, it's situated on forty acres bordering the Chesapeake and has its own private beach with a view of the Chesapeake Bay Bridge-Tunnel. As for the rooms, they're small but comfortable. The food is ghastly.

Eastville

Holly Brook Plantation, Route 13, Eastville 23347. Phone: 678-5057. Rates: From about $150 for a double, including breakfast and dinner. No credit cards.

A bed and breakfast that is owned by the Association for the Preservation of Virginia Antiquities (APVA), of all people. Set on 130 acres, it is a delight. This typical Eastern Shore 1735 manor house was left, with its antique furnishings, to the APVA, who came up with this ingenious way of using the property. The only drawback is that it's about an hour from Chincoteague, but if that doesn't bother you, this would be a prime choice.

Chincoteague

Miss Molly's, North Main Street, Chincoteague 23336. Phone: 336-6686. Rates: June–August, from about $55; September–May, from about $48. Includes breakfast and tea. Shared baths. Credit cards accepted.

Another bed and breakfast, this one right in the heart of Chincoteague. It's called Miss Molly after a character in the Misty books, and indeed she lived in this house. Her photograph now decorates the staircase. The couple who own it, James and Priscilla Stam, were both college educators and originally came looking for a summer retreat. They've carefully restored this pleasant Victorian home in the best of taste and have created a pleasant ambience for their guests. Reserve well in advance.

The Channel Bass Inn, 100 Church Street, Chincoteague 23336. Phone: 336-6148. Rates: February–November, from about $50. Closed: December and January. Credit cards accepted.

More formal than Miss Molly's and, if you desire privacy, better suited to your needs. Attractively furnished. For the food here, see below. Reserve well in advance.

WHERE TO EAT

Onancock

Hopkins & Brother Store, 2 Market Street. Phone: 787-8220.

Credit cards accepted. (See page 251.) Very good and moderately priced. April 15–December 31: Hours are geared to the times that the store's ferry to Tangiers operates; call for times. Closed: January 1–April 14. Reservations unnecessary.

Accomac

The Owl, Route 13 North of Accomac. Phone: 665-5191. Credit cards accepted.

On my 0–10 Crabcake Scale, devised as an infallible quality measure for the Chesapeake Bay area—if they can't make good crabcakes, don't even think of darkening their door—this is between 8 and 8.5. Not bad. Not bad at all. And their spoonbread rates among the top ten in Virginia, while the panfried chicken is impeccable. For dessert, have the ambrosial chocolate rum pie, worthy of a great patisserie. As for the prices, to say moderate is to overstate the case. Dinner: Daily, 7–11. No reservations necessary.

Chincoteague

Landmark Crab House, Landmark Plaza. Phone: 336-5552. Credit cards accepted.

The setting is all-American fishing village, with the docks seen through the windows, the oyster boats tied up for the night. After dinner, a little stroll to help the digestion can be very pleasant. The dining room is large and has some unfortunate "cute" touches, viz. the salad bar, a converted crab float, while on the ceiling a clam boat is suspended upside down. But the seafood is tops; Chincoteague oysters are worth a trip to the Eastern Shore in themselves, and here they're served plain and simple, on a bed of ice or steamed to exactly the right moment and then served with all the crackers and melted butter you can ask for. Crab dishes are good—particularly one with Smithfield ham. The bread is lousy, the salad bar standard, and it's very crowded, but I'd still make this my first choice on the island for a seafood dinner. Moderate. Dinner: Monday–Saturday, 5–9; Sunday; 1–9. Closed: Monday in winter. Reservations suggested.

Channel Bass Inn, 100 Church Street. Phone: 336-6148. Credit cards accepted.

This restaurant is so pompous that the phone number is unlisted. And when you make a reservation, you must give a credit card number; no show, you still pay, a policy I can understand, but the unlisted phone number is really too much.

The food has received lavish praise, and I expect the praise has fed on itself, for although the food *is* good, it certainly is not among the top ten restaurants in Virginia, as some critics have alleged. The chef-owner quite naturally specializes in seafood and has added a Spanish twist to some of his recipes that often gives his creations an interesting fillip. One last comment: I think the prices are unmercifully high, bordering on outrageous. Dinner: 6–9 in season. Closed: December and January; Monday–Wednesday, February–April and October–November. Reservations required.

THE
NORTHERN NECK

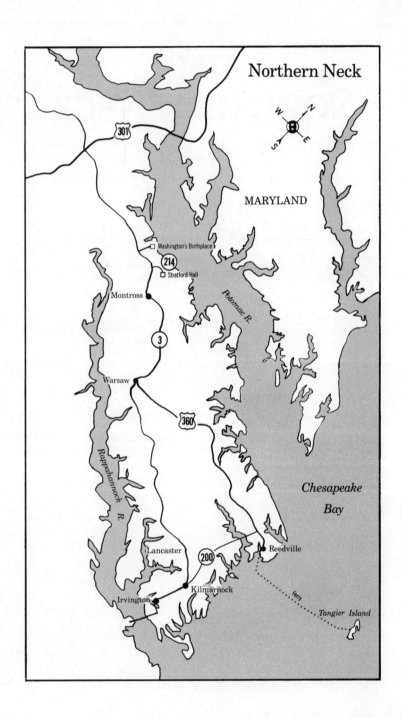

Northern Neck

MARYLAND

301

214
Washington's Birthplace
Stratford Hall

Montross

3

Potomac R.

Warsaw

360

Rappahannock R.

Chesapeake
Bay

Lancaster

200

Reedville

Kilmarnock

Irvington

Ferry

Tangier Island

THIS small but wonderful land that time and technology have thankfully passed by—the area between the Potomac and Rappahannock Rivers—has a mood and atmosphere all its own. Laced with waterways, its dominant theme, the area has a primordial richness that is deeply satisfying to the visitor, as a good hearty stew is to the psyche and stomach. It's robust, beautiful, straightforward and, above all, very real—an impression enhanced by the limpid clarity that the abundant water gives to the light. Driving in the Northern Neck can be a delight, for the variety of scenery—wheat fields and harbors, woods and small towns with names like Hyacinth, Lively, Ophelia, Nuttsville—lends a motley enchantment that surprises and charms. Make it a point to get off the main roads to enjoy any of the dozens of smaller ones.

With the exception of Tangier Island, none of the places mentioned in this section is more than an hour's drive from any of the others.

IRVINGTON

The Tides Inn   If you plan to stay in the Northern Neck, this is far and away the most pleasant place to be. In fact, it is good enough to be considered on its own merits as one of the premier resort facilities in Virginia.

The setting is particularly appealing, for the Inn is on a high point of a peninsula, eight miles up the Rappahannock from the Chesapeake Bay. Most of the rooms offer delightful views, and all of them are nicely appointed and of generous size. An agreeable private beach with a salt-water swimmingpool and an attractive, informal room called the Summer House that serves lunch and drinks is at the tip of the peninsula, and a private pier harbors some boats that belong to the Inn—and guests— including the yachts that are available free for cruises in the creek, the nearby river and the Chesapeake Bay. The landscaping surrounding all this adds luxuriant color to the scene.

Within a two-mile drive is superb golfing at the Golden Eagle Golf Course. All told, the Tides Inn offers two eighteen-hole courses and one nine-hole, three-par course as well as a putting green and a practice fairway. (The Golden Eagle Golf Course has a rating of 73; the Tartan Course, 70.1.) The Golden Eagle embraces four hundred acres of lake and woods; and the clubhouse, known as the Gallery, has a very good restaurant called Cap'n B's (see page 269) that specializes in New Orleans–style food. It is open for lunch only.

In addition to golf, the Inn also offers four tennis courts, two fast-dry and two all-weather, a vast array of boats ranging from canoes to paddleboats to the aforementioned yachts, and dancing four nights a week, including weekends, in the Chesapeake Club, the Inn's comfortable lounge that has something of the inimitable feel of an ocean liner.

In short, this is a special place. As headquarters for visiting the Northern Neck, it is ideal, and it's also pretty nice if you don't want to do anything else but play golf and tennis, swim and relax. I highly recommend it with only one caveat; the food, which is uninteresting. It's not bad, mind you, just eminently forgettable. (For rates and other information, see page 268.)

Christ Church (1732) Just a few miles from the Inn, this is the only colonial church in this country that has remained virtually unchanged; many critics and historians also feel that it is the most beautiful church from the period. I tend to agree, if only because the exterior is flawless in its simple, perfect and inspired design and in its very subtle detail and execution.

First, some background. The church was the gift of Robert "King" Carter of nearby Corotoman, which has long since disappeared. His descendants certainly haven't, and among them are eight governors of Virginia, three signers of the Declaration of Independence, two presidents of the United States (the Harrisons), Robert E. Lee, bishops, judges and a host of others. Carter was one of the wealthiest men of his time; at the end of his life he held 300,000 acres of land. He and his family were long connected with this church—his father and four of his father's five wives were buried here, and when the parishioners decided to replace the 1669 building and move it closer to the town of Kilmarnock, Carter offered to pay the entire cost of the new

Many scholars feel that Christ Church is our most beautiful church from the colonial period. Make a special effort to see it.

building if they would agree to leave the old one in place where the graves of his father and his father's wives would be assured protection. Not surprisingly, the vestry agreed.

The church wasn't finished until shortly before Carter's death, but while he lived, he used it in as regal a manner as possible. No one could enter until he and his retinue were inside, where a quarter of the church was reserved for his family, servants and guests. His pew—like all the others, a rectangular affair with a high back—was large enough for him to have his own chair inside it, and above hung a damask valance from a brass rod to protect him from the stares of the vulgar. When Carter died, his tomb and those of his three wives were placed behind the church. His is very much larger and more ornate than was usual in the Virginia of his day—a tomb befitting a king.

The exterior of the church is breathtaking. It is cruciform, 140 feet wide, with the transept four feet off center. Each of the three arms is 68 feet wide. The building is topped with four hipped roofs with two pitches that end with a slight upturn at the eaves. The result is a delightfully unexpected pagoda look.

The exterior is of brick set in Flemish bond with glazed headers. The entrances carved in the three arms—all with their original and very beautiful doors—are singularly effective. The bricks framing them (and the round arched windows) have a warm orange tinge achieved through a rubbing process that distinguishes them from the rest of the brick, a subtle touch that gives further variety to the walls. The overall design of these entrances, each topped by a striking oeil-de-boeuf, give relief and a feeling of plasticity, while the perfection of the proportions gives the building a monumental presence.

The interior is ablaze with natural light—in addition to the oeils-de-boeuf, there are twelve other windows, each five by fourteen feet. In the chancel you will find the early Carter tombs. The pulpit, a triple-decker affair with a walnut sounding board, is quietly but elegantly carved, as is the walnut communion rail. It is an airy, even soaring space—the ceiling is 33 feet above the floor—a great building, well suited to the worship of God, that lingers in the mind's eye and casts a sense of deep, contemplative satisfaction.

Next door is the Carter Reception Center, which offers a slide show and has a little museum displaying artifacts dug up at Corotoman as well as from the church. The church is open daily, 9–5. Closed: December 25. The reception center is open: April–Thanksgiving, Monday–Friday, 10–4; Saturday, 1–4; Sunday, 2–5. Admission: Free. Phone: 804-438-6855.

STRATFORD HALL

This early Georgian house (1725–1730) is unique in Virginia, and uniquely beautiful. I would rank it as one of my three favorite houses for architecture, setting and furnishings. See it if at all possible.

Stratford Hall is as distinguished for its history as for its beauty. It was built by Colonel Thomas Lee, and among the distinguished men who were either born or lived here were several members of the Governor's Council, burgesses, two signers of the Declaration of Independence, a governor of the state, members of the Continental Congress, diplomats and, in starry culmination, Robert E. Lee.

The main house is H-shaped, ninety feet in length, and stands in the center of a square with dependencies at the four corners. The features that immediately strike the eye: The chimney groupings, each made up of four clustered chimneys whose caps are connected by arches and between which are balustrated platforms. (It has been speculated that the platforms were used to watch for ships approaching up the Potomac.) They are an extremely dramatic and virile touch, reminiscent of the great

English architect Sir John Vanbrugh. The other stunning feature is the monumental entrance staircase, with its massive balustrades, that sweeps dramatically up to a rather simple but beautifully proportioned second-story door, narrowing as it ascends so that it draws the eye upward in a rush.

The exterior is further distinguished by the treatment of the brick. All of it is laid in the Flemish bond pattern, but the brick on the ground floor and chimneys has glazed headers. A further touch is the rubbing of the brick around the corners and the jambs on the second floor, and the chimneys, which gives it a different color from the rest.

The resulting impression is of a great, massive building with exquisite sensibility. It is the kind of building that the eye delights in roving over and around, absorbing its visual sophistication. I find approaching the house and wandering about it an intensely rewarding experience; it's hard not to revel in such focused brilliance.

The interior, I am happy to say, does not disappoint. In fact, the restoration has been superbly accomplished and is itself worth the trip. Downstairs are bedrooms, the schoolroom, the winter kitchen, and so forth. Upstairs, at the dead center of

In many ways Stratford Hall, the Lee ancestral home, is my favorite house in Virginia, and I particularly like this side view of it. From the house you can go down to the banks of the Potomac for panoramic scenery of great romantic beauty.

the house and at the head of the outside staircases is one of the glorious rooms of this country—the Great Hall, 29 feet square, with impeccably carved wall paneling and a tray ceiling seventeen feet above the floor. It is one of the finest entrance rooms you will ever see and has been furnished with splendid pieces, all of museum quality. Through the doors flanked (as are the windows) by Corinthian pilasters can be seen the Potomac to the north and, to the south, the plantation fields. It is perfection (perfection brushed with tragedy, though, for two Lee children were killed here over the years in falls from the stairs).

I'm also particularly fond of the two other rooms on this floor, the mother's room and the adjoining nursery at the southeast corner of the house. The bedroom, filled with light and perfectly furnished, is a respite after the grandeur of the rest, while the nursery exudes domesticity, with its delightful collection of eighteenth-century toys scattered about.

The 1,600-acre estate is preserved as a working plantation. Cattle graze as grain ripens in the fields. Elsewhere on the land a tree farm thrives. Nearer to the house are wonderful gardens to explore. The West Garden has vegetables, flowers, herbs, trees and shrubs, including espaliered apple and pear trees. Homely in the best sense of the word, friendly and informal, it invites you to linger among its earthly pleasures. The East Garden, restored by the Garden Club of Virginia, is a typical eighteenth-century English formal garden with brick walls, oyster-shell paths, boxwood and specimen trees. There's a wildflower walk, too—leave the East Garden by the north gate and follow it along the north side—and while you're on this part of the grounds, be sure to explore the north vista, a view that extends almost a mile to the Potomac.

And now for the final delight of your visit. I almost hate to tell you about it and ruin the surprise, but if I didn't you might just miss it. What I'm referring to is the drive down to the old mill, a romantically pretty building rebuilt on the original foundations, with an equally pretty and romantic millpond behind it. You continue down to the shores of the Potomac, which is seven miles wide here, and look at the great and glorious cliffs that rise, serrated sentinels, from the shore. It is a great landscape, grand enough to have inspired one of the more ambitious members of the Hudson River School had he but been aware of it.

No doubt about it, a visit to Stratford Hall is one of the
highlights of anyone's trip to Virginia. No wonder Robert E. Lee
never forgot it; during the Civil War he wrote to his daughter
Annie, "I am pleased at your description of Stratford and your
visit. It is endeared to me by many recollections and it has
always been a great desire of my life to be able to purchase it.
Now that we have no other house, and the one we love has been
so foully polluted [Arlington], the desire is stronger with me
than ever. The horse chestnut that you mentioned in the garden," he adds, "was planted by my mother." I wonder if it's still
there.

Stratford Hall, near Montross on Route 214, is open daily,
9:00–4:30. Closed: December 25. Admission: $3; children 6–high
school, $1. In addition to the standard tour, special decorative
arts and garden tours are also available. Each lasts about two
hours and is limited to four or five people. They cost $6 apiece,
and reservations must be made in advance. Phone 804-493-9720
for the special tours. The plantation number: 804-493-8038. A
plantation lunch is available, April–October, 11:30–3:00, and the
Visitor Center offers a slide presentation on the Hall, as well as
a small museum.

George Washington Birthplace National Monument

Four miles beyond Stratford you'll first encounter a monument
commemorating this site. George lived here exactly three and
a half years. When his father died, the house passed to his
half-brother Augustine. It burned to the ground on Christmas
Day 1779, and was never rebuilt. The site of the original house
is indicated; the house you actually see is the Memorial House,
called Wakefield, which was built in this century to represent
a typical plantation house of the time George lived here. It is
moderately interesting. More appealing are the walks along
Popes Creek and the active farm with livestock and gardens
that is operated according to eighteenth-century methods. This
is well suited to children. The birthplace is open daily, 9–5.
Closed December 25, January 1. Admission: Free. Phone: 804-
224-0916.

TANGIER ISLAND

Virginia is full of unique communities and special places, but this surely is one of the most unusual. Tangier Island, an hour and three quarters by boat from Reedville, sits alone in the Chesapeake Bay, the home of a hardy breed that have lived here since the end of the seventeenth century.

Discovered by Captain John Smith in 1608, the island was later bought from the Indians for the munificent price of two overcoats. But it wasn't settled until 1686, when John Crockett arrived with his eight sons and their families. By the beginning of the nineteenth century, approximately one hundred people lived here, about half of them Crocketts and the remainder the ancestors of the people who inhabit the island today. (As for the name, no one really knows where it came from. One theory is that Captain Smith named it after Tangier, Morocco, where he had once been imprisoned.)

The island's moment in the sun came during the War of 1812, when the British Navy landed troops here in preparation for the assault on Fort McHenry. When they left, Francis Scott Key went with them and wrote our National Anthem during the famous bombardment. After the occupation, the island quickly fell back to its prewar ways of life—fishing, crabbing and oystering—and today little has changed.

But I'm getting a little ahead of myself. First you have to get there, and the most pleasant way to do this is aboard the *Captain Thomas*, which operates out of Reedville, a small but bustling fishing port filled with Victorian houses. (**Tangier and Chesapeake Cruises, Inc.,** Warsaw. Operates: May, weekends, June–September, daily. Departs: 10. Returns: 4:15. Fee: $16; children, $8. Phone: 804-333-4656.) This venture is owned and operated by a family as pleasant as you could ask for, which of course makes sailing with them a distinct pleasure. The trip is narrated—unobtrusively—and the information is interesting and well presented. Getting there, in this case, is definitely half the fun.

As you approach the dock, you'll notice soft-shell crab farms: Tangier proudly boasts that it is the soft-shell capital of the world. Peelers (see page 249) are placed in wooden floats to shed;

Weatherbeaten but proud: That description of the house could also apply to the residents of Tangier Island.

then they are packed and shipped to (I hope) wherever I am.

When you leave the boat you will have lunch at Tangier Island's most famous landmark, the **Chesapeake House**, a gastronomic delight founded in 1940 by Hilda Crockett and now run by her two daughters, Betty Nohe and Edna Moore. Inside the house, you are seated at long communal tables to enjoy a parade of food that includes clam fritters, crabcakes (7.8 out of a possible 10 on the all-important Mulligan Crabcake Scale), homemade breads, ham, potato salad, corn pudding and all-butter pound cake. Down-home eating like this would be the envy of many a restaurant, and makes for a memorable meal.

After lunch you have plenty of time to explore the odd little island, only two and a half miles long and less than a mile wide, where about 850 people live in tightly packed white frame houses. (Note the graves in the yards, by the way.) Little bridges over the canals connect the different sections, and there are even "taxis"—golf carts are more accurate—to haul you about. The people are very friendly, like all islanders I've met, but it is a bit disconcerting to see in all of them a faint resemblance. As you talk to them, you'll quickly notice that many of them have a lingering accent reminiscent of their English roots; if you overhear them speaking the local dialect, you won't be able to understand one word in twenty.

I should also tell you that the island has an airport that is used by hunters, among others. The island is right in the middle of the Atlantic Flyway, and the hunting is superb.

WHERE TO STAY AND EAT
Area Code: 804

WHERE TO STAY

Irvington

The Tides Inn, Irvington 22480. Phone: 438-5000 or, for reservations made from outside the state, 800-446-9981; inside the state, 800-552-3461. Rates: American Plan, April–October, for a single, from about $95; for a double, from about $178. Weekly rates, golf package plan. Closed: January–mid-March. Credit cards accepted. (See page 259.)

Tides Lodge, Irvington 22480. Phone: 438-6000. Rates: End of March–November, varying widely according to length of time spent and accommodations chosen. A single begins at about $108; for a double, from about $138. Weekly rates, golf package plan. Closed: December–March 15. Credit cards accepted.

Owned by the Stephens, the same family that owns and operates the Tides Inn, this is the motel version. It offers the same service and attention that you will find at the Inn for a little less money. It is less formal, as well, and there's enough Campbell plaid used in the décor to make you think the decorator must have been a homesick Scot. Actually, it's to honor Sir Guy Campbell, the famous golf architect.

Lancaster

The Inn at Levelfields, P.O. Box 216, Lancaster 22503. Phone: 435-6887. Rates: For a single, from about $35; for a double, from about $55. Breakfast included. Credit cards accepted.

This antebellum house (c. 1857) with a typical double-tiered portico makes a very pleasant bed and breakfast. There is a swimming pool, guest rooms all have a working fireplace, and all rooms have a private bath. Lunch (11:30–2:00) and dinner (6:00–9:30) are served here Wednesday–Saturday. Sunday brunch: 11:30–2:00.

Tangier Island

Chesapeake House, Tangier Island 23440. Phone: 891-2331. Rates: April 15–October 15, about $25. Includes breakfast and "family-style big seafood dinner." Closed October 16–April 14. No credit cards. (See page 267.)

That's right, the price is unbelievable. Nothing fancy, but clean and comfortable.

WHERE TO EAT

Irvington

Tides Inn. Phone: 438-5000. Credit cards accepted. Moderately expensive. Lunch: 12–3:30. Dinner: 7–9. Reservations required. (See page 259.)

The Tides Lodge. Phone: 438-6000. Credit cards accepted.

The dining room here is a little more informal than at the Inn. The food isn't bad and the atmosphere is pleasant. Moderate–moderately expensive. Lunch: 12–3. Dinner: 7–9. Reservations required.

Cap'n B's. Phone: 438-5000. Credit cards accepted. (See page 260.)

It's the best of the three and moderately priced. Too bad it's lunch only, 11:30–3:30. Reservations unnecessary.

Tangier Island

Chesapeake House. Phone: 891-2331. No credit cards. (See page 267.)

The best eating in this area, and it's downright cheap. Family-style meals served from 11:30–6:00 (last seating). Reservations required.

A SHORT GLOSSARY OF ARCHITECTURAL TERMS

Baluster

A short upright post supporting a railing.

Balustrade

The ensemble of balusters and rail.

Brickwork
  English Bond

Alternate rows of headers (the end of a brick) and stretchers (the side of a brick).

  Flemish Bond

Bricks laid with headers and stretchers alternating in the same row.

Capital

The head of a column.

Classic Revival architecture

Replaced Georgian architecture about the end of the Revolution. See Greek and Roman Revival. Also Federal, which was influenced by Classic Revival.

Cornice

The crowning, projecting ornamental molding along the top of a building.

Dentils

A small series of ornamental blocks set in a row to form dentil molding.

Diaper Work

A brick work surface decoration that forms a repeated pattern.

Fanlight

A window, usually semicircular and set over a door.

Federal Style	Generally speaking, its period is from the end of the Revolution into the 1830's. Similar to Georgian but more restrained and elegant. See Point of Honor, Lynchburg.
Flemish Gable	Also called stepped gable and Dutch gable. A gable that ascends in steps rather than in a straight or curved line. See Bacon's Castle.
Georgian Style	In this country the period roughly beginning with George I (1714) to the end of the Revolution. Most commonly—and incorrectly—called Colonial. Characterized by strict rules of design and proportion derived from classic buildings. See Carter's Grove, Williamsburg.
Gothic Revival Style	A movement derived from the Gothic of the Middle Ages. Popular here from about 1845 throughout the nineteenth century. Based, among other things, on emotions and imagination, it is quintessentially romantic. See Virginia Military Institute (VMI), Lexington.
Graining	A painting technique that imitates the grain of wood.
Greek Revival Style	From about 1800 to the Civil War, with some examples into the twentieth century. A style based on classic Greek architecture. See Arlington House, Arlington.
Hyphens	In Georgian architecture, the links connecting the main house with the dependencies.

Keystone	The central stone at the crown of an arch.
Lintel	The horizontal beam that bridges an opening or two or more columns.
Oeil-de-Boeuf	Literally, bull's eye. A small circular or oval window.
Orders	In Classical architecture, a column, composed of base, shaft and capital, and its principal horizontal member, the entablature (lintel). Mentioned in this text:
Doric	Simplest of the three. Greek version has no base.
Ionic	The capital has two volutes or spiral scrolls.
Corinthian	The most complex capital, with stylized acanthus leaves the primary decoration.
Palladian	Architecture influenced by Andrea Palladio (1508–80), the most influential of all Italian architects. Characterized by symmetry and, often, flanking dependencies. A Palladian window is an arrangement with a rounded window flanked by two lower square-headed ones, the three separated by columns or pilasters. See Monticello, Charlottesville.
Pediment	The triangular space above a portico or, much reduced, over doors or windows.
Pilaster	The projecting part of a shallow pier or square column that is at-

tached to a wall. It usually conforms with one of the orders. (See above.)

Portico

A columned porch, the centerpiece of a façade.

Portland Stone

A light-colored limestone from England's Isle of Portland.

Pulpit
  Wineglass

Shaped in the classic stem-and-bowl pattern.

  Sounding Board

The acoustic canopy over the pulpit.

Quoins

The prominent dressed stones at the corners of a building.

Roman Revival Style

Jefferson was its prophet in this country. A style originally adapted to create a monumental architecture that would reflect the best qualities of the new republic. From about 1800 to the Civil War, but never as pervasive as Greek Revival. See the Virginia State Capitol, Richmond.

Roof Types
  Gambrel

A roof with a double slope on each side, the lowermost sharply pitched.

  Hipped

A roof with four sloping planes.

  Mansard

Double-sloped, like the gambrel, but the lower slope is even more sharply pitched. Named for François Mansart (1598–1666), the great French classicist.

INDEX

About the Author

TIM MULLIGAN was educated at Phillips Academy, Andover, Yale University and the University of Paris. He has been both an editor and a writer for several national magazines and the author of *The Hudson River Valley: A History & Guide.* He is currently at work on a book about the construction of the first transcontinental railway.